International Immigration Policy

International Immigration Policy: A Theoretical and Comparative Analysis

Eytan Meyers

palgrave
macmillan

INTERNATIONAL IMMIGRATION POLICY

First published 2004 by
PALGRAVE MACMILLAN™
175 Fifth Avenue, New York, N.Y. 10010 and
Houndmills, Basingstoke, Hampshire, England RG21 6XS
Companies and representatives throughout the world

PALGRAVE MACMILLAN is the global academic imprint of the Palgrave Macmillan division of St. Martin's Press, LLC and of Palgrave Macmillan Ltd. Macmillan® is a registered trademark in the United States, United Kingdom and other countries. Palgrave is a registered trademark in the European Union and other countries.

ISBN 0–312–23143–1 hardback

Library of Congress Cataloging-in-Publication Data
Meyers, Eytan
International immigration policy : a theoretical and comparative analysis / by Eytan Meyers.
p. cm.
Includes bibliographical references and index.
ISBN 0–312–23143–1
1. Emigration and immigration—Government policy. 2. Immigrants—Government policy. 3. Illegal aliens—Government policy. 4. Refugees—Government policy. 5. Asylum, Right of. I. Title.

JV6271.M49 2004
325'.1—dc22 2003058845

A catalogue record for this book is available from the British Library.

Design by Newgen Imaging Systems (P) Ltd., Chennai, India.

First edition: April, 2004
10 9 8 7 6 5 4 3 2 1

Printed in the United States of America.

Dedicated to my grandmother

Dr. Rose Mushin, a woman ahead of her time

Table of Contents

List of Figures and Tables

Figures

Tables

Introduction

Migration is a growing global phenomenon, which has a tremendous impact on the demography, culture, economy, and politics of the state. In 2000, an estimated 175 million people lived outside their country of birth, an increase of 46 percent since 1990, and double the number in 1975. Of these, about 159 million were considered international migrants, approximately 16 million were recognized refugees fleeing a well-founded fear of persecution, and about 900,000 were asylum seekers.[1] On January 1, 1998, the total foreign or non-national population of the 15 European Union (EU) Member States was 19.1 million of the total population of 375 million.[2]

Immigration is now the key demographic factor responsible for population growth in most Western societies. In the United States, immigration accounts for more than half the population growth (when U.S.-born and naturalized children of recent immigrants are included), and according to some projections, about 93 percent of the population growth in the year 2050 will result from immigration that has occurred since 1991.[3] In 2001, the EU's population rose by 1.6 million, with 75 percent of the growth due to net migration (immigration minus emigration).[4] In the future, the importance of immigration in demographic terms will further increase. Since the birth rate in EU countries does not reach the replacement level, their population would decline if not for immigration.[5]

Immigration also has a tremendous impact on the composition and culture of the countries of destination. Europeans are attempting to cope with the transformation brought about by immigration, from relatively homogenous to multicultural societies. Cultural conflicts with regard to the position of Muslims in predominantly Christian societies have further intensified following the September 11, 2001 terrorist attacks. In the United States, the Hispanic community just turned into the largest ethnic minority, surpassing the Afro-American one.[6]

During the past two decades, immigration has become a prominent political issue in most Western democracies. The growing economic and demographic disparity between North and South, the civil war in the former Yugoslavia, the collapse of communist regimes in Eastern Europe, and wars and natural disasters in other parts of the world have sent hundreds of thousands of asylum seekers into Western Europe. They have joined millions of foreign residents already living in Western Europe, many of them former migrant workers with limited political rights, which undermines European ideals of democracy and equality. In addition, an estimated 500,000 foreigners a year enter the EU illegally, and there are believed to be three million unauthorized foreigners living in Europe. The host of the EU 2002 summit in Seville, Spanish Prime Minister Jose Maria Aznar, said that reducing illegal immigration was "the most important question in European politics at the moment." His comment was largely in response to xenophobic tensions, anti-immigrant violence, and extreme-right anti-immigrant parties that have spread throughout Europe. In France, Le Pen reached the second round of the 2002 presidential elections, where he won 18 percent of the vote. The Pim Fortuyn party received 18 percent of the vote in the May 2002 Dutch elections, and became the second largest party in Parliament. In Austria, Haider's Freedom Party won 26.9 percent of the vote in the October 1999 national elections, and joined the ruling coalition. And the Swiss People's Party (UDC), headed by Christopher Blocker, gained 22.5 percent of the vote in the October 1999 Swiss national elections.

Meanwhile, in the United States, there has been a continuing debate over how to handle the surge of illegal immigrants—particularly from Mexico—and how to cope with Haitian and Cuban refugees. In 1993, President Clinton asserted that one of the biggest domestic challenges the United States will face in the 1990s will be how to stem the increasing flow of illegal immigrants while maintaining the American commitment to legal immigration and legitimate political refugees.[7] In 1996, the INS (Immigration and Naturalization Service) estimated that there were five million unauthorized foreigners living in the United States, which was about 2 percent of U.S. population. Another estimate, in 2002, put the number of unauthorized immigrants in the United States at nine million.[8]

The growing immigration also became a source of friction as well as of cooperation in the international arena. For example, fear of Turks pouring into the EU in search for jobs has been one of the main reasons for the delays in accepting Turkey into the Union. But the shared immigration pressures have also contributed to the gradual movement toward a common EU migration and asylum policy.

Immigration policy is the crucial element determining immigration patterns. Given the large number of people who would like to emigrate to the industrialized countries for economic or political reasons, and the strictly limited opportunities to do so, it is immigration control policy that mainly determines the scope of global migration (including, it could be argued, illegal migration).[9] As Aristide R. Zolberg wrote: "All the countries to which people would like to go restrict entry. This means that, in the final analysis, it is the policies of potential receivers which determine whether movement can take place, and of what kind."[10] In 1976, 7 percent of the 150 UN member-nations had policies to restrict immigration. Today, 40 percent of the UN's 193 member-nations have policies aimed at restricting immigration.[11]

This book offers a theory of international immigration policy. It explains how governments decide on the number of immigrants they will accept; whether to differentiate between various ethnic groups; whether to accept refugees and on what basis; and whether to favor permanent immigration over migrant workers.

Chapter 1 briefly analyzes the major theories of immigration control policy, and presents the main themes and hypotheses of this study. Chapters 2–5 examine the aforementioned hypotheses in four case studies: chapter 2 deals with the United States, chapter 3 with Britain, chapter 4 with the Netherlands, and chapter 5 with Germany. Each chapter offers a historical description of the country's immigration control policies, followed by an analysis of the factors determining these policies. Chapter 6 explains the similarities and differences between immigration control policies of various countries. Chapter 7 summarizes the arguments and findings of the book, and briefly discusses the influence of regional integration on the immigration policies of the member states.

Part of chapter 6 was first published as "The Causes of Convergence in Western Immigration Control," *Review of International Studies*, 28(1), pp. 123–41, 2002, and was reprinted with the permission of Cambridge University Press. Several paragraphs of chapter 1 first appeared in "Theories of International Immigration Policy," *International Migration Review* 34(4), pp. 1245–82, and were reprinted with the permission of the Center for Migration Studies of New York.

All four countries examined in the study are important countries of immigration, and, at the same time, they vary with regards to the type of immigration received. The United States has been the largest recipient of immigrants globally and has the largest foreign population. Germany has received more refugees and asylum seekers than any other European country, and in 1998 it had over half of the EU's non-EU foreign residents.[12] In proportion to the size of the local population, the Netherlands is dealing with the second largest number of asylum seekers in the EU, preceded only by Sweden. At the same time, the countries examined vary with regards to the type of immigrants received. Britain and the Netherlands accepted large colonial immigration, while Germany and the United States have not. Many immigrants to Germany and the Netherlands were originally viewed as temporary migrant workers, and only later became permanent residents. In contrast, Britain mostly accepted permanent immigration, and the United States admitted both migrant workers and permanent immigration, but did not naturalize most of the migrant workers.[13]

Work on this book was supported by grants from the MacArthur Foundation received through the University of Chicago and from the Pacific Council on International Policy/The Center for International Studies at The University of Southern California. I would like to thank Gary Freeman, James Hollifield, David Laitin, Douglas Massey, Duncan Snidal, Adam Przeworski, and Gerald Rosenberg who read parts of the draft and gave me valuable comments. I particularly want to thank my father, Nechemia Meyers, and my wife, Avital Meyers, without whom this project would not be possible.

CHAPTER 1

A Theory of Immigration Policy

This book has two goals: to offer a theory of the socioeconomic and foreign policy factors shaping immigration control policy, and to describe and analyze the immigration control policies of the United States, Britain, Germany, and the Netherlands between the late nineteenth and the early twenty-first centuries.

Chapter 1 starts with a review and a critique of current theories about racism and immigration control policy. It then presents the main themes of the study, the types of immigration policy analyzed (i.e. the dependent variable), and the socioeconomic and foreign policy factors shaping immigration control policy (hypotheses 1–7). The third part of the chapter describes how the type of immigration determines the relative influence of the aforementioned socioeconomic factors on immigration control policy (hypotheses 8–11 and table 1.1). The fourth part notes two factors rejected by the theory, and adds a short discussion of illegal/undocumented immigration. Finally, it offers an explanation for the similarities and differences between immigration policies of the major receiving countries (hypotheses 12–14).

Theories of Immigration Control Policy: A Review and Critique

Theories explaining racism and immigration control policy can be categorized into three major groups: theories that focus on the economic competition between the native-born and the immigrants; theories that highlight the cultural discord between the two groups; and studies that deal with the impact of international relations and multilateral agreements on immigration control policy.

The first group of theories focuses on the economic competition between the native-born and the immigrants. According to Husbands, theories of this kind explain racism by competition between ethnic groups for a scarce resource, for example jobs, housing, private and public welfare benefits.[1] According to Money, theories of economic interests view immigration policy as an outcome of the preferences of economic actors within the host society.[2] These preferences are attributed to the differential economic impact of immigrants on groups in the host society. And according to Fetzer, theories of "class politics" or "economic self-interest" point to immigration's supposed threat to natives' economic well-being.[3]

Theories of economic competition include a Marxist and a non-Marxist/pluralist variants. *The Marxist approach*—presented by Beard and Beard, Gorz, Marshall, Marx, Castells, Nikolinakos, Castles and Kosack, Miles, and Bovenkerk et al.—argues that economic factors and a class-based political process shape immigration policies.[4] It asserts that capitalists import migrant workers in order to exert a downward pressure on wages and thereby increase their own profits, and in order to divide the working class. They achieve the latter by encouraging racism among the working class. *Domestic politics and pluralist models* assume that the state serves as a neutral arena for societal interests: interest groups and parties. Policymaking is the result of bargaining as well as of compromises between these interests, or sometimes it reflects the fact that one or more of these actors has succeeded in capturing the state.[5] In the context of economic competition, the two prominent interest groups are the employers and the unions. Both the Marxist and the pluralist approaches argue that employers' demand for labor, and fluctuations in the economy and in the labor market influence immigration control policy.

The second group of theories highlights the cultural discord between the native-born and the immigrants. According to Husbands, such theories see racism as a spontaneous response to what is strange and unfamiliar, and in later stages as based upon negative responses to customs and habits of the arriving groups.[6] Another variant of that theory explains racism as based on moral and symbolic challenges to the racial status quo in society generally. According to Money, these theories emphasize the primacy of cultural values, and often consider national identity a primary determinant of immigration policy.[7] Fetzer analyzes two approaches that mostly relate to the this group of theories: marginality theory, which emphasizes the impact of cultural differences between immigrants and natives of dominant ethnicity, waves of culturally different immigrants, and recessions; and contact theory, which emphasizes the impact of the percent of foreign-born.[8]

Some variants of the culture-based theories explain changes in immigration control policy as a response to the size of immigration and to the cultural differences between immigrants and natives. Another variant—the national identity approach—argues that the unique history of each country, its conceptions of citizenship and nationality, as well as debates over national identity and social conflicts within it, shape its immigration policies (see Higham, Jones, Herbert, Brubaker, Leitner, Kurthen).[9] In comparison to the other theories delineated here, the "national identity" approach downplays the importance of external and "situational" factors. Instead, it explains the timing of immigration policies on the basis of social conflicts and debates over national identity. It relates variations in immigration and citizenship policies between countries of destination to their different conceptions of national identity or different characteristics. Three such distinctions, which partially overlap, are (a) between settler societies, which accept large-scale immigration, and ethnic states, which tend to reject such immigration; (b) between homogeneous and heterogeneous countries; and (c) between countries whose citizenship laws tend toward *jus sanguinis* and those countries whose citizenship laws tend toward *jus soli*.[10]

A third group of studies focuses on the impact of international relations and multilateral agreements on immigration control policy (see Miller, Miller and Papademetriou, Teitelbaum, Weiner, Loescher and Scanlan, Mitchell, Bach, Tucker, Salomon, Hollifield, Miller, Zolberg, Hartigan, Loescher, Skran, Teitelbaum and Weiner, Koslowski).[11] Some studies, which relate to the realist approach, argue that actual or potential conflicts among states, including military ones, have influenced immigration policies. Others, adopting a neoliberal institutionalist approach, argue that international institutions and regimes facilitate cooperation between countries with regard to immigration control policies.

I describe the aforementioned theories in detail, and analyze their main strengths and weaknesses, elsewhere.[12] To summarize, each of these approaches contributes to our understanding of immigration policy or specific types of such policy. The economic competition theories correctly predict the short-term correlation between the economic cycle and immigration policies. In particular, they shed light upon policies regarding migrant workers and in some cases illegal immigrants. The culture-based theories spotlight importance of the cultural differences between immigrants and natives. Theories of international relations and of multilateral institutions particularly contribute to our understanding of refugee policies and of immigration policies within the EU.

However, each of these approaches also suffers from certain weaknesses. With regard to the Marxist approach:

(a) Its prediction of long-term growth in immigration as a structural part of capitalism is debatable. It may be argued that illegal migration and asylum seekers have replaced the traditional labor migration in terms of its role in the labor market. But it is not clear why the capitalists would resort to such replacement given their alleged control of the state.
(b) The Marxist approach fails to explain the tendency to impose restrictions on immigration of dissimilar ethnic origin. According to the Marxist approach, the state (in the service of the capitalists) encourages the importation of immigrants of dissimilar racial and ethnic composition in order to expand the labor force and cause racial tensions between immigrants and local labor. In practice, however, immigration policies have discriminated against immigrants of dissimilar racial and ethnic composition.
(c) The exclusive focus of the Marxist approach on the economic motive lessens its ability to explain refugee policies and other permanent immigration policies that are influenced by foreign policy considerations.
(d) The Marxist focus on the economic motive also prevents it from explaining restrictions on permanent immigration, passed in various countries during major wars (e.g. World War I), despite a growing demand for labor.

The main weaknesses of the "national identity" approach are its inability to explain concurrent immigration policies in various countries, and its vaguely defined explanatory variables. First, the "national identity" approach is unable to explain the fact that various countries have adopted similar immigration policies at the same time (see chapter 6). Such resemblance undermines the argument that immigration policies are shaped by each country's unique history, social cleavages, and perception of national identity. And second, the approach is vague with regard to identifying social conflicts and debates over national identity. For instance, there is no doubt that the Civil War constituted a major social conflict in U.S. history, and the same is probably true of the civil rights movement of the 1960s. But it is hard to reach a consensus on whether other historical events can be seen as social conflicts and signify a "loss of national confidence," including these presented by Higham and Jones. Vague definitions of this type risk being tautological, where the independent variable (social conflicts and debates over national identity) are chosen according to the dependent variable (restrictions on immigration).

Finally, with regard to theories of international relations, neither realist nor neoliberal institutional approaches have significantly contributed to the study of immigration control policies. With regard to realism:

(a) The theory emphasized security, while viewing social issues as less important. Consequently, realist works tended to neglect the issue of immigration.
(b) Realism defines the state as a unitary rational actor. But such a perspective cannot explain why some scholars (notably economists) criticize immigration policy for being inefficient or irrational.[13]
(c) Realism focuses on power as a key concept; but global power relations usually do not determine immigration policy.

With regard to the neoliberal institutionalist approach, most studies conclude that supranational organizations and international regimes have had little impact on the immigration policies of individual countries, with the partial exception of the EU and the refugee regime.

However, the greatest weakness of most literature on immigration control policy is that it does not relate to any theoretical approach. Numerous studies explore immigration policies of individual receiving countries. But these studies are (a) empirically oriented and lack a general theory, and (b) they mostly examine the policy of a single country during a limited period or, in a few cases, are volumes in which each country is analyzed independently. Zolberg notes that immigration policy literature tends to be a-theoretic, focusing on specified periods and particular countries, and constitutes an array of discrete bits.[14] Myron Weiner writes:

> High on a list of priorities for future research should be the study of determinants of exit and entry rules. While the policies of some individual countries have been studied, except for the recent work by Aristide Zolberg, Astri Suhrke, and Michael Teitelbaum there is little systematic comparative and theoretical work on such issues as how and why states make their access rules, the interplay between domestic and international considerations, the relationship between regime type and access rules, and how the rules are affected by internal political transformations.[15]

This study offers such a theory of international immigration policy. It explains how governments decide on the number of immigrants they will accept; whether to differentiate between various ethnic groups; whether to accept refugees and on what basis; and whether to favor permanent immigration over migrant workers. The theory does not belong to any one group of theories, but rather combines elements from all three groups. It refers to economic recessions (hypothesis 1), which are identified with the economic competition theories; to immigration of dissimilar racial or ethnic composition (hypothesis 2), and liberal/racist ideological trends (hypothesis 7), which relate to culture-based theories; and to the impact of wars, external threats, and considerations of foreign policy (hypotheses 3–6), which are part of the international relations literature. At the same time it rejects the influence of social conflicts and industrial unrest, which are identified with the national identity approach. But most importantly, the study attempts to present a set of socioeconomic and foreign policy factors that determine immigration control policy, and to demonstrate the relative importance of each factor under various circumstances.

The Main Themes of the Study

The main themes of this study are:[16]

- Immigration control policy is determined by an interaction between (a) socioeconomic and foreign policy factors and (b) the type of immigration.
- Immigration control policies of various countries are determined by the same set of socioeconomic factors.
- The type of immigration—for example temporary labor migration, permanent dissimilar immigration, permanent similar immigration, refugees and illegal immigration—determines the relative influence of the various socioeconomic and foreign policy factors on immigration control policy.
- The type of receiving society—that is settler societies versus ethnic states—mainly influences immigration control policy in an indirect fashion, through the type of immigration accepted by the country. In other words, the socioeconomic factors leading to labor migration policy in settler societies will *resemble* those leading to labor migration policy in ethnic states. The socioeconomic factors leading to labor migration policy in settler societies will *differ* from those leading to permanent immigration policy in the same societies.
- Interdependence between the socioeconomic and foreign policy factors that lead to immigration control policies in various countries explains most of the similarity among the immigration control policies of these countries.

- The structural factors of each country (i.e. population density, geo-political position, and economic structure) affect the preference for specific types of immigration, and consequently, which socio-economic and foreign policy factors will influence immigration policy the most. Thus, they are the "basic" factors causing the differences between immigration control policies of various countries at any given time.

The Dependent Variables

The study seeks to explain how governments decide on the number of immigrants they will accept, whether to differentiate between various ethnic groups, and whether to favor permanent immigration over migrant workers. The three dependent variables are:

- The number of immigrants accepted: "liberal policies" indicate a decision to accept more immigrants, while "restrictive policies" indicate a decision to accept fewer immigrants;
- Which immigrants to accept: "liberal policies" indicate a greater willingness to accept immigrants of dissimilar racial, ethnic, and cultural composition, while "restrictive policies" indicate a lesser willingness to accept such immigrants, instead favoring immigrants of similar composition.
- The decision of whether to favor permanent immigration over migrant workers.

In practice, the first two decisions are closely linked because (a) most immigration to Western societies during the past century and a half has been regarded as dissimilar;[17] and (b) countries tend to apply more liberal policies toward permanent similar immigration (see hypothesis 10). Consequently, policies with regard to the size of immigration, and those dealing with its composition, tend to converge, and the main decision most countries make is *how many immigrants of dissimilar composition to accept*. For example, according to hypothesis 2, immigration of dissimilar composition causes countries to restrict immigration in term of composition (i.e. to limit the number of dissimilar immigrants), which in turn decreases in the overall number of immigrants. According to hypotheses 6 and 7, considerations of foreign policy and general liberal attitudes cause countries to liberalize immigration policy in terms of composition, which in turn increases the number of immigrants. At the same time, recessions have led countries to limit the number of immigrants, which in practice mainly affected dissimilar immigrants, thus influencing the composition of immigration.

The Socioeconomic and Foreign Policy Factors Shaping Immigration Control Policy

I argue that immigration control policy is determined by five factors: the state of the economy, the volume of immigration of dissimilar composition, wars, foreign policy considerations, and ideological cycles. Policies on different types of immigration are influenced by these factors to varying degrees, a topic which is dealt with in the section that follows.

Hypothesis 1 Recessions cause countries to accept fewer immigrants (i.e. to restrict immigration), while economic prosperity causes them to accept more immigrants (i.e. to liberalize immigration control policy).

The state of the economy influences immigration policy through the interest group channel, and, under certain circumstances, also through the partisan channel. In times of economic decline, when people are unemployed or earn lower wages, pressures to restrict immigration mount. Workers view the immigrants as competitors for scarce employment opportunities and as the cause for stagnant or declining wages because immigration expands the supply of labor. The worse the state of the economy, the more workers will invest resources in fighting immigration. The employers, who face a reservoir of workers willing to work for lower wages, limit their investment in immigration advocacy because the marginal utility of such an effort declines. The government, whose aim is to maximize votes, as well as support from interest groups, faces growing pressures for restrictions on immigration on the part of the workers, and declining pressures for immigration liberalization on the part of the employers. Consequently, it restricts immigration. In contrast, during economic prosperity, employers are desperate for additional manpower, and they invest resources in promoting liberal immigration policies. The workers in low-paying jobs limit their opposition to immigration because the inflow of immigrants into these jobs allows them to climb the social and professional ladder. The government, faced with pressures for additional migrants on the part of the employers, liberalizes immigration policy.

The state of the economy sometimes also influences immigration policy through the partisan channel. Economic crises produce dissatisfaction with government policies and increase the support for extremist parties, including (but not restricted to) anti-immigration parties. The latter especially benefit from such protest voting during periods of large dissimilar immigration.

The state of the economy, and in particular the state of the labor market, will be measured in this study in terms of the annual unemployment rate.

Hypothesis 2 Large-scale immigration of dissimilar racial or ethnic composition contributes to restrictions on immigration (in terms of size and composition of immigration).

The second important factor contributing to restrictions on immigration is opposition to large-scale immigration of dissimilar racial/ethnic/cultural composition (when compared to the racial/ethnic/cultural composition of the receiving society or of its dominant element).[18] This hypothesis relates to culture-based theories, which see racism as a response to what is strange and unfamiliar, and as challenges to the racial status quo in the society. Studies have demonstrated that the native population tends to judge immigrants according to the degree to which they diverge from the dominant norm according to racial, ethnic, and cultural terms. In the United States, for example, the dominant norm has been WASP, leading to a preference ordering: Anglo, Germans, Slavs, Southern Europeans (French, Italians, and Spaniards), Jews, Latinos and Asians, African.[19] The WASP norm was also dominant in Australia, New Zealand, and the British part of Canada, producing a similar racial/ethnic/cultural ordering in these countries. Several scholars add that a process of cultural coding and racial prejudice developed during the era of imperialism in order to legitimize inequality, and later encompassed nonwhite immigration.[20] And Zolberg contends that receiving countries reject groups who are thought to jeopardize national integration and regime maintenance, although he also recognizes the influence of aggregate individual prejudice.[21]

The volume of immigration also relates to competition-based theories, because the greater the volume of immigration (especially during recessions), the greater will be the competition between the native-born and the immigrants for scarce resources. In addition, while culture-based theories tend to depict racism as a spontaneous response to what is strange, it can also be depicted in more rational-choice terms of competition. The founders and core supporters of anti-immigration movements are mainly a segment of the majority ethnic group, which expects to lose some of its social, cultural, and political prominence to the new ethnic groups. In the United States, for instance, the leaders and followers of anti-immigration movements were usually Protestants who feared

Catholic and Jewish immigration, and the founders of the 1890s nativist movement were from rich Protestant families in the Northeast. The anxiety felt by the supporters of anti-immigration groups with regard to the political impact of immigration has also led some of these groups to demand restrictions on the political and naturalization rights of foreigners. In other cases, founders of anti-immigration movements are political entrepreneurs, who act according to their self-interest while exploiting more spontaneous xenophobic feelings of the public.

The size of immigration will be measured in this study according to the annual number of aliens admitted for legal permanent residence as a percentage of the local population.

Hypothesis 3 Wars facilitate the establishment of migrant worker programs.

Hypothesis 4 Wars, external threats, and domestic threats linked to external sources foster a tendency to associate dissimilar immigrants with external threats and contribute to restrictions on permanent dissimilar immigration (in terms of size and composition of immigration).

Hypothesis 5 Wars and external threats contribute to the encouragement of permanent immigration of similar composition.

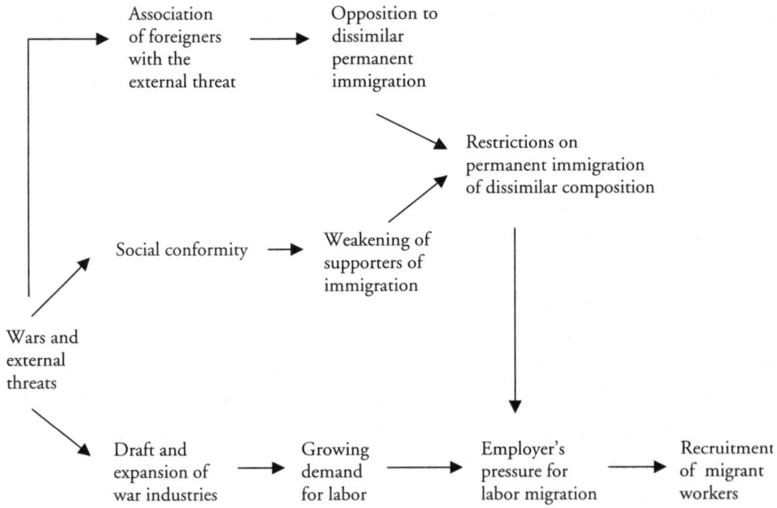

Figure 1.1 The dual impact of wars on immigration policy

Wars and external threats have a dual impact on immigration control policy (described in figure 1.1). On the one hand, wars, external threats, and domestic threats linked to external sources cause the countries of destination to associate dissimilar immigrants with external threats, and consequently to restrict permanent immigration of dissimilar composition. Such threats also contribute to social conformity, which weakens the supporters of dissimilar immigration and facilitates the passage of anti-immigration measures. Finally, wars sometimes cause countries that feel demographically inferior to their potential enemies, to encourage permanent immigration of similar origin.

On the other hand, wars facilitate the establishment of migrant worker programs in what can be termed "the war—migrant labor link." Wars produce demand for manpower because part of the labor force is mobilized and another part is employed in war industries.Consequently, employers pressure the government to approve the recruitment of migrant workers. In cases where permanent immigration is restricted, the impetus for recruitment of temporary migrant labor is especially strong. In the long run, the recruitment of temporary migrant workers produces an increase in permanent migration through "chain-migration."[22] Thus, wars produce conflicting outcomes: in the short run, they lead to restrictions on permanent immigration of dissimilar immigration; in the long run, they facilitate an increase in dissimilar permanent immigration.[23]

Hypothesis 6a Considerations of foreign policy tend to facilitate the liberalization of immigration control (in terms of size and composition of immigration).

Receiving countries tend to accept immigrants from specific countries in order to advance foreign policy goals, such as improving military and trade relations with allies, demonstrating opposition to adversaries, gaining international respectability, and sustaining political links that evolved in the past (usually during their colonial era). The impact of foreign policy considerations on immigration policies is particularly strong in countries that seek leadership status.

Hypothesis 6b Regional integration schemes are likely to influence the immigration control policies of their member states in several ways:

(a) Regional integration liberalizes the policies of the member states toward immigration from the others.
(b) By facilitating free, or freer, movement of labor and people among the member states, regional integration decreases the degree of

control that states have over their own labor migration policies and their borders.

(c) Where free movement is achieved, regional integration contributes to harmonization between immigration control policies of the member states, and to the formation of a common "external immigration policy" toward immigrants from outside the region.

(d) This common external immigration policy is likely to be relatively restrictive.

Regional integration liberalizes, on the one hand, the immigration policies of the member states toward immigrants from member states. But on the other hand, it is likely to make external immigration policy more restrictive by pressuring the countries with relatively open external borders to restrict immigration from outside the region in order to prevent the immigrants from moving to other member states.

Hypothesis 7 General racist attitudes facilitate restrictions on permanent immigration of dissimilar composition, while general liberal attitudes promote the liberalization of immigration control policies.

Attitudes with regard to equality and minority rights, which change over time, influence immigration control policy toward permanent immigration of dissimilar composition. In particular, racist theories and terminology were prevalent in various Western societies prior to World War II, and facilitated the passage of restrictions on dissimilar immigration, which were based on ethnic selection criteria. The war against the Fascist powers, the impact of the Holocaust, and the civil rights movements of the 1960s–1970s delegitimized the use of overt racist terminology and policies, and produced the abolition of ethnically explicit selection criteria.

It should be noted that the influence of these attitudes is limited in three ways. First, the delegitimization of racist policies has caused receiving countries to virtually end ethnic-based selection systems. But it has not established the freedom of entry, and thus it has had only indirect influence on the number of immigrants accepted. Second, policymakers who come under domestic pressures to restrict immigration of dissimilar composition have found ways to do so without using overt racist terminology. Finally, the extent to which this aforementioned ideological cycle has an independent influence over immigration policies, one distinct from that of the economic cycle, migratory pressures, and foreign policy considerations, is an open question, one dealt with in chapter 6.

The Type of Immigration and the Influence of the Socioeconomic and Foreign Policy Factors

One of the main themes of this book is that that the type of immigration—that is permanent immigration, temporary labor migration, refugees and illegal immigration—determines the relative influence of the aforementioned socioeconomic and foreign policy factors on immigration control policy. More specifically, I argue:

Hypothesis 8 Labor migration policy is mainly determined by the state of the economy. It is also influenced by the "war–migrant labor link" and by foreign policy considerations (regarding the character of the program). Labor migration policy is influenced to a lesser degree by the volume and composition of immigration and by racist/liberal ideology.

The state of the economy is the main determinant of labor migration policy. Labor migration policy is administered by the government, which responds to pressures from economic interest groups. Alternatively, where the government loses control, it is *de facto* shaped by the employers. As noted in hypothesis 1, during recessions, workers will oppose immigration, while employers will limit their investment in immigration advocacy. During periods of prosperity, employers will recruit foreign workers and invest resources in promoting liberal immigration policies, while workers will limit their demands for restrictions on immigration. Thus, the state of the economy directly influences labor migration policy.

Wars also facilitate the establishment of migrant worker programs (see hypothesis 3). In contrast, foreign policy considerations rarely cause the establishment of migrant worker programs, but they influence the character of those programs: from which countries the workers will be recruited, and sometimes the nature of their employment. The impact of foreign policy considerations is facilitated by the fact that labor recruitment contracts are usually signed between the country of origin and the country of destination, or between companies and individuals with the approval of the respective governments.

The volume of dissimilar immigration and racist/liberal general attitudes has a limited influence on labor migration policy, for two reasons. First, countries of origin and those of destination often sign agreements for the recruitment of labor. In some of these cases the volume of immigration is predetermined by the policy, and is less likely to produce substantial opposition.[24] And second, unlike permanent immigrants—who are expected to become citizens, and thus influence the ethnic and political character of the receiving society—temporary migrant workers are *expected* to return to their country of origin and not have a lasting effect on the ethnic, cultural, and political character of the receiving society. Therefore, attitudes toward these immigrants are only influenced to a limited degree by their racial and ethnic characteristics, and by the prevailing liberal/racist ideology.

In two cases the volume of dissimilar immigration does influence policy with regard to migrant workers. First, when the state loses control over labor migration, it may attempt to *regulate* migration and enforce immigration and labor laws. But as long as the economy is thriving, and the demand for manpower surpasses the supply of local labor, the state is unlikely to *halt* the recruitment of migrant labor. Second, many "temporary migrant workers" eventually stay in the country of destination. As the permanency of their stay becomes evident, their racial/ethnic composition influences immigration policy to a greater degree.

Hypothesis 9 Immigration control policy with regards to permanent immigration of dissimilar composition is influenced by all five factors, in the following order of importance: the volume and composition of immigration, the state of the economy, racist/liberal general attitudes, wars and external threats, and considerations of foreign policy. The racist/liberal general attitudes influence the selection of immigrants, and consequently the numbers accepted.

In contrast to labor migration, permanent migrants settle in the country of destination, compete for social services, and influence the ethnic and political character of the receiving society. Their impact is especially notable when they are of a different racial, ethnic, or cultural background than the native population. Consequently, immigration control policy with regard to permanent dissimilar immigration is influenced first and foremost by the volume and composition of immigration (according to hypothesis 2).

In countries where permanent immigrants, rather than temporary migrant workers, are the main source of foreign labor—that is in settler societies—the state of the economy also influences immigration control policy (hypothesis 1).

According to hypothesis 4, wars, external threats, and domestic threats linked to external sources foster a tendency to associate dissimilar immigrants with external threats and contribute to restrictions on permanent dissimilar immigration.

According to hypotheses 6a and 6b, considerations of foreign policy tend to facilitate the liberalization of immigration policy with regard to permanent immigration of dissimilar composition. But multinational organizations, which remove obstacles to free movement, tend to contribute to restrictions on such immigration.

Finally, according to hypothesis 7, general racist attitudes facilitate restrictions on permanent immigration of dissimilar composition, while general liberal attitudes promote the liberalization of immigration control policies.

In terms of relative consistency and importance, the volume and composition of immigration has the most consistent impact on policy toward permanent immigration. The state of the economy also substantially influences immigration control policies in those countries where permanent immigration is the main source of labor. The impact of wars, external threats, domestic threats linked to external sources, and foreign policy considerations is weaker and less consistent than the previous two factors. Racist/liberal general attitudes influence the selection criteria of immigrants, and consequently the numbers accepted.

Hypothesis 10a Immigration control policy with regard to permanent similar immigration tends to be more liberal than the policy with regard to permanent dissimilar immigration.

Hypothesis 10b Wars and external threats may cause countries to encourage permanent immigration of similar origin. Neither large-scale immigration nor mild recessions are sufficient to produce restrictions on permanent immigration of similar composition. Doubts with regard to the degree of similarity between the immigrants and the dominant element of the receiving society, or, at times, severe depressions, are necessary in order to generate such restrictions.

In sharp contrast to dissimilar permanent immigration, permanent immigration of similar composition is usually welcomed by the receiving countries. There are several sub-categories in this context. First, people who hold the nationality of a country usually cannot be excluded.[24] Thus, former emigrants, who retained their citizenship, can reenter the country without restrictions. Second, descendants of former immigrants who wish to return are sometimes viewed as "repatriates," and are eligible to return with few or no restrictions. Finally, immigrants who share ethnic and cultural characteristics with the indigenous population face less animosity from that population than do dissimilar immigrants, and thus immigration control policy toward them tends to be more liberal. As a result, the volume of immigration, moderate changes in the state of the economy, general racist/liberal attitudes, and considerations of foreign policy have little impact on such immigration policy.[25]

Three factors that do, occasionally, influence policy with regard to permanent similar immigration are:

(a) Wars and external threats, which sometimes cause countries that feel demographically inferior to their potential enemies to encourage permanent immigration of similar origin (hypothesis 5).
(b) Severe depressions, which contribute to restrictions on permanent immigration of similar origin. These restrictions are usually implemented by use of administrative means rather than by the enactment of legislation.
(c) Doubts with regard to the degree of similarity between the immigrants and the dominant element of receiving society contribute to restrictions on such permanent immigration.

Hypothesis 11 Refugee policy is mainly influenced by foreign policy considerations. It is influenced to a lesser degree by the volume of immigration, the state of the economy, wars and external treats, and by racist/liberal general attitudes.

Refugee policy is influenced first and foremost by foreign policy considerations. Receiving countries accept refugees in order to (a) demonstrate their opposition to the regimes of the countries of origin or to a third country that occupies the countries of origin; (b) demonstrate their sense of responsibility toward former allies; (c) demonstrate their cooperation with current allies; or (d) gain international respectability.

In contrast to regular/non-refugee immigrants, where a global regime does not exist, the refugee regime does influence international norms and country immigration policies to some degree.[26] But its influence is limited. The norms of the international refugee regime do not compel countries to accept permanent residents. Most scholars of international law agree that the right of asylum refers to the right of each country to grant asylum, and that states are not under an obligation to grant refugee status—the obligation is only to consider a person's claim for protection.[27] The main norm widely accepted is that of non-refoulment, where a country is prohibited from forcibly returning the refugee to a country of persecution. The conventional interpretation is that a refugee has the right for temporary asylum pending resettlement, if nonadmission is tantamount to surrender to the country of persecution.[28] This means that no economic or political rights are conferred on the refugee beyond providing for his basic needs as a temporary resident. The difference between the right for asylum and that of non-refoulement is demonstrated by a phenomenon known as "refugees in orbit," where a country returns an asylum seeker from its territory to a state other than that of his nationality, which in turn returns him whence he came or sends him on to another state. In addition, Hartigan's analysis of a case where the UN was instrumental in pressuring Mexico and Honduras into accepting refugees for temporary settlement reveals that it did so by influencing the short-term self-interest of the receiving countries rather than appealing to international norms based on long-term interests.[29]

Beyond their refugee status, refugees resemble non-refugee permanent immigrants because they are expected to remain for long periods of time or even permanently in the country of destination, receive social services, and potentially influence the ethnic, cultural, and political character of the receiving society. In addition, and with the exception of Germany and Israel, most post–World War II refugees to the West have been of dissimilar composition. Therefore, the factors specified here influence refugee policy in a similar manner to the way they influence policy toward permanent dissimilar immigration. But the influence of these factors on refugee policy is frequently weaker than in the case of non-refugee permanent immigrants because domestic opposition to refugees is mitigated by foreign policy considerations, and in particular by the linkage made between the immigration of refugees and security interests of the state. Racist general attitudes have influenced refugee policy, although their exact impact is somewhat harder to estimate because the current refugee regime was created after World War II.

Asylum seekers wait for a decision on their application, and thus their status—both in theoretical terms and in practice—is somewhat ambiguous. In most countries of destination, the majority of asylum seekers of dissimilar composition are judged to be "economic" immigrants rather than *bona fide* political refugees, and their claims for asylum are rejected. Yet many of them do stay in the country of destination either legally or illegally. Thus, asylum seekers fall in-between the aforementioned categories of permanent immigrants of dissimilar composition and refugees.[30] As permanent immigrants of dissimilar composition, the model expects policy to be influenced first and foremost by the volume and composition of immigration. But the decision of whether to define them as refugees is also influenced by foreign policy considerations.

In fact, much of the influence of the various explanatory factors on refugee policy is brought to bear at an early stage, when deciding on whether to define the asylum seekers as refugees. Frequently, defining the asylum seekers as refugees indicates that considerations of foreign policy have been more influential than have been racist attitudes and the dissimilar composition of immigration, and that pressures by the executive and by pro-immigration ethnic groups to liberalize immigration control policy have overcome domestic pressures to restrict it.

The hypotheses of the theory are summarized in table 1.1:

— A higher value for the "type of immigration control policy" (the dependent variable) denotes a more liberal policy.
— Higher values for the independent variables denote: economic prosperity, a larger volume of immigration of dissimilar composition, an involvement in wars, the influence of foreign policy considerations, and general liberal attitudes.
— A plus sign denotes that an increase in the independent/explanatory variable produces a liberalization of immigration control policy. A minus sign denotes that an increase in the independent/explanatory variable produces restrictions on immigration.
— "Strong" versus "weak" denotes the relative influence of each socioeconomic and foreign policy factor on each type of immigration control policy.[31]

Social Conflicts and Industrial Unrest

Two partially overlapping factors that the theory rejects are social conflicts and industrial unrest. The "national identity" approach explains the timing of immigration control policies on the basis of social conflicts and debates over national identity. Higham and Jones, in particular, argue that social cleavages, social unrest, and industrial unrest within American society fostered fears of losing national identity and of a national breakdown. This, in turn, produced nationalism and nativism (xenophobia).

Social conflicts are hard to define, which is one of my criticisms of the "national identity" approach. Industrial unrest will be measured according to the number of workers involved in strikes as a percentage of employed workers. But this argument suffers, in my opinion, from another difficulty. When large numbers of local workers are involved in strikes, employers are likely to recruit foreign workers in order to break the unity among local ones.

It should be noted that this argument, which I reject, does not focus on conflicts between the native population and the immigrants as the cause of restrictions, but rather on social cleavages within the receiving society—for example the Civil War and the class cleavage of 1886–1896 in the United States. In contrast, I accept the argument that a substantial involvement of immigrants in industrial unrest might contribute to

Table 1.1 The socioeconomic and foreign policy factors influencing immigration policy

Type of immigration control policy	*Relative influence of the explanatory factors*				
	The state of the economy	*Volume of immigration of dissimilar composition*	*Wars the country is involved in and external threats*	*Foreign policy*	*Liberal/racist general attitudes*
Labor migration policy	Strong (+)	Weak (–)	Strong (+): the war–migrant worker link	Relatively weak with regards to the initiation of programs; stronger with regards to which countries of origin, the nature of employment, and labor mobility in regional organizations	Weak (+)
Policy on permanent dissimilar immigration	Strong (+) in countries where permanent immigrants are the main source of foreign labor, weaker in others	Strong (–)	(–) with regard to migrants associated with external threats	Weaker (+)	Strong (+) with regard to the composition of immigration, consequently influencing its size
Refugee policy	(+) but weaker than in the case of regular permanent dissimilar immigration	(–) but weaker than in the case of regular permanent dissimilar immigration	Wars produce refugees but sometimes hinder international migration; (–) with regard to migrants associated with external threats	Strong (+)	(+)
Policy on permanent similar immigration	(+) only severe depression	Doubts with regard to degree of similarity influence policy	Strong (+) in some cases where countries feel demographically inferior to potential enemies	Weak	Weak

restrictions on immigration. Castles and Kosak, for example, argue that the leading role of migrant workers in the 1973 strikes in Germany contributed to the ban on the entry of migrant workers.[34] I find this argument more compelling because (a) immigrant militancy frightens the employers; (b) in some cases it is perceived as a domestic threat linked to external sources (hypotheses 4); and (c) migrant involvement in strikes highlights the issue of immigration, and focuses public attention on the increasing permanency of the migrants.

Illegal (Undocumented) Immigration

Policy on illegal immigration is a complex issue, which is not analyzed in this book. But based on a theoretical comparison to other types of immigration policy, I offer the following arguments, which should be explored further.

The fact that illegal/undocumented immigration is prohibited, does not mean that there is no variation in immigration control policy. In this case, rather than dealing with how many immigrants to accept, policy deals with how many resources should be allocated in order to prevent such immigration, what means should be used in order to prevent illegal immigration, whether to grant amnesty to the immigrants, and whether to grant or to deny them social services.

In addition, illegal immigration undermines the sovereignty of the state, which contributes to restrictions. But countries do not always invest heavily in stopping such migration. The inclination of the country of destination to block illegal immigration depends on the aforementioned factors, such as the state of the economy, the composition of immigration, and external threats.

Illegal immigration has some characteristics of permanent immigration, and others of labor migration. The relative influence of the socioeconomic factors on policy with regard to illegal immigration depends, in part, on the presumed permanency of that immigration. If the immigrants are expected to stay in the country, and in the long term become citizens, the composition of immigration and the ideology factors are likely to influence policy—as they do when permanent immigration is concerned. If, on the other hand, the illegal immigrants are expected to return to their country of origin, the composition of immigration and the ideology factors are less likely to influence policy—as is the case with labor migration policy. Where illegal immigration is composed of families, their usage of social services falls between that of permanent immigration and labor migration. On the one hand, the families consume more social services (education, health care, etc.) than do unmarried migrant workers. On the other hand, illegal immigrants might not be eligible for certain social services that are available to legal migrant workers.

External threats are likely to influence policies with regard to illegal immigrants, particularly when the government fears that people representing these threats (e.g. terrorists or spies) will infiltrate the country as illegal immigrants. In contrast, considerations of foreign policy are unlikely to substantially influence the basic components of immigration control policy: the decisions of how many resources should be allocated in order to prevent such immigration, and of whether to grant an amnesty to the immigrants. This is because the countries of origin would find it hard to justify illegal immigration. But considerations of foreign policy might influence the implementation of policies, as the countries of origin ask for the humane treatment of the immigrants. Considerations of foreign policy may also contribute to the legalization of undocumented immigration by replacing it with a labor migration program.

Global Patterns in Immigration Policies

The following three hypotheses attempt to explain the similarities and differences among immigration policies of the major receiving countries. The hypotheses are elaborated and tested in chapter 6.

Hypothesis 12 There has been an extraordinary similarity between the immigration policies of the major receiving countries for over a century.

Hypothesis 13 The interdependence between socioeconomic and foreign policy factors that lead to immigration policies explains this similarity in immigration policies of the major receiving countries. This explanation is superior to alternative explanations, including (a) a global hegemon that forces or persuades various countries to act in unison; (b) global or regional migration regimes and organizations; (c) interdependence between the immigration policies of various countries; (d) the emulation of immigration policies of one country by others; and (e) the world system approach.

Hypothesis 14 Structural factors of each country and its preference for permanent or temporary immigration, both of which are relatively stable, produce the differences between immigration policies at any given time.

In order to clarify the focus of the study, several parameters should be noted. First, the study focuses on immigration control (i.e. the rules and procedures governing the selection and admission of foreign citizens) rather than on immigrant policy or immigrant integration (i.e. the conditions provided to resident immigrants).[35] Second, it only examines policies of receiving countries, not those of sending countries. Third, it only explores the policies of the United States, Britain, Germany, and the Netherlands. While these countries have accepted the majority of immigration to industrialized countries during the past century, further studies are required in order to determine the degree to which the processes described here also fit other societies, in particularly non-Western ones. Fourth, the study only deals with immigration policies, not with the consequences of these policies (which at times differ from the original intent), or with the motives of the migrants themselves. Fifth, the analysis is based on the UN categorization of immigration into four types: permanent immigration, labor migration, illegal migration, and refugees.[36] The term "permanent immigrants" denotes those immigrants who are accepted at the country of destination as settlers and eventual citizens. In contrast, the term "migrant labor" or "temporary migrant workers" indicates those who are supposed to work in the country of destination for a limited period and then return to their country of origin. In practice, the distinction is an oversimplification. Many "temporary migrant workers" stay in the country of destination, while many "permanent immigrants" end up returning to their country of origin. Thus, the two terms refer only to the original intention and perception of the country of destination with regard to the immigrants.[37]

Finally, most chapters of this book explain variations in immigration control policy *over time*. Only in chapter 6 do I discuss global patterns in immigration policy, and explain the similarities and differences between immigration control policies of *various countries at any given time*. The structural factors causing the differences between immigration control policies of various countries at any given time—population density, geopolitical position, and economic structure—are relatively stable in any given country over time. Thus, I refer throughout the book (with the exception of chapter 6) to the type of immigration and to the socioeconomic and foreign policy factors (which, in fact, are influenced by the structural factors) as independent variables rather than as intervening ones.

CHAPTER 2

Immigration Policies of the United States

During the past two centuries, the United States has admitted more immigrants than any other country. In accordance with the theory advanced here, policies on different types of immigrants were influenced by socioeconomic and foreign policy factors to various degrees. Labor migration policy—regularizing the recruitment of Chinese and European migrant workers in the nineteenth century, and of Mexican and Central American migrant workers in the twentieth century—was mostly influenced by the economic factor and by the "war–migrant labor link." Refugee policy was primarily shaped by foreign policy considerations, and to a lesser degree by other factors. Policy on illegal immigrants was chiefly influenced by the economic factor and by the volume of illegal immigration, and to a lesser extent by the other factors. Policy on permanent immigration was shaped by the state of the economy, large-scale immigration of dissimilar composition, wars, foreign policy considerations, and liberal/racist ideological trends.

LeMay divides American immigration policy into four phases, labeled the "Open-Door Era," the "Door-Ajar Era," the "Pet-Door Era," and the "Dutch-Door Era."[1] During the "Open-Door Era," between 1820 and 1880, there were virtually no restrictions on immigration. The "Door-Ajar Era," from 1880 to 1920, saw the beginnings of restrictions, even while the door was still open to most would-be immigrants. During the "Pet-Door Era," from 1920 to 1950, the national origins quota system formed the basis of American immigration policy, and a restrictive approach allowed only a favored few to enter. Finally, during the "Dutch-Door Era," since 1950 (or 1965 according to other students of U.S. immigration history), the United States has allowed total immigration to increase, but favored certain categories of immigrants. The analysis here mostly follows that division, although it also elaborates on the post-1945 and post-1965 changes in U.S. immigration policy.

U.S. Immigration Policy Prior to the 1840s

Prior to the 1840s, the United States welcomed newcomers to its shores almost unequivocally. In 1783, George Washington proclaimed America's open-door policy. In 1841, President John Tyler, after referring to America's vast resources of unoccupied or under-populated land, invited people from other countries to "come and settle among us as members of our rapidly growing family."[2] An exception to this generally liberal policy was the restrictions on immigration and naturalization implemented during the 1790s. They were chiefly in response to the French revolution and fears of French agents introducing radical ideas.[3] In 1790, Congress passed the first Naturalization Act, requiring a two-year period of residency and the renunciation of former allegiances. In 1795 a second naturalization act increased the period of residency to five years. In 1798, Congress passed the Alien and Sedition Acts, giving the President powers to expel aliens who posed a danger to national security or who were suspected of subversive activities, and raising the residency period to 14 years. The Alien and Sedition Act applied for only two years, and was not renewed at the end of that period. Moreover, during the term of the act, President John Adams appears to have made little or no use of the power granted to him.

The restrictions of the 1790s were limited to a specific group of immigrants who were associated with an external threat. The 1796–1798 economic recession may have also facilitated the passage of the 1798 Aliens and Sedition Acts. But overall, the United States did not significantly restrict immigration between 1776 and 1850. The need for immigrants to settle the South and the Midwest, to construct the railroads, and to defend the country overshadowed any temporary economic downturns. The similarity between the composition of immigration—most immigrants were English or of other Western European origins—and of the local population also contributed to the absence of substantial restrictions on immigration during that period.

U.S. Immigration Policy, 1840s–1874

The first major anti-immigration movements emerged in the 1840s and 1850s. Anti-Irish and anti-German sentiment sprung up in the mid-1840s and reached its peak between 1855 and 1860. The leading nativist movement during that period was the "Know Nothing," or the American Party, whose membership was limited to native-born Protestant Americans. In 1855, the American Party gained 8 percent of seats in the Senate and 18.4 percent of those in the House; in 1856 it lost seats in the House while keeping its share in the Senate; in 1858 it lost in the Senate but gained in the House; and in 1861 it gained 14 percent of the Senators elected in the North and 15.9 percent of the Representatives elected in the North.

The second anti-immigration movement to emerge in the 1850s targeted the Chinese and was centered in California. Chinese immigration to the West Coast surged after the discovery of gold in California in 1848–1849 and met the need for labor to build the railroads. The Chinese—immigrants of dissimilar racial composition—constituted only a small part of total immigration to the United States. But their presence was felt in the lightly populated West Coast, were they comprised between 10.4 and 17.3 percent of the California population. Throughout the 1850s and 1860s, the Chinese in California encountered mob violence as well as discriminatory laws imposed by the California legislature. Already in 1849, a Know-Nothing judge serving on California's Supreme Court ruled that the Chinese were forbidden to testify against white people. In 1855 the California legislature passed a Foreign Miners Tax. And in 1867, the Democratic Party won the California elections by running on an anti-Chinese platform.[4] But the West Coast anti-Chinese movement only led to federal restrictions in the mid-1870s.

The anti-immigration sentiment of the 1850s, particularly that aimed at the German and Irish, was produced by a combination of factors, including: (a) a surge in immigration of dissimilar racial and religious composition; (b) the association of immigrants with external threats and foreign radicalism; and (c) a weak economy. Between 1846 and 1857, annual immigration to the United States was between 0.7 and 1.6 percent of the American population, an all-time high (percentage-wise). The composition of immigration became predominantly Irish and German, and often Catholic. Moreover, some of these immigrants were associated with external threats, although the accusations against them may partially have been a pretense for ethnic or religious-based xenophobia. The Irish belonged to the Catholic Church, an old nemesis of the English Protestants in the United States. In an earlier period the Catholic church was identified with rival Catholic powers, such as Spain and France. Later, it was argued that Catholic traditions clashed with the concept of individual freedom.[5] Some of the German immigrants were associated with the 1848 radicalism in Europe. According to Jones, the suspicions of the nativists were intensified by the prevalence of foreign nationalistic organizations, membership in which implied a divided allegiance and perhaps involvement in revolutionary activity.[6] The growing immigrant population with voting rights seemed to threaten the American political structure and the political balance of power. The Irish gained leadership positions in the Democratic Party in the Northeast. They were blamed for encouraging immigrants to vote as a block and for vote fraud. The Germans were instrumental in establishing the Republican Party, and played an important role in liberal groups and in the abolitionist movement. Both the Irish and Germans were active in the labor movement.

The third factor that contributed to the restrictionist movement was the weak economy. The United States experienced economic recessions in 1854–1855 and 1857–1858, the years when the Know Nothing group had its greatest success. In comparison, the Know Nothing's representation in Congress declined in 1856, when the economy revived.

The Civil War led to the encouragement of immigration. The war was a domestic conflict that did not suggest an association between immigrants and an external threat, and thus did not lead to restrictions on immigration. At the same time, in what is termed here the "war–migrant labor link," the war generated demand for immigrants to work in the war industries and agriculture, and to replace workers who were mobilized. During the 1860s, the per capita GNP of the north grew tenfold, and the number of factories increased by 80 percent. President Lincoln stated in 1863, "there is still a great deficiency of laborers in every field of industry, especially in agriculture and our mines, as well as of iron and coal."[7] The following year he added: "I regard our immigrants as one of the principal replenishing streams which are appointed by Providence to repair the ravages of internal war."[8] The economic expansion continued after the war. The discovery of natural resources such as oil and coal, together with the Homestead Law of 1862, facilitated the westward movement and created a demand for labor to work in the mines and on the railroads. Immigration, including temporary labor migration, was encouraged during this period, both by the federal government and by the states. The Contract Labor Act of 1864 authorized employers to contract for the services of prospective migrants and to pay for their passage. In addition to the prosperous economy, the similar composition of immigration—most immigrants arriving between 1863 and 1873 were British and Scandinavian—contributed to the positive attitudes toward the newcomers.

U.S. Immigration Policy, 1875–1916

The United States started to move toward the "Door-Ajar" approach in the 1870s. A surge in Chinese immigration to the West Coast led to an anti-Chinese movement, which successfully promoted restrictive laws in California and other western states during the 1860s and 1870s. The nation-wide economic depression between 1873 and 1877/1878, and again between 1882 and 1885, coupled with peaks in immigration in 1873 and 1881–1882, facilitated the passage of restrictive legislation at the federal level. In 1875, Congress passed the first restriction, prohibiting the immigration of Chinese women for the purpose of prostitution and of convicts. In 1879, the House and Senate passed a bill limiting Chinese immigration, but President Hayes vetoed it. In 1882, the Chinese Exclusion Act suspended the entry of Chinese workers for ten years, barred all foreign-born Chinese from acquiring citizenship, excluded convicts, lunatics, idiots, and persons likely to become public charges, and placed a head tax on immigrants. In 1885, Congress approved the Foran Act, which prohibited the admission of contract laborers. Two years later the Payson Act was passed, prohibiting aliens from acquiring or holding land. The same year, the American Protective Association—an anti-Catholic nativist group—was formed. The Chinese Exclusion Act and the Contract Labor Act were amended several times between 1887 and 1893.

While a weak economy and increasing immigration (especially Chinese) led to restrictions on immigration, foreign policy considerations delayed the implementation of these restrictions. The executive attempted to block, or ameliorate, restrictions on Chinese, but in most cases only succeeded in delaying rather than eliminating the restrictions. In February 1876, the Senate received a resolution of the California legislature calling for a revision of treaties with China. Between February and May 1876, Senator Sargent and Representative Page—both from California—submitted resolutions that the president should renegotiate the treaty with China in order to allow for restrictions on Chinese immigration.[9] Neither of these resolutions passed Congress, and President Grant did not act on this matter. In 1878, Senator Sargent of California called on President Hayes to change the international treaties in order to prevent Chinese immigration to the United States, but to no avail. In January–February 1879, both houses passed a bill to restrict the number of Chinese passengers on board American vessels headed for the United States, a bill which was then vetoed by President Hayes. In 1881, President Arthur asked Congress to take into account the interests and susceptibilities of the Chinese government in any modification of the immigration laws. In April 1882, Arthur vetoed a Chinese exclusion bill because he saw it as a repudiation the Burlingham Treaty obligations and as contrary to good foreign policy. And in 1888, the Committee on Foreign Affairs opposed a bill to repeal the Chinese Exclusion Act because of a pending treaty with China.[10]

The "Door-Ajar" policy gained momentum after 1890. Restrictions and attempts to impose restrictions were the product of a fluctuating economy, the highest level of immigration in U.S. history (until the 1980s), a dramatic change in the composition of immigration, and, in some cases, an association of immigrants with external threats. The United States experienced unemployment of more than 5 percent between 1891 and 1899, in 1904, from 1908 to 1911, and from 1914 to 1916. Over one million immigrants per annum arrived between 1905 and 1907, in 1910, and in 1913–1914, which equaled over 1 percent of U.S. population. But the major reason for the growing opposition to immigration was its composition. Whereas the majority of the "old" immigrants came from Western Europe, most of the "new" immigrants came from Eastern and Southern Europe. The British, Scandinavian, and German immigrants, most of them Protestant, were replaced by Russian, Polish, Austo-Hungarian, and Italian immigrants, the majority of whom were Greek-Orthodox, Catholic or Jewish. The cultural impact of the "new" immigrants was intensified by their large number, which enabled them to preserve their cultural and social identities within the ethnic enclaves of the big cities.[11] The turning point in the composition of immigration to the United States occurred in 1897, when, for the first time, "new" immigrants from Southern and Eastern Europe outnumbered the "old" immigrants. The share of the "new" immigrants among America's foreign-born population grew from 1 percent in 1860 to over 38 percent in 1910.

The recessions and large immigration of dissimilar composition led to restrictions on specific groups of immigrants. The Immigration Act 1891 excluded people likely to become public charges, those suffering from different diseases, and polygamists. It also prohibited advertisements that encourage immigration and authorized the deportation of illegal immigrants. The acts of 1892 and 1893 extended the Chinese Exclusion Act and the Contract Labor Act. The 1893 act also gave the president the power to prohibit immigration from countries with cholera and other infectious diseases. In 1894 Congress increased the authority of the Treasury Department by making its decisions final, thereby preventing Chinese immigrants from seeking redress through the courts. The Immigration Act of 1903 excluded anarchists, saboteurs, epileptics, and professional beggars and reaffirmed the contract labor law. In 1907, an economic recession and a surge in Japanese immigration to the West Coast led to the signing of a "Gentlemen's Agreement" between the United States and Japan, which restricted Japanese immigration.[12]

But the most important aspect of American immigration policy between 1893 and 1916 was the unsuccessful attempt to block immigration from Eastern and Southern Europe. Exclusion efforts were based on the perceived characteristics of the new immigrants, such as their poverty and higher illiteracy rate, rather than on a blunt ethnic-based quota. One such measure was the exclusion of immigrants who were likely to become public charges. Another measure increased the head tax. The third was the literacy test, which required prospective immigrants to read and write a short passage. Senator Henry Cabot Lodge asserted that the literacy test would bear "most heavily on Italians, Russians, Poles, Hungarians, Greeks, and Asians, only lightly on the English-speaking peoples, Germans, Scandinavians, and French." He added that the test was aimed at "races whose traditions and inheritances, whose thoughts and whose beliefs are wholly alien to ours."[13] Literacy test bills passed one or both Houses of Congress in 1895–1898, 1907, and 1912–1916, but were blocked either by the other House or by a presidential veto.

An association of immigrants with external threats facilitated restrictive immigration policies. Japan's victory over Russia generated anxiety about a possible Japanese threat, which combined with growing Japanese immigration, produced the 1907 "Gentlemen's Agreement." Fears of European radicalism—following President Mckinley's assassination by a European anarchist—contributed to the 1903 Immigration Act. In contrast, foreign policy considerations mitigated these restrictions: the "Gentlemen's Agreement" between the United States and Japan prevented a blatant act restricting Japanese immigration; citizens of Mexico, Cuba, and Canada were exempted from increases in the head tax; two of President McKinley's messages to Congress deplored outbreaks of mob violence against foreigners and recommended legislation for the protection of foreigners; and several members of the Industrial Commission stated that the Chinese Exclusion Act should be carefully adjusted in order "not to seriously interfere with commerce with China."[14]

U.S. Immigration Policy, 1917–1941

The shift toward the more restrictive "Pet-Door Era" started in 1917, when, after numerous futile attempts, Congress finally passed the literacy test bill over President Wilson's veto.[15] In addition to the literacy test, the Immigration Act of 1917 also excluded immigrants from an "Asiatic barred zone," added excludable classes, raised the head tax, and introduced the power to deport aliens convicted of certain offenses. The following year, immigration acts authorized the president to control the immigration of persons whose presence was deemed contrary to public safety in time of war or national emergency, and required U.S. citizens to carry a valid passport in order to enter or depart the United States. The 1918 acts also removed time limits on the deportability of anarchists and made the return of those deportees a felony. In 1919–1920, over five hundred aliens suspected of being radicals were deported to Russia during and after the "Palmer Raids." In 1920 the House passed a bill to suspend immigration for 14 months, but the bill died in a Senate committee. Finally, Congress passed the national origins quota acts of 1921 and 1924, which sharply curtailed immigration from Eastern and Southern Europe and halted Asian immigration. The act of 1921 limited the number of immigrants of each nationality to 3 percent of the number of foreign-born persons of that nationality living in the United States in 1910 and confined European immigration to 350,000 per annum. The 1924 act further limited the number of immigrants of each nationality to 2 percent of the number of foreign-born persons of that nationality living in the United States in 1890 and confined European immigration to 150,000 per annum.[16] In practice, the impact of the quota system was even greater because Western European immigrants did not fill their quota, while most potential immigrants from Eastern and Southern Europe were rejected.

Economic recessions (11.7 percent unemployment in 1921, 5 percent in 1924) and large-scale Eastern and Southern European immigration (a total of 805,000 immigrants in 1921 and 707,000 immigrants in 1924) facilitated the passage of the quota acts. Congressman Albert Johnson justified the quota bill by noting that immigration was increasing in volume and that a large percentage of the immigrants were Jews.[17] The use of an ethno-centric selection system revealed that the large dissimilar immigration caused the restrictions. In contrast, the state of the economy did not contribute to the passage of the 1917 literacy bill, as unemployment was relatively low during the war. Immigration, too, was low in 1917, but the supporters of the bill warned of renewed immigration from Eastern Europe once the war ended.

An association of European immigrants with external threats and imported subversion, especially in the context of World War I and the Bolshevik revolution, contributed to the passage of the literacy test and the quota acts. Between 1914 and 1917, prior to America's direct involvement in the war, German Americans campaigned for an embargo on the export of war supplies. Many Americans interpreted the agitation as an attempt to undermine the nation's neutrality. An outburst of anti-German feelings followed, with the *New York Times* describing the German Americans as "completely subservient to foreign influence and a foreign power."[18] The accusations against German Americans intensified after German agents were identified as responsible for sabotage in American industry and shipping. Rumors circulated about the disloyalty of German Americans and their activities against the American war effort. The war heightened the fear and suspicion of the American public toward aliens and naturalized citizens, especially those from enemy countries. During the war, the government arrested more than 1,200 German aliens, required aliens to register, and prohibited the employment of aliens and naturalized citizens in certain occupations.

The Bolshevik revolution in Russia and the peace agreement between Russia and Germany strengthened the association between foreigners, external threats, and subversion, and diverted xenophobia toward Eastern European immigrants. Radical activities in the United States—including the 1917–1918 strikes (led by the IWW) that targeted several industries vital to the war effort, the industrial unrest of 1919, the establishment of two communist parties, and the flourishing of radical newspapers inspired by the Bolshevik revolution—heightened the public's suspicion of radical movements and radical immigrants. The outcome of these feelings was the "Big Red Scare," the Palmer raids of 1919–1920, and restrictions on Eastern European immigration.

World War I and its aftermath brought a peak in nationalism and social conformity, which allowed for the suppression of dissenting voices and for restrictions that would not have been imposed in calmer times. This conformity found its expression in the "100 percent Americanism": "Above all, 100 per centers belligerently demanded universal conformity organized through total national loyalty . . . This new nationalism outlawed many kinds of deviation."[19] While growing immigration, economic recessions, and an association of immigrants with external threats generated support for the advocates of restrictions, social conformity and anti-German attitudes silenced groups that previously prevented restrictions on immigration, that is the liberals and the old immigrants from Germany and Ireland. The only pressure groups left to oppose restrictions on immigration were composed of immigrants from Southern and Eastern Europe, but they were too weak to succeed on their own.

Restrictions on permanent immigration reached a peak during and after World War I. However, wars also generate support for temporary migration, in what is termed here the "war–migrant labor link." World War I created a demand for additional manpower because part of the labor force was drafted, another part was employed in war industries, and the supply of permanent immigration dried out due to restrictions on permanent immigration and obstacles to travel. Between 1915 and 1918, unemployment dropped from 8.5 to 1.4 percent. Consequently, employers pressured the government to approve the recruitment of temporary migrant labor. Several months after passing the restrictive Immigration Act of 1917, Congress granted entry to temporary workers from the Western Hemisphere, that is Mexicans. The program was originally a response to pressures from agricultural employers in the Southwest, but was later extended to permit the employment of laborers in nonfarm work. The temporary-worker scheme ended in 1919/1921.[20] Hutchinson also notes that wartime labor shortages reversed the previous attitudes toward Chinese labor. Congress received a resolution from the Pasadena Board of Trade in favor of the importation of Chinese workers under suitable restrictions, and both Senate and House received resolutions to direct their committees on agriculture to look into the importation of Chinese farmers during the war.[21]

The Great Depression led to the broadening of the restrictions imposed by the 1921 and 1924 quota acts. European immigration was already limited by the absence of economic opportunities and by the quota acts. Therefore, further restrictions focused on Mexican and Filipino immigration, not regulated by the quota acts. In 1929, a bill aimed at restricting Mexican and Latin American immigration failed to pass Congress. The same year, the previously temporary national origins quota system was made permanent. In 1930 a bill applying quotas to Mexico passed the Senate, but was not reported out of a House committee. Two other bills, to suspend all immigration except for immediate family members of U.S. citizens and to restrict Filipino immigration failed to pass the Senate. Instead of formally restricting Mexican immigration through legislation, the government utilized administrative measures and legislation of a general character to limit Mexican immigration and deport Mexicans living in the United States. In 1929, consular officers began to enforce provisions of the Immigration Act of 1917, which effectively denied entry to most Mexicans applying for a visa. The same year, Congress passed a law making illegal entry a punishable crime. Between 1929 and 1937, the United States repatriated approximately 500,000 illegal Mexican immigrants.[22] In 1929–1930, repatriations of Mexicans were voluntary, while between 1931 and 1932/1933, local public and private welfare agencies organized large-scale repatriations of Mexicans.[23] In addition, the federal government used a campaign of threatened deportation to promote the departure of Mexicans. Repatriations continued until 1937, although on a smaller scale.

The deteriorating economy drove the U.S. government to restrict Mexican immigration and further limit European immigration. In 1930 President Hoover told Congress: "There is need for revision of our immigration laws upon a more limited and more selective basis, flexible to the needs of the country. Under conditions of current unemployment it is obvious that persons coming to the United States seeking work would likely become either direct or indirect public charges. As a temporary measure the officers issuing visas to immigrants have been . . . instructed to refuse visas to applicants likely to fall into this class."[24] Consequently, the State Department decided on a strict interpretation of the "public charge" clause with regard to applicants for visas. Within five months, it succeeded in cutting European immigration by 90 percent. The strict interpretation of the "public charge" clause by consular officers continued throughout the decade, causing immigration to exceed repatriation by only a small margin.[25]

During the 1930s, Congress also restricted the immigration of specific ethnic groups (e.g. Filipinos) and professional groups (e.g. traders and musicians). A compromise act, combining independence to the Philippines with restrictions on Filipino immigration, passed in 1933–1934. Between 1933 and 1939, attempts to allow for the entrance of Jewish refugees from Nazi Germany failed in Congress, and the few refugees who were accepted came under the national origins quota. Congress even defeated a refugee bill that would rescue 20,000 children from Nazi Germany, despite the willingness of American families to sponsor them.

During the 1917–1941 period, foreign policy considerations mediated or delayed restrictions on Western Hemisphere immigration; but domestic pressures for restrictions eventually prevailed. The Wilson administration managed to exclude Japan from the Asiatic "barred zone" created by the 1917 Immigration Act. But Japanese immigration to the United States was banned in 1924, and the secretary of state, who opposed that ban, stated, "our friends in the Senate spoiled years of effort in a few minutes and caused the U.S. unrepairable damage."[26] During the 1920s, Pan-Americanism and regional economic concerns prevented Congress from restricting Western Hemisphere immigration. Such immigration (especially from Mexico, Cuba, Canada, and Newfoundland) was exempted from an increased head tax, the quota acts of 1921 and 1924, and Health and "public charge" provisions. Later, during the Great Depression, the administration applied the "public charge" clause and other informal administrative procedures to curtail immigration from Mexico. But it did so in order to prevent formal anti-Mexican legislation that would damage the relations with that country. And there are strong indications that President Hoover would have voted the 1930 Harris Bill limiting Mexican immigration, if it passed Congress.[27]

U.S. Immigration Policy During World War II

World War II, like World War I, had a dual impact on immigration policy. On the one hand, the war increased conformity and anti-immigration sentiment, leading to some restrictions on freedom of expression, potential immigrants, and foreign-born citizens. On the other hand, the wartime need for manpower generated the recruitment of migrant workers.

During World War II, external threats to the United States produced a limited reemergence of nationalism, conformity, and anti-immigrant sentiment. After a short period of liberal legislation during the early New Deal, the war generated some restrictions on the freedom of expression, including: the Smith (sedition) Act; the granting of permission for wiretapping by federal officials; the Rapp-Coudert Committee on "subversives" in government; the 1942 amendment to the Foreign Agents Registration Act; and a few prosecutions under the Smith Act. However, as Dorsen notes: "During World War Two there was no repetition of the excesses of the World War One period. The nation remained relatively calm, and expression in opposition to the war was not suppressed."[28] Moreover, liberal decisions continued in the High Court throughout the war.

The main restriction on foreign-born citizens of the United States was the infamous evacuation of Americans of Japanese ancestry from the West Coast, and their detention in relocation centers. But immigration control restrictions were limited to the decisions to fingerprint and register arriving aliens (1940), allow consular officers to refuse visas to aliens who endangered the public safety (1941), and the addition of new groups subject to deportation (1943). According to the theory advanced here, restrictions on permanent immigration during World War II were less far-reaching than during World War I because of a weaker drive for conformity and limited dissimilar immigration prior to the war. Between 1932 and 1945 immigration to the United States ranged from 23,000 to 83,000 per annum in comparison to over one million immigrants per annum prior to World War I. Moreover, the share of Asian and Eastern and Southern European immigrants was much smaller prior to World War II.

The second consequence of the war was the recruitment of temporary migrant workers. The rapid mobilization and the expansion of war industries generated acute manpower shortages. Southwestern growers and other pressure groups pushed for the recruitment of temporary laborers. The administration responded to these demands by signing the 1942 Bracero agreement with the Mexican government, and similar agreements with several British possessions in the West Indies in 1943.[29] In addition, the United States employed German prisoners of war, some of whom were in prison camps whose location was determined by local demands for labor.

But the most important development during World War II was the growing influence of foreign policy considerations, which led to the liberalization of U.S. immigration policy. In 1943, Congress repealed the Chinese Exclusion Act and replaced it with a small quota. It did so, following a request by the administration, in order to counteract Japanese propaganda that emphasized America's racist policy toward its wartime ally. While the numerical impact of that change was minuscule, it signaled the growing influence of the executive, driven by foreign policy considerations, on immigration policy.[30]

U.S. Immigration Policy, 1945–1965

The three trends that emerged during World War II continued after the war. The first was the renewed emphasis on social conformity and restrictions on freedom of expression, combined with an association of foreigners with external threats and imported radicalism. The second was the growing demand for foreign labor, and the third was the expanded influence of foreign policy considerations on the liberalizing immigration policy. American immigration policy between World War II and 1965 allowed for greater immigration to the United States. The association of immigrants with the Soviet/communist threat produced restrictions, but these had a limited numerical effect. In contrast, economic and foreign policy considerations facilitated the acceptance of immigrants, many of whom came outside the framework of the quota system.

The first trend, which accelerated during the Cold War, included an increase in social conformity, restrictions on freedom of expression, and an association of foreigners with external threats and imported radicalism. The Soviet expansion in Eastern Europe, the outbreak of the Korean War, the detonation of the Soviet atom bomb, and the successful launching of "Sputnik" produced public anxiety over the Soviet threat. Fears of the external threat and of "imported" subversion reached a peak between 1950 and 1954, with the 1950 Internal Security Act, the 1953 Rosenberg and Sobell execution, the 1954 Communist Control Act, and "McCarthyism" between the 1951 and 1954. As during World War I, Cold War fears led to social conformity and to the silencing of dissenting opinions. Kairys notes: "In the 1950s . . . the judiciary essentially collapsed. Unpopular ideas and associations again became illegal, dissenters were jailed and lost jobs. The courts abdicated in the face of a reactionary media blitz."[31] The combination of social conformity and an association of subversion with foreign influences set the ground for restrictions on immigration. The 1950 Internal Security Act facilitated the exclusion and deportation of foreign subversives, and required aliens to report their addresses annually. The 1952 McCarran-Walter Act retained the tough national origins quota system, despite economic and foreign policy considerations that called for a liberalization of the system. The McCarran-Walter Act also included security provisions aimed at screening immigrants who were possible security risks. Finally, in 1954–1955, over one million people—most of them illegal Mexican immigrants—were deported under the quasi-military "Operation Wetback." The deportation of Mexican immigrants was not a direct outcome of the fear of communist subversion. However, I believe that it was related to the xenophobia of the time, and that such violations of civil liberties could only have been carried out because of the social conformity and the restrictions on the freedom of expression that characterized the Cold War period.

Despite the xenophobia, the U.S. government did not impose substantial restrictions on Eastern Hemisphere immigration (except regarding security provisions) for two reasons. First, immigration to the United States was still limited to one-seventh (as a share of American population) of its volume prior to the 1917–1924 restrictions. Second, the growing influence of foreign policy considerations, the demand for manpower and the impact of the horrors of World War II pushed immigration policies in the direction of liberalization.

The second postwar trend was the growing demand for foreign workers. The prosperous economy produced low unemployment rates and a shortage of manpower, especially in the agricultural sector. The Korean War made the problem more acute, and agricultural employers in the Southwest pressured the administration for the expanded recruitment of Mexican workers. In 1951, the number of migrant workers employed in the United States almost tripled from 76,525 to 203,640, and it increased to a peak of 459,850 in 1956.[32]

Foreign policy considerations also fostered the liberalization of immigration policy. Following World War II and the emergence of U.S. global hegemony, the focus of American foreign policy shifted toward the containment of communism. The United States started accepting refugees from communist countries, first from Eastern Europe and later from Cuba and South East Asia, as a symbol of its ideological commitment. That commitment was expressed by a representative of the U.S. Coordinator for Refugee Affairs, who stated that "ally responsiveness" obliges the United States to grant asylum only to ". . . people who come from fallen allied democratic regimes or who served as support troops in conflicts to preserve Western values."[33] The first President to respond to the refugee problem was President Truman, who in 1945 admitted Jewish refugees from Europe under a presidential directive. This initial directive was primarily a reaction to the impact of Holocaust horrors, but the legislation and directives that followed mainly concerned refugees from communism. Forty percent of the 1948 and 1951 Displaced Persons Acts quota was allocated to refugees whose homelands had been annexed by a foreign power. They included ethnic Germans, Poles, Russians, Greeks, Yugoslavians, Czechoslovakians, and refugees from the Baltic countries. In 1952, President Truman declared: "The countries of Eastern Europe have fallen under the Communist yoke . . . We do not need to be protected against immigrants from these countries; on the contrary, we want to stretch out a helping hand . . . to succor those who are brave enough to escape from barbarism, to welcome and restore them against the day when their countries will, as we hope, be free again."[34] President Eisenhower called on Congress, as part of American foreign policy, to revise U.S. immigration laws so as to make special provisions to admit escapees from behind the Iron Curtain. Congress enacted the Refugee Relief Act of 1953, which admitted over 200,000 refugees outside the existing quota, including German, Greek, and Yugoslavian refugees. Following the failed Hungarian revolution, President Eisenhower used the parole status to admit Hungarian refugees, and later Congress enacted the Hungarian Refugee Adjustment

Act to grant those refugees immigrant status.[35] President Eisenhower also used the parole status for Chinese arriving from Hong Kong. The Refugee-Escapee Act of 1957 reallocated unused immigrant visas for German expellees, Dutch refugees, and refugee-escapees from communist-dominated countries in the Middle East. In 1958 Congress passed the Azores and Netherlands Refugee Act, which granted admission to persons displaced as a result of the earthquake in the Azores and to nationals of the Netherlands displaced from Indonesia, following the Sukarno revolution there. Starting in 1961, Cuban refugees received parolee status, and they were then granted immigrant status by the Cuban Adjustment Act of 1966. The 1965 immigration act once again defined those fleeing communism as refugees.

Several elements characterize American refugee policy during the Cold War. First, the influence of the American executive on immigration policy increased substantially. While the majority of immigrants to the United States continued to come under the regular quota, presidential directives, as well as legislation on refugees that was fostered by the president, produced the most fluctuations in the number of immigrants admitted. Second, the influence of anticommunist ideology on immigration policies was common to all American presidents, regardless of their partisan affiliation. Third, the preference for refugees from communist countries went against the numerical and ethnic limitations of the 1920s national origins quota system, and contributed to the system's downfall. Fourth, while the executive played an active role in shaping American policy, it was mainly reacting to events in the global arena, that is to the defeat of anticommunist movements and to communist takeovers. Fifth, the preference for refugees from communist countries discriminated against refugees from other countries, including refugees from right-wing dictatorships such as Haiti. Finally, while American foreign and immigration policies moved toward a global perspective, the special status for Western Hemisphere countries was slow to disappear. Western Hemisphere immigration continued to be exempted from quota restrictions until 1965, because the executive opposed the imposition of a quota. In 1976, When Congress finally set a quota of 20,000 on immigration for Mexico, it was in the face of opposition from President Ford.[36]

In addition to increasing the number of immigrants admitted, the United States also broadened the ethnic composition of immigration. This was for two reasons. First, the Holocaust, the conflict between democracies and Fascist powers, and the civil rights movement delegitimized the use of racist or even ethnic-based terminology in immigration policy. Second, the shift in American foreign policy toward a global anti-communist perspective prompted the United States to offer asylum to Eastern European and Southeast Asian refugees, thereby undermining the national origins quota system.

The repeal of the Chinese Exclusion Act for reasons of foreign policy in 1943 signaled the first breakdown of the ethnic- and race-based quota system. Filipinos and Indians became eligible for admission to the United States in 1946. The impact of the Holocaust and of anticommunist ideology facilitated the admission of European Jews and Eastern European refugees under the Displaced Persons Act of 1948 and its 1951 amendment. The 1952 Walter-McCarran Act avoided much of the overt racial discrimination of the original quota system and annulled the exclusion of Asian-Pacific immigration, although in practice it granted only token quotas. During the debate over that act, the anti-restrictionist forces equated the quota system to Nazi Germany's racist philosophy.[37] The refugee acts of 1953, 1956–1957, and 1958, which admitted refugees from Eastern Germany, Hungary, and Indonesia, further contributed to the collapse of the ethnically explicit selection system. Finally, the national origins quota system was eliminated by the Nationality and Immigration Act of 1965, which was influenced by the civil rights movement. The national origins quota system was replaced by a new selection system, which gave preference to relatives of U.S. citizens and resident aliens, to professionals, scientists, artists, persons alleviating labor shortages, and to refugees from communist or certain Middle Eastern countries. The 1965 Act also: (a) set a limit of 170,000 immigrants per annum from the Eastern Hemisphere; (b) placed a limit of 120,000 immigrants per annum from the Western Hemisphere, which was to take effect after June 30, 1968; (c) set a limit of 20,000 immigrants from any single foreign state in the Eastern Hemisphere; and (d) repealed the Asia-Pacific triangle restrictions.

U.S. Immigration Policy Since 1965

American immigration policy has been characterized by five major themes since 1965: (a) a continued preference for refugees from communism until the collapse of the USSR, and a gradual shift toward a broader definition of refugees since then; (b) a gradual introduction of a uniform system for the selection of permanent immigrants; (c) a limited attempt to control the growth of permanent immigration, especially that of relatives of U.S. citizens; (d) an attempt to encourage the immigration of highly skilled workers and of investors; and, perhaps the most prominent theme (e) an effort to stop illegal immigration. In addition, the September 11, 2001 events caused a shift toward more rigorous screening of prospective immigrants, and a transfer of certain functions from the INS to the newly created Department of Homeland Security.

The anticommunist ideological commitment of the United States continued to drive its refugee policy until the collapse of the USSR. The 1965 act formally defined refugees as those fleeing communism or coming from the Middle East. After the fall of Saigon, and throughout the 1970s and early 1980s, the United States accepted roughly 400,000 Vietnamese, Cambodian, and Laosian refugees.[38] The Indochinese Refugee Resettlement Program began in 1975, and the status of those refugees was adjusted by the 1977 Indochinese Refugee Act. During the 1970s, the attorney general also granted parolee status to Soviet immigrants. In 1980, the United States took in 125,000 Cuban refugees during the Mariel boatlift. The 1980 Refugee Act allocated 50,000 visas for "normal-flow" refugees, and permitted the president, after consultation with Congress, to increase the annual allocation.[39] The wording of the 1980 Refugee Act deviated from the Cold War ideological definitions in order to conform with the 1967 United Nations Protocol on the Status of Refugees, but the majority of refugee migration continued to originate from communist countries in Europe and Asia.[40]

The favorable treatment of refugees from communist regimes stood, until recently, in sharp contrast to the attitude of the United States toward refugees from noncommunist dictatorships. Most applications of Haitians, Guatemalans, and El Salvadorans for political asylum in the United States were denied, while Cubans and Nicaraguans were granted asylum. In 1985, the American Baptist Churches (ABC) filed a class action suit on behalf of Salvadorans and Guatemalans in the United States against the INS. It accused the INS of following State Department policies in deciding not to grant the Salvadorans and Guatemalans asylum because the United States was supporting the governments in the civil wars of these countries.[41] It is plausible, however, that the racial character of the Haitians (i.e. black) and their low socioeconomic status, further hindered their acceptance.

The collapse of the USSR and the end of the Cold War generated a change in U.S. refugee policy, which has gradually shifted from an emphasis on refugees from communism to a broader definition of refugees:

- In 1994, an agreement between the United States and Cuba called for the United States to accept 20,000 Cubans annually, and for

Cuba to prevent the exit of other Cubans trying to leave for the United States.

- In 1994, the United States recognized persecution because of homosexuality as grounds for asylum, although in practice only a small number of foreigners have been granted asylum on that basis.
- The 1996 Illegal Immigration Reform and Immigrant Responsibility Act (IIRIRA) expanded the grounds for granting asylum to include up to 1,000 persons who have suffered from a country's restrictive policies on childbearing.
- In 1990, The United States settled the ABC lawsuit, granting temporary protected status to some 236,000 Salvadorans and Guatemalans, and directing the INS to reconsider their petitions for asylum. The 1996 IIRIRA tightened the procedures dealing with foreigners living unlawfully or in a TPS in the United States, which could have led to the deportation of up to 400,000 Central Americans.[42] But pressures from the Clinton administration and from domestic groups led Congress to pass the Nicaraguan Adjustment and Central American Relief Act (NACARA). This act, signed on November 19, 1997, still favored Nicaraguans and Cubans, but it also permitted Salvadorans and Guatemalans who applied for asylum before April 1, 1990, to have their applications for residence in the United States considered under pre-IIRIRA rules.[43]
- In 1997, the bipartisan Commission on Immigration Reform (CIR) urged Congress to recommend that priority in admission be given to persons who satisfy the 1951 UN definition of a refugee.
- In 1998, Congress passed the Haitian Refugee Immigration Fairness Act, which was expected to grant immigrant status to an estimated 50,000 Haitians who had been in the United States since 1995.
- The majority of countries from which citizens are eligible for refugee or TPS status—including Liberia, Bosnia, Kosovo, Somalia, Sierra Leone, Sudan, and Burundi—suffer from civil wars.[44]
- During recent years, the largest quotas were awarded to refugees from Africa. For example, the 2002 quota of 70,000 was divided between Africa (22,000), the former USSR (17,000), Southeast Asia (15,000), Europe (9,000), East Asia (4,000), and Latin America (3,000). Most of these immigrants gained refugee status because of ethnic cleansing, political and religious persecution, and anti-Semitism.

But while U.S. refugee policy has changed since the end of the Cold War, this transformation has been gradual:

- The new quota for Cubans still gives them preferential treatment over immigrants from other countries, and Cuban immigrants are still treated more favorably than Haitian ones. Under the so-called wet-foot, dry-foot policy, which was put in place by President Clinton after the 1994 exodus, if Cubans are intercepted at sea, they are returned to Cuba. But if they make it to U.S. shores, they are paroled into the United States, which allows them to become immigrants one year after arrival.[45]
- The 1997 Nicaraguan Adjustment and Central American Relief Act eased the situation of various groups of Central Americans who faced probable deportation, but it still favored Nicaraguans and Cubans. The latter were permitted to obtain immigrant status, while El Salvadorans and Guatemalans, who applied for asylum before April 1, 1990, could only have their applications to remain in the United States considered under pre-IIRIRA rules, and they still had to prove individually that they would face hardship if deported. This situation changed later, in May 1999, when the Clinton administration announced revised regulations under which the INS would presume that certain Salvadorans and Guatemalans would face "extreme hardship" if they were deported from the United States. Under this new plan, Salvadorans and Guatemalans who were in the United States by 1990 were also presumed to be entitled to legal immigrant status.[46]
- To some degree, the overall distribution of refugees admitted continues patterns of the Cold War period. In 1993, 41 percent of the refugees admitted to the United States were Jews or Evangelical Christians from the former USSR, and 32 percent were from Vietnam and Laos.[47] The planned distribution of 78,000 refugees for 1999 included 48,000 from Europe and the former Soviet Union. And the second and third largest quotas in 2002 were awarded to the Balkan states and to refugees from the former USSR. The continued preference for European refugees has been a product of the war in Bosnia and of domestic pressures: the Lautenberg Amendment, originally enacted in 1989 and later extended, permits "historically persecuted groups," including Jews and Evangelical Christians from the former Soviet Union, to enter the United States if they can show a "credible basis for concern" about the potential for persecution, a lower

standard than the normal refugee requirement to show a "well-founded fear of persecution."[48]

The second theme of U.S. immigration policy has been the gradual introduction of a uniform system for the selection of permanent immigrants.[49] In 1968, the government set the quota of 120,000 immigrants per annum from the Western Hemisphere. In 1976, Congress established a limit of 20,000 immigrants per country from that Hemisphere. Two years later, an amendment to the Immigration and Nationality Act combined the ceilings of both hemispheres to a worldwide total of 290,000, with the same seven-category preference system and the 20,000 per-country limit. The 1965–1978 legislation, and later the addition of a lottery, created a relatively impartial selection system of permanent immigrants. This system does not apply, of course, to family members of American citizens, whose numbers have grown substantially since 1965, and to refugees.

The third theme of U.S. immigration policy has been the limited attempt to control the growing permanent immigration, mostly composed of relatives of U.S. citizens. While the global permanent immigration *quota* has not changed much since the 1920s, staying at about 300,000 per annum, the number of *out-of-quota* immigrants—mostly family members of American citizens—has grown substantially since 1965. Thus, in practice, the expected normal intake was already 750,000–1,000,000 by the 1990s. The composition of permanent immigration to the United States has also changed, from predominantly European to mostly Asian and Latin American origin. By the late 1970s, European immigration had fallen to 13 percent of the total.[50] This development was not anticipated by the framers of the 1965 Act, as is evident in Attorney General Robert Kennedy's assessment in 1964: "I would say for the Asia-Pacific triangle it would be approximately 5,000, Mr. Chairman, after which immigration from that source would virtually disappear; 5,000 immigrants could come in the first year, but we do not expect that there would be any great influx after that."[51]

Several attempts have been made to limit permanent immigration to the United States during the past three decades. The 1976 Immigration Act, which set a limit of 20,000 immigrants per country from the Western Hemisphere, was in response to the growing permanent immigration from Mexico. The original aim of the 1990 Immigration Act was to set a ceiling on permanent immigration by bringing in fewer family members, but this attempt failed because of pressure from ethnic groups. And in 1995, the bipartisan Commission on Immigration

Reform recommended a 30 percent reduction in legal immigration, from 675,000 per year to 550,000. This recommendation was originally endorsed by the Clinton administration, and included major House and Senate immigration bills in 1996. But later, the recommendation lost its support because of (a) efforts by the administration to separate legal and illegal immigration proposals in Congress; (b) opposition of Asian pressure groups; (c) a reluctance on the part of the Republicans to alienate Hispanic voters; and (d) the selection of Senator Spencer Abraham—an opponent of such a reduction—to chair the Senate immigration subcommittee.[52]

The United States has also had a long history of restricting the permanent immigration of the poor. The 1996 welfare law added to this tendency by (a) making most legal immigrants ineligible for means-tested benefits for their first five years in the United States; (b) requiring U.S. sponsors of immigrants to demonstrate that their income is at least 25 percent above the U.S. poverty level; (c) requiring the U.S. sponsors to sign a legally binding affidavit that they have the resources to support the immigrant in the United States, and permitting the government agency to sue the sponsor to recover any benefits paid to the immigrants sponsored; and (d) until naturalization or ten years of work in the United States, the law makes many immigrants ineligible for welfare benefits by assuming that the immigrant has access to the income and assets of his sponsor.[53]

The fourth theme of American immigration policy has been an attempt to encourage the immigration of the highly skilled in order to reverse the perceived decline in the skill level of immigrants and to compete for skilled labor with other receiving countries such as Australia and Canada.[54] Since the 1960s, the United States has issued visas that admitted foreign professionals, including nurses, scientists, and programmers. The Immigration Act of 1990 increased the number of visas available to immigrants with required skills from 54,000 to 140,000 annually, and created five major preferences. The first employment preference admitted up to 40,000 "priority workers" and their families—persons of extraordinary ability, outstanding professors and researchers, and multinational executives and managers—as immigrants. Another 40,000 visas were allocated to immigrants with advanced degrees or "exceptional ability" and concrete offers of employment. An additional 40,000 visas went to an assortment of skilled workers, professionals, and "other workers." Finally, the fourth and fifth preferences provided visas for "special immigrants" (including religious workers, those with foreign medical degrees, etc.) and investors.[55] The 1990 Act also established an investor immigrant visa, like those of Canada and Australia, which grants permanent residence to foreigners and their families who are willing to invest at least $500,000 in the United States and create at least ten U.S. jobs for non-relatives.[56]

The H-1B program was created in 1990 in order to help U.S. employers facing temporary labor shortages to admit foreigners with at least a B.A. degree for up to six years. The program differed from a previous guestworker program in that it limited access to 65,000 foreign workers a year, put a cap on the number of visas, and ended the requirement that temporary workers leave the United States when their visas expired. In 1998, the American Competitiveness Act increased the annual number of H-1B nonimmigrant visas for foreign high-tech workers from 65,000 to 115,000 in 1999 and 2000. This increase took place despite growing opposition, which challenged the need for additional foreign high-tech workers.[57] In 2000, the annual number of H-1B visas was raised again to 200,000, with universities and nonprofit organizations excluded from the cap. According to government data, there were about 400,000 H-1B workers in the United States in March 2001. But the sharp slowdown in the computer industry since the spring of 2001 caused employers to request fewer H-1B workers.[58]

The United States has also admitted a relatively small number of foreign farm workers.[59] The H-2A program allows farm employers facing labor shortages to individually apply for foreign farm workers. In practice, U.S. farm employers continued to rely mostly on illegal immigrants, and the number of H-2A admissions dropped from 30,000 in 1989 to about 15,000 in 1995. In 1995, California farm organizations failed to include a guestworker program in immigration reform legislation moving through Congress.[60] U.S. employers and the Mexican government continued to advocate an expansion of the guestworker program, but the September 11 terror attacks stalled discussions on that matter. During the November 2002 APEC meeting, Mexican President Vicente Fox and U.S. advocates of the guestworker program hoped to restart immigration talks. U.S. ambassador to Mexico, Antonio Garza Jr., also supported including a guestworker program as part of discussions between the two countries. And Secretary of State Colin Powell said that the U.S.–Mexican immigration discussions would start with the issue of an expanded guestworker program.[61]

Perhaps the most prominent theme of American immigration policy since 1965 has been the attempt to solve the problem of illegal immigration. According to the number of illegal immigrants apprehended, illegal immigration has rapidly increased since 1965.[62] The INS estimated that there were five million unauthorized foreigners living in the United States in October 1996, up from 3.9 million in October 1992, and that their number was going up by 275,000 per year. This suggested that about 2 percent of all U.S. residents were unauthorized foreigners/illegal immigrants.[63] Another estimate, in 2002, put the number of unauthorized immigrants in the United States at nine million.[64]

Pressures to control illegal immigration mounted in Congress and at the state level. Some of the means suggested included: high-technology equipment along the borders; ditches and triple fences along parts of the Mexican border; a tripling of the number of Border Patrol agents; a border crossing fee; fraud-proof, machine-readable visas, social security cards and even identity cards; denying citizenship to American-born children of illegal immigrants; and making illegal immigrants ineligible for health, education, and other benefits.[65] The bipartisan U.S. Commission on Immigration Reform (CIR), established by the 1990 Immigration Act, also recommended several measures to deter illegal immigration, including: the issuance of a magnetic Social Security card that would also include other personal information; the establishment of a national registry of the names and social security numbers of all persons authorized to work in the United States in order to deter illegal aliens from obtaining U.S. jobs; the reinforcement of border control; and the exclusion of illegal aliens from various benefits not including health care in emergencies and public education for their children.

Arizona, California, Florida, Illinois, New York, New Jersey, and Texas sued the federal government to reimburse them for funds they spend on the education, medical care, and incarceration of illegal immigrants. The strongest pressure came from California, where voters approved Proposition 187, known also as the "Save Our State" Initiative. The initiative called for the exclusion of illegal aliens from the state's public education systems, nonemergency health care, and other benefits. It also required all service providers to report suspected illegal aliens to California's attorney general and to the INS, and would have made the use of false documents a state felony. Proposition 187 was declared unconstitutional by a federal district court judge, who argued that "California is powerless to enact its own legislative scheme to regulate immigration," and that regulating immigration is strictly federal business. Eventually, in 1999, a mediated settlement was achieved, where California dropped its appeal of the aforementioned judge's ruling, and opponents of Proposition 187 agreed to permit its provisions making it a state crime to manufacture and distribute false documents to go into effect. Similar initiatives in Arizona and Florida failed to win a place on the ballots of these states.[66]

Such pressures led the federal government to adopt tougher measures against illegal immigration. The Farm Labor Contractor Registration Act was amended in 1974 to prohibit employers of migrant farm-workers in the United States from "recruiting, employing, or utilizing, with knowledge, any illegal immigrants."[67] In 1986, after eight years of debate, Congress passed the Immigration Reform and Control Act (IRCA), based on the Simpson-Mazzoli bill. The 1986 act provided for fines on employers of illegal immigrants, and granted an amnesty to illegal immigrants who had resided in the United States continuously since January 1, 1982 or who had worked there for 60 days since 1984 (in the context of the Special Agricultural Worker Program). The act has since been deemed ineffective by the Commission on Immigration Reform (CIR) and by various scholars because it contained loopholes that enabled the employers to evade the law if the immigrant presented forged documents, and because of the amnesty program, which legalized the residency of 2 to 3 million Mexicans and led to large-scale fraud.

In 1996, Congress passed the Illegal Immigration Reform and Immigrant Responsibility Act (IIRIRA). The act covered various aspects of illegal immigration, including border control, enforcement inside the country, alien smuggling, document fraud, apprehension, detention and removal, as well as restrictions on employment and on public benefits. It required the INS to document foreigners entering or leaving the United States and to develop pilot verification programs. It also significantly toughened penalties on unauthorized immigrants and increased the size of the Border Patrol. The IIRIRA allowed the INS to summarily exclude or return aliens who arrive in the United States without documents, and it ruled that foreigners who overstay their visas and remain in the United States for six to 12 months illegally are barred from the United States for three years, and that those who overstay for a year or more are barred for ten years.[68]

Under the 1996 IIRIRA, the INS has introduced voluntary pilot programs to test ways of providing effective and nondiscriminatory verification procedures, with a focus on electronic means of checking employment eligibility. One of these has been the Employment Verification Pilot system in which employers send I-9 information on aliens to the INS via modem. The entries are checked against the Alien Status Verification Index, a database with 50 million immigration records. In 1998, the INS also started issuing new Permanent Resident Cards (i.e. green cards), which include secret security features and holograms in an effort to thwart the now-widespread counterfeiting. And the INS has implemented the IDENT system, which photographs and fingerprints most persons apprehended along the Mexico–U.S. border, and electronically stores them. By the end of 1997, according to the INS, this system had 1.4 million records, including 150,000 "lookouts," often persons that are thought to be smugglers because of the number of times they were apprehended and the number of those apprehended with them. Finally, the INS has constructed various physical barriers, such as an "electronic wall," which augments the steel fences and Border Patrol agents in place along the Mexico–U.S. border. Cameras and heat sensors are mounted on 60-foot high platforms and underground sensors detect entrants, whom Border Patrol agents can then apprehend.[69]

The pressures to restrict illegal immigration also led Congress to allocate more resources for enforcement, and the INS to conduct highly publicized operations against such immigration. A provision of the 1996 Illegal Immigration Reform and Immigrant Responsibilities Act required the INS to hire 1,000 new Border Patrol agents a year until 2001. The budget of the INS grew from $372 million in 1981, to 1.5–1.6 billion in 1993, $3.1 billion in 1997 and $3.8 billion in 1998. It had 2,100 Border Patrol agents in 1982, 4,000–4,200 agents in 1993–1994, and 8,000 by the end of 1998.[70] The INS concentrated many agents along border stretches where crossing is feasible—in order to deter illegal entry—near El Paso, Texas in 1993 ("Operation Hold the Line"), near San Diego in 1994 ("Operation Gatekeeper"), in Arizona in 1995 ("Operation Safeguard"), and near Brownsville, Texas ("Operation Rio Grande") in 1997. The programs reduced the number of illegal immigrants entering the United States in these areas, but in some cases their success was temporary, or they diverted illegal immigration to other locations.[71]

During recent years, there have been attempts to legalize the status of some of the illegal immigrants.[72] The 245(i) program would have allowed foreigners illegally residing in the United States, for whom immigration visas become available, to pay a $1,000 fine to the INS and adjust their status in the United States, rather than returning to their countries of origin for interviews with the State Department. The 245(i) program was resurrected for a few months under legislation enacted at the end of the Clinton administration, and Congress was in the process of extending the program in late 2001–early 2002. The United States also conducted discussions with Mexico with regard to an "earned legalization" for unauthorized foreigners in the United States who had jobs and paid taxes.

On September 5, 2001, President Bush said that "the United States has no more important relationship in the world than our relationship with Mexico," and President Fox made the legalization of the unauthorized Mexicans residing in the United States his top priority in foreign policy.

These U.S.–Mexico discussions and the 245(i) program were stalled following the September 11 terror attacks. But efforts to legalize illegal immigrants continued. In the fall of 2002, the Mexican government launched a campaign on that matter, and President Fox asserted that it was time to reach an agreement on legalization. The response of the U.S. administration was ambivalent. The new ambassador to Mexico, Antonio Garza Jr., said the United States "should recognize the contribution of undocumented Mexicans and open the door for them to earned legalization. Talks should center on the criteria that will allow people to obtain this status." In contrast, Secretary of State Colin Powell said that the United States would start with less controversial issues, such as temporary work visas and an expanded guestworker program, rather than with legalization. In October 2002, House Minority Leader Richard A. Gephardt (Democrats) introduced the Earned Legalization and Family Reunification bill that would allow unauthorized foreigners who had been physically present in the United States for at least five years, and who had worked and paid taxes for at least two years, to become legal residents if they demonstrated some knowledge of English and passed a federal security check. While the terror attacks contributed to the suspension of the U.S.–Mexican discussions with regard to legalization, Gephardt argued: "Our proposal will bring undocumented immigrants out of the shadows and into the light of accountability and greater cooperation in our fight against terrorism."

The latest development in U.S. immigration control policy has been a shift toward more rigorous screening of immigrants, especially those coming from the Middle East, and a transfer of certain functions from the INS to the newly created Department of Homeland Security, following the September 11, 2001 terror attacks:[73]

- Since September 11, 2002, a new program requires visitors from Libya, Syria, Sudan, Iraq, and Iran to be photographed and fingerprinted. U.S. Attorney General John D. Ashcroft said the system would be expanded by 2005 to improve the government's tracking of "virtually all of the 35 million foreign visitors who come to the United States annually."
- The rigorous screening decreased the number of refugees accepted in 2002 to 27,113, far below the quota of 70,000.

- After September 11, some 1,200 foreigners were arrested and detained in secret. Of those, three were charged with terrorism-related crimes, but over 400 were deported for violating immigration laws.[74] These violations were frequently overlooked by the authorities prior to September 11, 2001.
- In July 2002 the INS began requiring legal immigrants to report changes of address within 10 days.
- Between late 2002 and April 2003 nearly 130,000 immigrants and visitors, predominantly Muslims, were questioned in immigration offices, airports, and border crossings—the largest effort to register immigrants in decades. Officials said they caught and detained 11 suspected terrorists and more than 9,000 illegal immigrants.[75]
- The INS required all U.S. schools that issue I-20 forms (that allow foreign students to obtain visas for U.S. study) to enter student information into the Student Exchange and Visitor Information System (SEVIS)—an electronic system aimed at tracking foreign students.
- In October 2002, the White House briefed Congress on a plan to scrutinize foreign students from countries that sponsor terrorism, who are interested in subjects such as bacteriology and nuclear technology, before giving them a student visa.

The 9-11 events also stalled negotiations between presidents Bush and Fox with regard to Mexican immigration, and border patrols along the Rio Grande were increased.[76] But the most far-reaching impact of the terror attacks in the context of immigration was probably an organizational one. In June 2002, President Bush proposed that the INS be transferred from the Department of Justice to a new Department of Homeland Security. On November 25, 2002, the president signed a bill creating a Department of Homeland Security, a Cabinet-level agency that will consolidate all or part of 22 federal agencies, including the INS. Its mission will be to guard U.S. borders against terrorists amid a flood of immigrants, visitors, ships, trucks, and planes.[77] The act "transfers from the Commissioner of Immigration and Naturalization to the Under Secretary for Border and Transportation Security all functions performed under the following programs, and all personnel, assets, and liabilities pertaining to such programs . . . [including] (1) The Border Patrol program; (2) The detention and removal program; (3) The intelligence program; (4) The investigations program; [and] (5) The inspections program."[78] The new under secretary for Border and Transportation Security will be responsible for "carrying out the immigration enforcement functions vested by statute in, or performed by, the Commissioner of Immigration and Naturalization" . . . "Establishing and administering rules . . . governing the granting of visas or other forms of permission, including parole, to enter the United States to individuals who are not a citizen or an alien lawfully admitted for permanent residence in the United States," and "Establishing national immigration enforcement policies and priorities."[79]

Factors Shaping U.S. Immigration Policy: An Analysis

The United States has admitted more immigrants than any other country. In accordance with the theory advanced here, policies on different types of immigrants were influenced by the socioeconomic and foreign policy factors to a varying degree. Labor migration policy was mostly influenced by the economic factor and by the "war–migrant labor link." Refugee policy was primarily shaped by foreign policy considerations, and to a lesser degree by other factors. Policy on illegal immigrants was chiefly influenced by the economic factor and by the volume of illegal immigration, and to a lesser degree by the other factors. Policy on permanent immigration was shaped by the state of the economy, large-scale immigration of dissimilar composition, wars, foreign policy considerations, and liberal/racist ideological trends.

The economic factor significantly influenced U.S. policy on permanent and temporary migration. The need for immigrants to settle the South and the Midwest and to construct the railroads contributed to the liberal immigration policy during the first century of the nation. Economic expansion also facilitated the admission of immigrants after the Civil War, between 1898 and 1906, and after World War II (in the latter case especially migrant workers). Economic downturns, on the other hand, led to restrictions on immigration. The financial panic of 1873 and the recession of 1873–1877 inspired an anti-Chinese movement in California. The 1882–1885 recession produced the 1882 Chinese Exclusion Act and the 1885 Contract Labor Act. The 1891–1897 depression and the 1893 financial panic generated the restrictive immigration acts of 1891 and 1893, an increase in the head tax, amendments to the Chinese Exclusion Act and the Contract Labor Act, as well as attempts to introduce a literacy test. The financial panic of 1907 and the recession of 1907–1908 contributed to the 1907 restrictions on Japanese immigration. The 1920–1921 depression, the decline of the war industries and the demobilization contributed to the passage of the 1921 quota act. The Great Depression produced restrictions on legal and illegal Mexican immigration, Filipino immigration, and the immigration of impoverished people. And a sluggish local economy generated attempts to restrict illegal Mexican immigration to California during the early 1990s.

I argued in chapter 1 that the state of the economy especially influences policy with regard to permanent immigrants in countries where such immigrants, rather than temporary migrant workers, are the main source of foreign labor. In the United States, up to the mid-1920s, permanent immigration was the main source of foreign labor, and thus fluctuations in the state of the economy substantially influenced policy on permanent immigration. In contrast, between 1942 and 1964, Mexican migrant workers became the prominent source of foreign labor. And after the Bracero program was terminated, illegal immigration to the United States increased, becoming the *de facto* main source of foreign labor. Consequently, in accordance with the theory, the state of the economy has had less of an influence on U.S. policies with regard to permanent immigration since World War II.

Large-scale immigration of dissimilar ethnic composition led to restrictions on permanent and on illegal immigration, but had a very limited effect on policies toward temporary labor migration. Chinese immigration to the lightly populated West Coast generated the 1875 and 1882 restrictions on such immigration. A surge in Japanese immigration led to the 1907 "Gentlemen's Agreement" between the United States and Japan, to the 1913 California anti-Japanese land law, and eventually to the total ban on Japanese immigration. The Greek-Orthodox, Catholic, and Jewish immigration from Eastern and Southern Europe at the turn of the century provided the impetus for the literacy test act and for the national origins quota acts. The use of a selection system explicitly based on the ethnic characteristics of the immigrants proves that the large dissimilar immigration was the cause for the restrictions. Furthermore, Senators William P. Dillingham and Henry Cabot Lodge, and Congressman Albert Johnson, who advocated restrictions, testified that they were aimed at limiting the new type of immigrants. Permanent Mexican immigration was restricted during the 1930s and by the 1976 act, although these restrictions were mitigated by foreign policy considerations.[80] The fear of Latin American population growth also contributed to the extension of quantitative limitations to Western Hemisphere immigration in 1965. Large-scale illegal immigration led to the 1930s repatriations of Mexican immigrants; "Operation Wetback"; the 1974 amendment to the Farm Labor Contractor Registration Act; the 1986 Simpson-Mazzoli (IRCA) act; and recent measures to block illegal immigration and to make such immigrants ineligible for public services.

Foreign policy considerations have been the main determinant of American refugee policy, and have influenced other types of immigration policy as well, particularly during the Cold War. Prior to World War II, American foreign policy focused on the Pacific and Latin America.[81] The American executive reacted to domestic pressures for restrictions. It attempted to block, or ameliorate, restrictions on immigration from the Western Hemisphere and the Far East, but in most cases only succeeded in delaying rather than preventing the restrictions. For example, Presidents Hayes and Arthur vetoed the Chinese Exclusion bill in 1879 and 1881, but the bill passed in 1882; President Roosevelt signed the restrictive 1907 "Gentlemen's Agreement" with Japan in order to prevent more blatant anti-Japanese legislation in Congress; and the War Department and the Department of State opposed restrictions on Filipino immigration, but such restrictions were implemented in 1934.

The emergence of U.S. global hegemony following World War II produced an expanded role for the executive and for foreign policy considerations in immigration policy. During the war, the INS was transferred from the Department of Labor to the Department of Justice (based on a recommendation from President Roosevelt) because of the supposed political threat represented by immigrants from enemy countries. As Sassen notes, this was meant to last only for the duration of war. But in the late 1940s and 1950s there was great concern over how immigration policy could be used to advance foreign policy objectives, and the INS was never returned to the Department of Labor.[82] During the Cold War, the executive branch initiated immigration policies rather than just reacting to domestic pressures. The rise of the United States to superpower status also shifted the focus of its foreign policy, and, consequently, its immigration policy, from the Western Hemisphere and the Far East to the global arena. The new focus was based on the ideological conflict with communism. In order to emphasize its anticommunist commitment, the U.S. executive used its parole powers and advanced refugee legislation on behalf of refugees from communist-controlled countries (usually following the failure of anticommunist movements), including the Soviet Union, Eastern Germany, Hungary, Czechoslovakia, Yugoslavia, China, Indonesia, Cuba, Vietnam, and Cambodia. While the majority of immigrants between 1945 and 1965 continued to come under the regular quota, most fluctuations in the number of immigrants admitted were due to refugee legislation and directives. The preference for refugees from communist regimes also eroded the numerical and ethnic limitations of the 1920s quota system.

According to hypothesis 8, foreign policy considerations rarely cause the establishment of migrant worker programs, but they influence the character of those programs: from which countries the workers will be recruited, and sometimes the nature of their employment. The Bracero program, between 1942 and 1964, was initiated in response to pressures from southwestern farmers, and was abolished mainly due to pressures from the unions. But the United States acceded to most of Mexico's demands, including guarantees of nondiscrimination, adequate housing, employment for at least three-fourths of the contract period, and so on. In a later stage, Mexico and the State Department became prime supporters of the program.[83]

The collapse of the USSR and the end of the Cold War generated a change in U.S. refugee policy, which has gradually shifted from an emphasis on refugees from communism to a broader definition of refugees. The United States has accepted fewer refugees from communist-controlled countries (most of which turned democratic) and more refugees from African ones. A relatively substantial number of refugees continued to come from the Balkans and from the former USSR, but they have gained refugee status because of ethnic cleansing, political and religious persecution, and anti-Semitism rather then for a clearly defined anticommunist ideology. And pressures from domestic groups contributed to the favorable policy toward Jewish and Cuban refugees. Nevertheless, post–Cold War foreign policy considerations do influence U.S. immigration and refugee policy. For example, pressures from Central American governments (e.g. El Salvador) combined with domestic pressures to prevent mass deportation of asylum applicants from these countries. The United States has admitted Kurdish and Iraqi refugees. And President Clinton extended TPS to Liberians, deferring their deportation, in order to promote stability in Liberia and West Africa. The September 11 events may have further facilitated the impact of foreign policy considerations on U.S. immigration policy.

The fourth factor shaping U.S. immigration policies has been *wars, external threats and domestic threats linked to external sources*, which produced social conformity and restrictions on immigration. Fears of French agents introducing radical ideas led to the passage of the 1790s restrictions. The 1901 assassination of President McKinley by a foreign-born anarchist led to an association of immigrants with imported radicalism, to a short-lived anti-anarchist hysteria, and to restrictions on immigration. Anxiety over Japan's emergence as a new world power contributed to the signing of the "Gentlemen's Agreement" in 1907, which restricted Japanese immigration. The World War I German threat and the Bolshevik revolution produced social conformity and an association of foreigners with the external threat. This contributed to the passage of the 1917 literacy test bill and to the 1920s quota acts restricting European immigration. The German and Japanese threat during World War II produced oppression of the Japanese minority in the United States, as well as some restrictions on the freedom of expression and on immigration.

The perceived Soviet threat during the peak of the Cold War also led to greater social conformity and to an association of foreigners with the external threat. Consequently, it contributed to the enactment of restrictions on immigration—including several provisions of the Internal Security Act, the McCarran-Walter Act, and possibly "Operation Wetback"—and delayed the elimination of the quota acts. Senator Pat McCarran, one of the two sponsors of the restrictive 1952 Walter-McCarran Act, argued that the quota system was favored by every authority in the field of immigration except for "a few on the pink fringe."[84] Representative Francis E. Walter, the second sponsor of the act, stated: "The immigration act excludes from the United States any alien whose presence would endanger the public safety . . . the more militant members of the Communist party . . . 91.5 percent of them were either of foreign birth, married to persons of foreign birth or born of foreign parents, and over half of them traced their origins either to Russia or to her satellite countries."[85] Another supporter of the Walter-McCarran Act, the Senate Immigration Subcommittee Staff Director Richard Arens, identified the four main groups opposing the act as "The out-and out communists; the Pinks and sincere but misguided and uninformed liberals . . . the professional immigration promoters . . . and professional vote solicitors who fawn on national groups, appealing to them not as Americans but as hyphenated Americans."[86] These quotes demonstrate how the Cold War fears and social conformity stigmatized and delegitimized the liberals and Eastern European immigrants who were the main supporters of immigration.[87]

Perceived external threats continued to contribute to restrictive immigration policies after the end of the Cold War. In 1993, when President Clinton asked Congress for more money and new laws to restrict illegal immigration and to speed interviews of people seeking political asylum, he indicated that his decision to push for this legislation was prompted in part by the World Trade Center bombing, which demonstrated how porous the American immigration system is.[88]

In 1995, the Oklahoma City bombing—initially thought to be the act of Middle Eastern terrorists—led to a spate of counterterrorist immigration proposals. Finally, the September 11 terror attacks caused several changes in U.S. immigration policy. The screening of prospective immigrants, especially those coming from the Middle East was tightened, which also decreased the number of refugees accepted. Negotiations between Presidents Bush and Fox with regard to Mexican immigration were stalled. And the Homeland Security Act of 2002 transferred various functions—including the Border Patrol program and the detention and removal program—from the INS to the newly created Department of Homeland Security. The act also stated that the under secretary for Border and Transportation Security will be responsible for "Establishing national immigration enforcement policies and priorities."

While external threats have generated restrictions on permanent immigration, wars also contributed to the recruitment of foreign labor, in what is termed here the "war–migrant labor link." Employers advocated the recruitment of European migrants during the Civil War, leading to increased immigration and to the Contract Labor Act of 1864. Employers again pressured the government to allow for the recruitment of Mexican workers during World War I, World War II, and the Korean War, producing the Bracero programs. During World War II, the United States also employed German prisoners of war, some of whom were in prison camps whose location was determined by local demands for labor. An interesting case is the Civil War, where (a) the demand for manpower increased, and (b) the permanent immigrants were not associated with an external threat. Consequently, permanent immigration rather than temporary migration was encouraged during the war.

Another factor that influenced American immigration policy has been the *fluctuations between racism and liberalism*. Conservatism and racism increased during the 1910s and 1920s, including the repression of radicalism, the imposition of Prohibition, Jim Crow laws, social discrimination against Catholics and Jews, and the rise of the Ku Klux Klan. This went hand in hand with restrictions on immigration.[89] World War II's Holocaust, the fight between democracies and Fascist powers and the civil rights movement of the 1960s delegitimized the use of racist terminology as the basis for immigration policy, thus contributing to the demise of the national origins quota system.

Finally, two partially overlapping factors that this analysis rejects as explanations for U.S. immigration policy are industrial unrest and social conflicts. For the period between 1890 and 1981 there was no correlation between the share of workers participating in strikes as a percentage of employed workers and immigration control policy. The peak years of strikes (over 8 percent of employed workforce) were 1916, 1919, 1922, 1941, 1945–1946, 1949, and 1952. No major restrictions were passed during any of these years (although the Walter-McCarran Act, passed in 1952, did retain the national origins quota system). On the other hand, the main restrictions—the 1917 literacy test act and the 1921 and 1924 quota acts—did pass during a period of industrial unrest (1916–1922), although not during the peak years of it, and this is also the period highlighted by Higham and Jones. So the data confirms Higham's and Jones's assertion with regard to that period, but it does not show a consistent impact of industrial unrest on immigration control policy over long periods. It also should be noted that immigrants (and particularly those in the IWW radical union) played an important role in the industrial unrest of the 1916–1922 period, a link I do find compelling.

It is hard to define the main *social conflicts* in U.S. history, but they surely include the Civil War and the 1960s civil rights movement.[90] In both cases immigration policy was mostly liberalized rather than restricted: permanent immigration was encouraged during the Civil War, and the civil rights movement facilitated the liberalization of immigration policy with regard to the volume and composition of immigration in 1965.[91] The Civil War is presented by the advocates of the "national debate" argument as the prime example for the influence of social conflicts on immigration policy. According to Higham and Jones, the American Party emerged on the eve of the Civil War because "a general crisis in American society" led to a lack of confidence in national identity and to restrictions on immigration.[92] This argument has three faults. First, the American Party, despite its electoral success, failed in its aim to have anti-immigration legislation passed: Congress did not pass bills introduced by the American Party that would have prohibited the immigration of criminals and paupers, restricted immigration, or extended the naturalization period.[93] The Senate did pass a restrictive measure, but that bill was submitted by a Whig Senator, and it failed in the House. Second, the Civil War cleavage in fact contributed to the fall of the American Party: after 1856, the party split over the slavery issue, with its southern wing going Democratic and the northern members joining the Republicans.[94] The North–South cleavage did contribute to the unparalleled political success of the anti-immigrant party in one respect: the collapse of the American party system during this period weakened partisan attachments and allowed for the rise of a major third party.[95] Third, "situational" factors alone explain the success of the anti-immigration movement of the 1850s: the economy was weak, the United States experienced an unprecedented number of immigrants of dissimilar ethnic and religious composition, and the immigrants were associated with external threats and imported radicalism. It seems likely that an anti-immigration movement would have emerged during the 1850s, propelled by the surge in German and Irish immigration and the declining economy, even without the North–South cleavage, although it would probably have operated within the major parties rather than form an anti-immigration party.

CHAPTER 3

Immigration Policies of Britain

Most immigration to Britain has been permanent. Thus, in accordance with the theory advanced here, British immigration control policy has been influenced by the volume of dissimilar immigration, foreign policy considerations, external threats, and wars. The state of the British economy affected immigration policy to some degree, although its impact was smaller than that of the other factors. Britain also experienced some temporary labor migration, which was primarily influenced by the state of the economy.

British Immigration Policy in the Eighteenth and Nineteenth Centuries

Until the early twentieth century, Britain had a liberal immigration policy. Only on two occasions, in 1793 and in 1848, did Britain regulate immigration. In both cases the controls were the result of an association of immigration with external threats. The 1792–1793 Aliens Act incorporated several regulations: it required ship captains arriving in Britain to give customs officers details of any foreigners transported by them; it ordered the arriving aliens to give the customs officer an account of their personal history and status; it enabled the King in Council to direct that aliens live in specific districts; and it allowed for the deportation of aliens who had been imprisoned. According to Plender, the immediate cause for the act was the flight of a small number of refugees from the French Revolution.[1] Their arrival coincided with the Francophobia that accompanied the deterioration in relations between Britain and France, and with fears that Jacobin agents had infiltrated the ranks of the refugees. The Aliens Act was phrased as a temporary measure, but although it was relaxed in 1802 and 1814, it was renewed at intervals until 1926. The act was also accompanied, during the national emergency preceding the outbreak of the Napoleonic Wars, by other restrictions on traditional freedoms, such as the Traitorous Correspondence Bill and Fox's Libel Bill.[2] This first restriction on immigration was the product of fears of an external threat, since the volume of immigration from France was very small, and the country experienced economic prosperity in 1792.

The other pre-1905 restriction on immigration was enacted in 1848, when political instability in Europe produced a flow of political refugees, whose presence in England generated fears of disturbances. As was the case in 1792, the external threat represented by those refugees led to the approval of the Aliens Removal Act, which provided the Home Secretary and the Lord Lieutenant of Ireland with power to deport any alien against whom written allegations had been made. The Act was not renewed in 1849.

British Immigration Policy, 1905–1938

Britain kept a liberal immigration policy until the early twentieth century. This policy was facilitated by the limited immigration into Britain, by the similarity between most of the immigrants and the local population, and by foreign policy considerations.[3] However, during the last two decades of the nineteenth century, an influx of Eastern European Jews generated local demands for restrictions on immigration. Between 1880 and 1914, pogroms led to a significant migration of Russian Jews to Britain, resulting in the quintupling of the Jewish population. The Jewish immigration was unprecedented in that it was largely composed of people who spoke no English, were poor, and whose occupation had been that of small artisans and traders in an agricultural society.[4] At first, there was limited support for restrictions. A 1889 Parliamentary Select Committee recommended against controls on immigration. But during the 1890s, the Trade Union Congress (TUC) passed several resolutions demanding the control of Jewish immigration.[5] In 1894 and 1898 the House of Lords approved Bills to restrict immigration, although neither of these Bills was passed by the House of Commons. In 1902 the Conservatives announced immigration control to be an element of the party's official policy. The same year, the government established a Royal Commission on alien immigration, which in 1903 recommended limited restrictions on immigration and on immigrant residence.[6] Finally, in 1905, Parliament passed the Aliens Immigration

Act. The act forbade the entry of certain types of criminals and of people who could not support themselves and their dependents. It also provided that no immigrant should land from any "immigrant ship" without the permission of an immigration officer. In practice, this latter provision was soon viewed as ineffective, since many alien immigrants evaded the authorities by travelling in boats too small to be classed as "immigrant ships."[7] Moreover, the 1905 Aliens Immigration Act was administered in a very liberal fashion by the Liberal government that came into power the following year. Nevertheless, the act stayed on the books, and its significance "lay in the breach with the principle of the previous eighty years that Britain should be freely open to immigration from overseas."[8]

The link between large-scale dissimilar immigration and restrictions on permanent immigration is evident from the developments that led to the 1905 act. The unprecedented influx of Jewish immigrants generated demands for restrictions on immigration. In contrast, relatively low unemployment rates in 1898 and 1902 weakened the demands for restrictions, and, as Rees notes, they probably prevented the passage of such restrictions during the last years of the nineteenth century. The act finally passed in 1905, a period of higher unemployment.[9] Finally, the "volume of strikes" variable (suggested by Higham in the American context) does not coincide with restrictive legislation, as strikes reached a peak in 1893 and 1912.

World War I produced the next restriction on immigration to Britain. In August 5, 1914, the day following the outbreak of the war, the House of Commons passed the Aliens Restriction Act. The 1914 legislation, which was much tougher than the 1905 act, gave the Home Secretary powers to prohibit the entry of immigrants and to deport them. For the first time all aliens had to register with the police.[10] The main object of the 1914 act, as presented by the Home Secretary, was to secure the detention and removal of spies. But although it was introduced for temporary security reasons, the 1914 act was renewed after the War by the Aliens Restriction Act of 1919. The main features of the 1914 and 1919 Alien Restriction Acts and of subsequent regulations were that immigration officers could refuse entry to aliens, and that immigrants without visible means of support could only stay in the United Kingdom for a short period, unless they secured a work permit issued by the Ministry of Labor. Until the Immigration Act of 1971, the system of control over the entry of foreign nationals (as opposed to Commonwealth citizens) was derived from the Alien Restrictions Acts of 1914 and 1919.[11]

The 1914 act was the product of wartime fears caused by an external threat. The bill passed in a matter of hours and received the royal assent that same day; unlike the 1905 bill, it was not preceded by a long debate. The 1914 act was also followed by a mass internment of Germans in Britain. Like the Aliens Act of 1793, it was considered a temporary measure, meant to deal with an emergency, but was subsequently amended to apply in period of peace.[12]

The 1919 act reaffirmed the 1914 act; thus it was also an indirect product of the wartime fears. In addition, the Act coincided with, and may have been facilitated by, an increase in unemployment, although unemployment was still relatively low. The 1919 act also coincided with a peak in strikes, but there is no evidence of any link between the two phenomena. Finally, it could be argued that the emergence of the labor movement as a political party facilitated the passage of the 1919 act. However, the act was passed by a liberal-conservative government, five years prior to the first Labor government.[13] The influence of foreign policy considerations on the 1914 and 1919 acts was evident in the exemption of Commonwealth subjects from the restrictions. Foreign policy considerations may also have prompted Britain to exempt political refugees from these restrictions.

During the 1920s and 1930s, the economic depression caused most receiving countries to restrict immigration. But Britain avoided restrictions on immigration, and even emphasized its commitment to free migration within the Commonwealth. One reason for this unique policy was foreign policy considerations. In 1922 and 1937, Britain signed the Empire Settlement Act, which empowered the government to assist emigrants from the United Kingdom who intended to settle in any part of the Commonwealth.[14] The premise behind these acts was that most migration would flow from Britain toward the colonies, and that free migration would strengthen the colonial links. The other reason was the limited dissimilar immigration: most immigration to Britain during the 1930s consisted of returning former emigrants and of Irish migrants.

British Immigration Policy, 1939–1962

The direction of migration—with more people leaving Britain than entering it—changed once Britain entered World War II and faced a shortage in manpower. During the war, colonial labor was recruited to work in forestry, munitions factories, and the services. In addition, some 10,000 West Indians were recruited to work as ground crews in the Royal Air Force, and considerable numbers of West Indians, Asians, and

Africans served the Allied forces.[15] These workers and soldiers formed the nucleus for a large-scale West Indian immigration that started in 1948, and for the Indian and Pakistani immigration that followed from 1955 onward—an example of the "war–migrant labor link" and the ensuing "migration chain."

Another group that arrived in the United Kingdom during World War II was composed of 120,000 Polish members of the Allied Forces, including some 70,000 members of the Polish Second Corps, known as "General Anders' Army," and 50,000 Poles who fought in France. They gained permanency through the Polish Resettlement Act, passed in 1947. The British unions initially opposed the Poles's settlement. But public sympathy for these wartime allies, labor shortages, the Poles's anti-Russian attitude and their unwillingness to return to Poland, and the fact that many of them had married British women contributed to the acceptance and integration of the Poles.[16] Thus, foreign policy considerations facilitated the acceptance of a group that otherwise might have been rejected because of its Eastern European origin.

After the war, Britain experienced low unemployment and a labor shortage, which (together with the consequences of World War II) led to the recruitment of foreign workers. In May 1947 the government announced its scheme for the recruitment of displaced workers in Europe. Within a two-year period, some 90,000 European Volunteer Workers (EVW's) (many of them displaced persons) came to Britain, as well as a smaller number of Ukrainian prisoners of war. Most of the workers were of Eastern European origin—Ukrainians, Poles, Latvians, Lithuanians, and Yugoslavs—who volunteered for jobs covered by short-term work permits.[17] They were expected to work in whatever job the Ministry of Labor deemed fit, after January 1948 they were not allowed to bring their dependents, and many of them left Britain for other countries. At a later stage, Germans, Italians, Austrians, and Spaniards were also recruited, but they faced shorter delays in winning the right to bring in their families. Thus, the permanent stay of migrants from Western, Central, and Southern Europe was facilitated to a greater degree than that of Eastern Europeans (other than the Poles).

But the main source of migrant labor in postwar Britain was New Commonwealth immigration (mostly from the West Indies, India, and Pakistan). The British government faced a dilemma with regard to these immigrants: on the one hand, the Royal Commission (1949) was concerned with assimilating immigrants of a different race; on the other hand, there was an acute labor shortage, especially of unskilled labor, which those immigrants could provide.[18] The British government continued its liberal immigration policy until the early 1960s because of foreign policy considerations. As Layton-Henry points out, Britain has traditionally favored the free movement of capital and labor within the Empire. The support for free movement of people, formalized by the 1922 and 1937 Empire Settlement Acts, was intended to sustain the links between Britain and its colonies.[19] Most migration traditionally flowed from Britain to the colonies, and the initial assumption after the war was that migration would continue in that direction. But the policy did not change even when it became apparent that New Commonwealth immigrants were now arriving in Britain. Immigration was still seen as a method of maintaining Britain's position in the world through its leadership of the Commonwealth. At the same time, the economies of West Indian countries were weak and they suffered from heavy unemployment. This caused West Indian politicians to lobby against controls on immigration, arguing that such controls would be economically disastrous for the islands and would undermine the Commonwealth and Britain's leadership role within it.[20] Britain's commitment to free Commonwealth migration was reaffirmed by the Nationality Act of 1948, and by a 1949 Conservative Party policy document. As a result, the postwar New Commonwealth immigration, remained unchecked. The immigrants first came from the West Indies, then from India and Pakistan, and finally from some African countries. During the 1955–1962 period nearly 500,000 New Commonwealth citizens settled in Britain, many of whom were later joined by their wives and other dependents.

The large-scale permanent immigration of dissimilar race composition produced racial riots and demands for restrictions on immigration. These demands fueled a political campaign against colored immigration, leading to the 1962 Commonwealth Immigrants Act, which restricted Commonwealth immigration. The Nottingham and Notting Hill race riots erupted in 1958, and opinion polls revealed public hostility to colored immigration. The British government pressured the Indian and Pakistani governments to restrict the issuing of passports, but this measure was relatively ineffective. In 1958–1959, New Commonwealth immigration declined temporarily, weakening the pressure for restrictions. But between 1959 and 1961 immigration surged to unprecedented highs, with West Indian immigration growing by a factor of four in comparison to the 1959 level, Indian immigration by a factor of eight, and Pakistani immigration by a factor of 30. As a result, the British government passed the 1962 Commonwealth Immigrants Act, requiring Commonwealth immigrants to obtain employment vouchers.

According to an Office of Information document, "In 1962, it became necessary to regulate entry in order to ensure that immigrants were admitted at a rate which the country had the social and economic capacity to absorb."[21]

British Immigration Policy, 1963–1971

The 1962 Commonwealth Immigrants Act was followed by further restrictive legislation. While the 1962 Act did cause a 50–60 percent decrease in immigration as compared to the 1961–1962 period, Commonwealth immigration in 1963 and 1964 still exceeded that of all other postwar years. Therefore, the political campaign for further restrictions on New Commonwealth immigration continued. In 1965 the Labor government responded to this pressure by restricting the number of employment vouchers to 8,500. It also abolished the Category C vouchers, which were on a "first-come, first-served" basis, and for which there was a waiting list of over 400,000.[22] In 1968, a flow of Indian refugees from Kenya generated renewed political pressure for further controls, which led to the Commonwealth Immigrants Act of 1968. That act introduced the concept of patriality (a term formally defined in 1971), which required all citizens of the United Kingdom and the colonies with no substantial connection to the United Kingdom (by birth, descent, adoption, or marriage) to obtain entry vouchers before arriving. According to Layton-Henry, Solomos, and Hansen, the clear intention of this concept was to control colored immigration from the Commonwealth while allowing unrestricted access to most white Commonwealth citizens of British descent.[23] Patrials, who are overwhelmingly white, have privileged access to the United Kingdom; they do not need work permits to take up employment or to settle permanently; they do not require resident permits for periods in excess of six months, nor do they have to register with the police. British immigration policy became even more restrictive and race-based with the Immigration Act of 1971, which (a) formally defined the concept of patrials; (b) ended the employment voucher scheme for Commonwealth citizens. Such citizens could now enter only on the basis of work permits that did not carry with them the right to permanent residency or the right to bring one's family, and would not automatically be renewed; (c) encouraged voluntary repatriation through financial incentives; and (d) strengthened the government's powers to prevent illegal immigration.[24] The Immigration Act of 1971 also replaced the Alien Restrictions Acts of 1914 and 1919 and the subsequent orders with one statue on the admission and stay of both Commonwealth citizens and foreign nationals.[25]

As immigration controls became harsher, immigrant policy and antidiscrimination laws have expanded. The Race Relations Act of 1965 was supposed to ensure equality of access to public facilities. The Local Government Act of 1966 provided for educational staff to teach English to immigrant children. And the 1968 Race Relations Act made it unlawful to discriminate on grounds of color, race, ethnic, or national origin in employment, housing, and the provision of services.[26]

Two factors led to the 1961–1972 restrictions on New Commonwealth immigration. First, the large-scale immigration of nonwhites produced political pressures at home. Second, Britain declined as a world power, which weakened its commitment to free migration.[27] The restrictions were not the product of economic decline, strikes, or social conflicts. While Britain's growth rate was lower than other Western European countries, its unemployment rate was low—below 3 percent throughout the 1946–1974 period (except for 3.1–3.8 percent in 1947). Strikes reached an all-time peak in 1962, but there is no evidence that they influenced immigration policies, or of an association between the strikers and immigrants. The 1950s and 1960 were not a period of social conflict or debate over national identity (other than that caused by immigration itself), except perhaps for the intensification of the conflict over Northern Ireland after 1968.

British Immigration Policy Since 1972

British legislation between 1962 and 1971—the 1962 Commonwealth Immigrants Act, the 1965 restriction of the number of employment vouchers, the 1968 Commonwealth Immigrants Act, and the 1971 Immigration Act—constituted the peak of restrictions on New Commonwealth immigration to Britain. Between 1972 and 1983 the British government continued to add legislation and regulations that further restricted such immigration: the 1973 immigration rules, the 1979–1980 immigration rules, the 1981 Nationality Act, and the 1982–1983 immigration rules. But these mostly implemented and revised restrictive legislation passed during the previous decade.

That legislation achieved its intended purpose. New Commonwealth immigration declined from 111,000–136,000 immigrants in 1961–1962 to 20,900–44,300 (with temporary surges to 68,500 in 1972 and 53,000–55,000 in 1975–1976) during the 1970s and 1980s. In addition, Britain reduced the number of work permits issued to non-EU foreign workers. The number of work permits reached a low point in 1976–1977, and subsequently remained at about the same level.[28]

But in the mid-1980s, a new type of immigration from the Third World started emerging—this time illegal/undocumented migration. Starting in 1989, the number of asylum seekers also substantially increased. In some cases, the two categories overlapped, because many illegal immigrants apprehended in Britain have applied for asylum in order to prevent their deportation, and because the authorities suspected that many of the asylum seekers are in fact economic migrants rather than genuine refugees escaping persecution. This phenomenon resembles the process that occurred in continental Europe, where the number of asylum seekers and illegal immigrants rose after the countries of destination halted their guestworker programs. Consequently, between 1985 and 1997, British policy focused on stemming the immigration of asylum seekers and illegal immigrants. When Labor returned to power, in May 1997, it abolished several restrictive policies enacted by the Conservatives. But overall, immigration control policy continued to concentrate on expediting the asylum process, and, in particular, on blocking illegal immigration and bogus refugees.

British Immigration Policy, 1972–1984

Certain sections of the 1971 Immigration Act—repatriation provisions and illegal immigration measures—came into force in October 1971. Other sections were designed to come into force on January 1, 1973, but their implementation was delayed because the Conservative government failed to pass the applicable immigration rules in October-November 1972 due to opposition by the Labor Party and by Conservative Party backbenchers. Eventually, the government succeeded in passing the revised immigration rules in 1973. One of the changes made was that anyone with a grandparent born in the United Kingdom would be exempted from the need for a work permit.

On August 4, 1972, General Idi Amin, president of Uganda, announced the expulsion of all Asians from his country. Most of the 50,000 Asians were British citizens, and it was clear that Britain would be primarily responsible for them.[29] The media warned of the expected arrival of the expellees, and some politicians—on the right-wing of the Conservative Party (such as the Monday Club and Powell), in the extreme-right, and at the local level—opposed their acceptance. But eventually the Conservative government accepted over 27,000 of the expellees, and induced other countries to accept the rest.

Between April 1974 and February 1975 the new Labor government moved toward a more liberal immigration control policy. It granted amnesty to certain illegal immigrants who were affected by the 1971 Immigration Act, it lifted the 1969 restrictions on the admission of husbands and fiancés of women settled in the United Kingdom, and it raised the quota for U.K. passport-holders from 3,600 to 5,000. In early 1976, the government also passed the Race Relations Act.[30]

However, starting in 1976 immigration control policy shifted again toward the restrictive pole. In March 1976, Home Secretary Roy Jenkins acknowledged the need to maintain a strict immigration control, and in April the Home Office minister responsible for immigration was dropped from the government for being too liberal with regard to immigration control.[31] In May 1976, the arrival of a small number of Asians from Malawi produced a media panic and an increase in support for the National Front. Its membership increased, and it gained between 15 and 19 percent of the vote in several municipal, county, and by-elections.[32] In July 1976, in response to mounting Conservative pressure over the Malawi Asian crisis, Jenkins announced the establishment of a parliamentary group to examine the possibility of creating a register of potential immigrant dependants. In October of the same year, the Conservatives annual conference was flooded with resolutions to control immigration, and the party's proto-manifesto stressed the need for an immediate reduction in immigration.[33] In February 1977, the Labor government decided that the register of dependants would not be feasible or desirable. In March 1977, the Labor government implemented a new Immigration Rule, under which men recently married to women already settled in the United Kingdom were no longer granted the right of immediate settlement. This measure led to a drop in the number of New Commonwealth citizens allowed to settle in the United Kingdom.[34] In April 1977 the government published its suggestions for the reform of the nationality and citizenship laws. It proposed two forms of British citizenship—one for those with close connections to the United Kingdom, and the other for those who were citizens of U.K. colonies.[35]

Margaret Thatcher's "swamping" statement of January 1978 highlighted the opposition of the Conservative Party to immigration. Mrs. Thatcher generated a controversy with her statement on television that people are afraid "that this country might be rather swamped by people with a different culture," and that "Britain should hold out the prospect of an end to immigration."[36] The Conservatives' manifesto for the 1979 general elections promised tough measures against immigration. When the Conservatives returned to power, they implemented some of their promises:

- Between November 1979 and March 1980, the Conservative government introduced new regulations restricting the admission for settlement of (a) husbands of women settled in Britain; (b) elderly dependants of sons and daughters settled in Britain; and (c) people who entered Britain as visitors or students. The regulations tightened family reunification overall, and introduced the controversial "primary purpose rule."[37]
- Between January 1981 and January 1983 the government passed the British Nationality Act, which differentiated between three major categories of citizenship: British citizenship, citizenship of the British Dependent Territories, and British overseas citizenship. The new nationality act also influenced immigration policy because only the first category—citizens of the United Kingdom, those whose parents or grandparents had been born, adopted, naturalized, or registered as citizens of the United Kingdom, and those who gained citizenship through permanent settlement in the United Kingdom—have the right of free access and settlement in the United Kingdom.[38]
- Between October 1982 and February 1983 the Home Secretary introduced changes in the immigration rules with regard to the admission of husbands and fiancés of British citizens.

British Immigration Policy, 1985–1996

As noted, since 1985, British policy has focused on stemming the immigration of asylum seekers and illegal immigrants:

- In 1985, an influx of Tamils from Sri Lanka, and perhaps also high unemployment and urban riots, led the Home Secretary Leon Brittan to announce that Sri Lankan Tamils would be allowed to remain only if they would suffer severe hardship if they returned. Ten days later new immigration rules required citizens of Sri Lanka to obtain visas in order to gain admission to the United Kingdom. According to Plender, this was the first occasion on which Commonwealth citizens were required to obtain visas.[39]
- The same year, the Conservative government also responded to a decision by the European Court of Human Rights by a rule change that (together with the 1988 legislation) removed the privileges enjoyed by pre-1973 male New Commonwealth migrants.[40]

- Between September 1986 and early 1987 the government, citing an increase in illegal immigration, imposed visa requirements on India, Pakistan, Nigeria, Ghana, and Bangladesh.[41] The government also used other methods to limit migration from the Indian subcontinent, including the strict enforcement of immigration rules at the ports, the deportation of people who broke the conditions of entry, and by requiring prospective immigrants to obtain entry vouchers at British High Commissions or Embassies in their country of origin.[42]
- The Immigration (Carrier's Liability) Act, passed in March 1987, gave the government the right to fine passenger carriers that brought people to the United Kingdom without proper documents. The Conservatives insisted that asylum rules had to be tightened in order to combat the rising number of bogus refugees.[43]
- In November 1987 the government introduced a bill repealing the absolute right of men and women settled in Britain before January 1, 1973 to be joined by their families. The bill, which went into effect in mid-1998 (the Immigration Act of 1988), also restricted rights of appeal against refusal of entry and against deportation.[44]
- In June 1989, the government imposed visa restrictions on Turkish Kurds.
- In 1989–1990 the government passed the British Nationality (Hong Kong) Act, which granted full British citizenship to 50,000 people from Hong Kong and their dependants, a maximum of 225,000.

Between 1988 and 1991 the number of asylum applications to Britain increased eleven-fold.[45] The number of illegal immigrants caught working in the United Kingdom increased from 4,000 in 1988 to 10,000 in 1995 and 1996. Parliament began debating a new asylum bill in 1991, but its passage was interrupted by the general election of 1992. A more moderate version of that bill eventually passed in 1993. The 1993 Asylum and Immigration Appeals Act was designed to give officials greater authority to prevent the filing of questionable claims and to deport those whose applications have been denied.[46] It included provisions that gave the authorities the right to fingerprint all asylum seekers as a means of confirming their identity where there was a suspicion that they had false papers. It also introduced the concept of "safe third country," and limited the right of appeal.[47]

The 1993 Asylum and Immigration Appeals Act sharply increased the proportion of asylum claims refused, from 14 percent in the six months before it came into force to 76 percent in the first nine months of 1994. Nevertheless, the number of asylum applications increased again in 1994–1995, producing a backlog of applications awaiting decision and allegations that many of the applications are bogus.[48] This, in turn, led to further restrictions on asylum applications and to controversies over the treatment of asylum seekers. The Asylum and Immigration Act of 1996 denied welfare benefits from asylum seekers who did not apply for asylum in Britain upon arrival. It also restricted council housing for asylum seekers and certain categories of immigrants, prevented them from working for six months and placed penalties on employers.

The government implemented several additional measures to stop illegal immigration and limit the number of asylum seekers: (a) DNA tests were conducted to see if a child brought into the country for family reunification is indeed the claimant's child;[49] (b) the home secretary offered to tighten marriage rules for potential immigrants in order to prevent "marriages of convenience"; (c) the government announced that it is considering plans to boost the deportation of asylum seekers by elevating the Home Office's Immigration and Nationality Department to executive agency status, and rewarding managers for meeting deportation targets; and (d) the home secretary visited Pakistan in order to talk to the government about trying to stem the flow of Pakistani asylum seekers.[50]

British Immigration Policy Since 1997

When the Labor government came into power in May 1997, it declared its intention to invalidate several restrictive immigration control policies enacted by the Conservatives. The changes included: eliminating the "Primary Purpose" rules, under which Britons marrying non-EU citizens had to prove that their marriage was not an attempt to avoid immigration controls; eliminating the so-called white list of countries whose citizens were regarded as facing no serious risk of persecution and thus could be returned before their applications for asylum were considered; and by not enforcing the 1997 employer sanctions laws. The government also increased the funds available to local councils to house and feed asylum applicants with no means of support.[51]

The government's second annual report, published on July 26, 1999, noted that it had already removed the primary purpose rule on immigration.[52] In February 1999, the government also announced that residents of 13 British Dependent Territories would be granted full citizenship and the right to migrate to the United Kingdom, thus reversing the elimination of these rights in the 1962 Commonwealth Immigrants Act and the 1983 British Nationality Act.[53] And a new law, effective December 4, 1999, extended the Race Relations Act to make police chief constables and senior immigration officials subject to prosecution if the staff they supervise are found guilty of racist acts.[54]

However, most immigration policies between 1997 and 2001 focused on expediting the asylum process, and in particular blocking illegal immigration and bogus refugees. Some of these policies had already been envisioned in the Labor's 1997 manifesto: the 1999 annual report argued that Labor's promises to streamline the system of visa appeals, ensure swift and fair asylum decisions, control unscrupulous immigration advisors, and crack down on fraud in birth certificates were all on course. But the growing numbers of asylum seekers and illegal immigrants caused the government to further emphasize these aspects of immigration policy. In late 1997, the Home Office announced measures aimed at restricting illegal immigration, such as beginning passport and identity checks on board *Eurostar* trains that pass through the Channel Tunnel from France and establishing a task force to deal with alien smuggling. In April 1998 it announced that the Carriers Liability Act would be extended to trains, so that the *Eurostar* would be liable for fines for passengers arriving in the United Kingdom without proper papers. The same year, the government also required nationals of the former Yugoslavia and Slovak citizens to have visas even if they were only on transit through the United Kingdom. The home secretary linked the visa requirement to "the abuse of the visa free arrangements by some passengers from the Slovak Republic. We must act to ensure the integrity of our asylum system."[55] On January 1, 1999, trucking firms were made liable for a 2000 pound fine per unauthorized foreigner brought into the United Kingdom. From February 2000, British authorities could require a 10,000 pound bond from visitors from high-risk countries including India, Pakistan, and Bangladesh. In August, 2000, the Britain started fingerprinting asylum seekers. And under the Immigration and Asylum Act, couples have had to personally go to the registrar at least 15 days prior to their wedding day, in order to prevent marriages of convenience, aimed at gaining a U.K. passport.[56]

The major immigration control act passed during the 1997–2001 period was the 1999 Immigration and Asylum Act, which went into effect in April 2000. Its main goals were to streamline the asylum system, and to reduce costs and abuse. The act limited asylum applicants to one appeal after rejection, extended carrier liability to truck drivers, speeded up the decision-making process to two months for a first decision and four months to handle any appeals, substituted vouchers for the cash assistance that asylum seekers received, and sought to disperse the asylum seekers around the country while their claims were being considered.[57]

The Recruitment of Foreign Workers Since 1996

After the European Volunteer Workers Program, and for over four decades (particularly after 1971), Britain did not implement substantial foreign worker programs. Instead, British employers used alternative sources of foreign labor: New Commonwealth migrants; EU workers; Irish workers;[58] young adults from Australia, Canada, New Zealand, and South Africa traveling the world; foreign professionals employed on an individual basis; and illegal migrants. In 1995, for example there were 200,000 Irish workers employed in Britain, as well as 15,000 Germans.[59]

But starting in the mid-1990s, and especially since 2000, Britain has renewed the state-controlled recruitment of non-EU foreign workers. In 1996, a Seasonal Agricultural Workers Scheme was added to the Asylum and Immigration Act of 1996 in order to permit British farmers to employ, from May through November, up to 10,000 Eastern Europeans as farm workers. In 2001, the government increased the number of permits for foreign farm workers from 10,000 to 15,200.[60] And in 2000–2001, the government announced, and started implementing, plans to simplify the procedures for admitting foreign professionals.

In May 2000, it was announced that Britain plans to simplify the procedures for admitting foreign professionals in order to reduce labor shortages in IT and health care. The pilot project, which aimed to attract non-EU skilled workers and professionals, was expected to draw workers mainly from India, Asia, and Eastern Europe. By that stage, Britain already eased the admission of foreign nurses, with 100 arriving by May 2000.[61] On September 11, 2000, Barbara Roche, the Home Office minister responsible for immigration, urged more flexibility in British immigration policy. Roche said that Britain is "in competition for the brightest and best talents-the entrepreneurs, the scientists, the high-technology specialists who make the global economy tick," so that the United Kingdom must make it easier for foreign professionals ("wealth creators") to enter and work. On September 29, 2000, new rules for foreign skilled workers were announced by the Department for Education and Employment.[62] In October 2001, Home Secretary David Blunkett announced that foreigners who are professionals would be allowed to enter the United Kingdom for one year under the Highly Skilled Migrant Program. The program, which was to begin in January 2002, was the first time in 30 years that immigrants without a prearranged job could enter the United Kingdom in search of employment. The aim of the program was to attract "highly mobile people with the special talents that are required in a modern economy." Their permits could be renewed indefinitely.[63]

The shift in Britain's skilled foreign labor policy is part of a larger, long-term move toward a system of work permits. This system might also include expanding the seasonal work program to nonfarm temporary workers, introducing work permits to help fill labor shortages in various industries, and letting foreign students who have been educated in the United Kingdom to apply for jobs without returning home.[64]

The main reason for this shift in policy was the shortage of labor in specific sectors (e.g. farm workers, nurses, and highly skilled workers in the IT industry), as well as the decline in unemployment rates in the labor market in general. In April 2000, unemployment rate fell to 3.6–3.9 percent, the lowest rate since the late 1970s. And in March 2001, the number of unemployed workers receiving UI benefits dropped to its lowest level since April 1975.[65] But the long-term move toward a controlled recruitment of non-EU foreign workers was also linked to the government's attempt to fight illegal immigration and its ramifications: the smuggling of people by "gang masters," the downward pressure on wages, and the proliferation of false asylum claims. In June 2001, Home Secretary David Blunkett announced that Britain would issue a limited number of visas for skilled and unskilled economic migrants to "pull the rug on the gang masters" who run the people-smuggling trade. Blunkett noted the impact of illegal immigration on lower-paid workers, and added that by opening up legal-entry options, there would be fewer false asylum claims by foreigners. And few months later, Blunkett told the Labor Party conference that he wants to deal with illegal immigration by introducing American-style work permits. "A properly managed system of legal migration," he argued, "would be a body blow to the gang masters and people traffickers who bring people to this country illegally."[66]

Factors Shaping British Immigration Policy—An Analysis

Most immigration to Britain has been permanent. Thus, in accordance with the theory advanced here, British immigration control policy has primarily been influenced by the volume of dissimilar immigration.

Restrictions on permanent immigration were passed in response to inflows of Eastern European (during the turn of the previous century), New Commonwealth immigrants (acts and regulations implemented between the early 1960s and the early 1980s), and illegal immigrants and asylum seekers (since the mid-1980s): the surge in Russian Jewish immigration after 1880 led to the 1905 Aliens Immigration Act; the arrival of almost 500,000 New Commonwealth immigrants between 1955 and 1962, especially in 1961–1962, generated the 1962 Commonwealth Immigrants Act; the continued large-scale New Commonwealth immigration after 1962 produced the 1965 restrictions; the 1968 flow of Indian refugees from Kenya led to the Commonwealth Immigrants Act of 1968; the arrival of a small number of Asians from Malawi in 1976 caused a flood of resolutions to control immigration in the Conservatives' annual conference and contributed to a more restrictive attitude by the Labor government; the 1985 influx of Tamils from Sri Lanka led to the imposition of a visa requirement for Sri Lankan citizens; the growing illegal immigration from Ghana, Nigeria, India, Bangladesh, and Pakistan generated the 1986 visa requirement for the citizens of these countries; the increase in illegal immigration also contributed to the enactment of the 1987 Immigration (Carrier's Liability) Act, to sanctions on employers of illegal immigrants, to the 1995 tightening of marriage rules for potential immigrants, and to the fines on trucking firms bringing unauthorized foreigners into the United Kingdom. Finally, the surge in Third World asylum applicants since 1989 led to the passage of the 1993 Asylum and Immigration Appeals Act, the 1996 Asylum and Immigration Act, the 1999 Immigration and Asylum Act, and to the implementation of additional restrictive regulations.[67]

The link between *the number of immigrants* and immigration control policy was frequently made explicit. For example, the home secretary justified the 1986 imposition of visa requirements on immigrants from India, Pakistan, Nigeria, Ghana, and Bangladesh by arguing that the number of people in the Third World who were seeking better prospects was large and growing. A statement issued by the Home Office maintained that the change became necessary in order "to maintain the effectiveness of immigration control in the face of pressures upon it."[68] The link between *the composition of immigration* and immigration control policy was also evident: the opponents of Russian Jewish immigration emphasized the ethnic and cultural characteristics of the immigrants; a Royal Commission on West Indian immigration stated its concern about the acculturation of immigrants of a different race; the opposition to colored immigration produced the distinction between "patrials" and "non-patrials," the former being overwhelmingly white; the Immigration Act of 1971 was rewritten after discovering that it made it just as difficult for Canadian, Australian, and New Zealandian to enter the United Kingdom as it did for colored Commonwealth citizens; Irish immigrants continued to be free of restrictions and to be accorded full citizenship rights.[69] Finally, the DNA tests with regard to family reunification are most frequently used for those coming from South Asia and Africa.

The state of the economy had a weaker influence on permanent immigration policy and asylum policy than the volume of dissimilar immigration. Most restrictions on immigration did not coincide with economic recessions: the restrictions of 1792, 1914, 1961–1962, 1965, 1968, and 1971 were passed during periods of relatively low unemployment (below 3.5 percent). Restrictions on asylum seekers continued after 1994, despite decreasing unemployment. But a labor shortage did facilitate the liberal immigration policy toward New Commonwealth immigrants during the 1950s. And higher rates of unemployment may have contributed to the passage of several restrictions, including the 1905 Aliens Immigration Act and those of the 1980s and early 1990s.

It should be noted that several studies did link the state of the economy with opposition to immigration at the local level. Foot describes the contribution of the 1961–1964 recession to anti-immigrant sentiments in Smethwick. According to Money, "recession in regions of rapidly expanding immigrant communities triggered growing opposition. The economic downturn in 1958 produced race riots in Nottingham (Birmingham) and London's Notting Hill district."[70] Money adds that the 1961 recession inspired broader-based opposition to immigration. The impact of the recession was uneven, and despite overall job creation, London and Birmingham (West Midlands), which were the only two cities to show a postwar decline in manufacturing employment, were also the center of opposition to immigration.

The state of the economy at the national level has had greater influence on British labor migration policy than on its permanent immigration policy, thus supporting the theory advanced here. In response to labor shortages, Britain recruited colonial labor during World War II and established the European Volunteer Workers program in 1947. A declining economy caused Britain to issue fewer work permits to non-EU workers during the 1970s, 1980s, and 1990s.[71] Labor shortages led to the establishment of foreign workers schemes in the farming, nursing, and high-tech sectors beginning in 1996. And the lowest unemployment rates in two decades contributed to plans for a renewed system of work permits, announced in 2001.

Foreign policy considerations have strongly influenced British permanent immigration policy. Until World War II, Britain supported free movement of capital, labor, and trade within the Empire in order to sustain its links with its colonies. As long as Britain aspired to world leadership, it refrained from restricting Commonwealth immigration. Even in the 1950s, when New Commonwealth immigration surged, Britain avoided restrictions because of opposition from West Indian politicians and its fear that such restrictions would undermine Britain's leadership role in the Commonwealth. Britain's loss of world power status, marked by the 1947 withdrawal of support from Greece and Turkey, the decolonization process, and the 1956 Suez operation, weakened its commitment to free immigration. As a result, domestic opposition to dissimilar immigration prevailed, leading to restrictions on immigration. Britain gradually eliminated its immigration links with the New Commonwealth, starting with the 1962 Act, which blocked most permanent immigration; continuing with the Nationality Act of 1981, which ruled that Commonwealth citizens were no longer automatically British citizens; and culminating with the 1985–1986 visa requirement for citizens of several New Commonwealth countries.

Foreign policy consideration also influenced Britain's refugee policy. The two major groups of refugees admitted by Britain were from New Commonwealth and communist countries. After World War II, Britain accepted 120,000 Polish veterans, most of them anticommunists. In 1956 it took in Hungarians, and later Vietnamese boat people. In 1972 Britain accepted Indian refugees from Uganda, and in 1974 it admitted Greek Cypriots.[72] Other examples of the impact of foreign policy consideration on immigration policy include the special allocation of vouchers to citizens of Malta, presumably because of the British and NATO defense facilities in that country, and the imposition of visa requirement on nationals of Cuba and Argentina.[73] According to one source, the 1985 restrictions on Tamil asylum seekers were influenced by considerations of foreign policy: "While there may be some evidence to suggest that part of the explanation of the home office's attitude towards Tamils was due to fear of 'bogus' refugee status being used to evade the strict immigration controls, an additional factor was the foreign office perception of the need to maintain good relations with the government of Sri Lanka, which holds a considerable strategic value in the Indian Ocean for the eastern Alliance."[74] But the relatively restrictive policy toward immigrants (and potential refugees) from Hong Kong demonstrates the declining influence of foreign policy considerations on British immigration policy: the British Parliament and government have refused to consider permitting more than 50,000 Hong Kong families to immigrate, despite heavy lobbying by Hong Kong Governor Chris Patten, because of their concern with reducing immigration.[75]

Wars and external threats have had the dual effect on British immigration policy described by the model. On the one hand, wars led to the recruitment of foreign workers. During World War II, manpower shortages in munitions factories and in forestry induced the recruitment of colonial labor. Those wartime migrants constituted the nucleus for the large-scale immigration from the West Indies and Asia during the next two decades. World War II also contributed to the recruitment of the European Volunteer Workers, many of whom were displaced persons, in the postwar period. On the other hand, external threats led to restrictions on permanent migration and on immigrants already settled in Britain. In 1792, Francophobia and fears of Jacobin agents led to the 1792 Aliens Bill. In 1848, fears that political refugees from Europe would cause disturbances prompted Britain to enact the Aliens Removal Act. In August 5, 1914, the day following the outbreak of World War I, the House of Commons passed the Alien Restriction Act. During the war, Germans in Britain were subjected to mass internment. The 1919 Act reaffirmed the 1914 Act, thus it was in part a product of the wartime xenophobia. In 1940, as Britain experienced military setbacks, it detained Jewish refugees from Europe. Finally, during the Gulf War, Iraqis and Palestinians in Britain were interned.[76]

Britain experienced a high level of *strikes* in 1912, 1919–1921, 1926, 1953, 1957, 1962, 1968–1974, 1979, 1981–1982, and 1984. The peak years of strikes were 1919, 1926, 1962, and 1979. Some of these years coincided with restrictive legislation: the 1919 Aliens Restriction Act, the 1962 Commonwealth Immigrants Act (although the bill was already introduced in 1961), the Commonwealth Immigrants Act of 1968, the Immigration Act of 1971, the 1979 immigration rules, the 1981 Nationality Act, and the 1982 immigration rules. However, I could not find any indications of a causal link between strikes and restrictions on immigration. In addition, other restrictions—in 1905, 1914, 1965, and after 1984—did not coincide with high levels of strikes. This factor warrants further examination.

Social conflicts and *debates over British or English national identity* have not influenced British immigration policies. With the possible exception of the Irish conflict, Britain hardly experienced serious social conflicts or debates over national identity during the past century.[77]

The main ethnic conflict, that is the Irish struggle for independence and later the Catholic–Protestant conflict in Northern Ireland, does not explain restrictions on immigration either. The 1919–1921 warfare partially coincided with the passage of the 1919 Aliens Restriction Act. But the 1914 Aliens Restriction Act preceded the Easter Rebellion of 1916, and the 1961 restrictions preceded the armed violence in Northern Ireland (which erupted after 1968). Moreover, while New Commonwealth immigration was restricted from 1961, Irish immigration was not. Welsh and Scottish nationalism, manifested by the Scottish National Party and the *Plaid Cymru*, has been on a rise since the 1970s. But this development, too, succeeded the main restrictions on immigration. Urban race riots, notably in 1958, 1976, 1980–1981, and 1985, are the only type of social conflict that may have contributed to restrictive immigration policies. However, this conflict did not evolve internally in British society, but rather was the result of dissimilar immigration, thus conforming to the model advanced here.

CHAPTER 4

Immigration Policies of the Netherlands

The Netherlands has admitted (or coped with) immigrants of six types:

(a) Migrant workers from neighboring Western European states—during the early twentieth century and then within the framework of the EEC/EC/EU;
(b) Migrant workers from outside the EEC/EC/EU—first, during the 1960s and 1970s, most migrant workers originated from Mediterranean countries (and were followed by family reunion and marriage migration during the 1970s and 1980s). Later, during the second half of the 1990s, labor migration from various countries increased again;
(c) Immigrants and refugees from Dutch colonies and former colonies in Southeast Asia, Latin America, and the Caribbean, mainly between 1946 and 1980;
(d) Asylum seekers/refugees—Jews fleeing Germany during the 1930s and later asylum seekers from the Third World and former communist countries since the mid-1980s;
(e) Illegal/undocumented immigrants;
(f) Returning Dutch nationals who had lived abroad.

In accordance with the model advanced here, as long as the stay of migrant workers was perceived to be temporary, Dutch labor migration policy was primarily influenced by the state of the economy, and to a limited degree by the composition of that migration. Policy with regard to colonial refugees and immigrants was mostly influenced by foreign policy considerations and later by the composition of immigration. Policy with regard to asylum seekers was primarily influenced by the volume and composition of immigration. Returning Dutch nationals faced no restrictions.

Dutch Immigration Policy Until World War II[1]

Until World War II, high population growth, high population density, and relatively late and limited industrialization made the Netherlands mainly a country of emigration.[2] The share of foreigners in the Dutch population was small during that period, constituting 1 percent of the population in 1900, 1.2 percent in 1910, 1.6 percent in 1921, and 2.2 percent in 1931. In comparison, foreign residents constituted 11.6 percent of Swiss population in 1900, and 10.4 percent in 1920.[3]

Most foreigners who lived in the Netherlands were similar to the local population in cultural terms. In 1921, only 1.1 percent of foreigners originated from Mediterranean countries, and their share grew to 3.5 percent in 1931. In 1930, 64.8 percent of foreign workers were German. In contrast, in 1972, 52.4 percent of foreigners originated from Mediterranean countries. In addition to the foreign workers, the Netherlands coped with inflows of refugees—particularly German Jews during the 1930s.

Until World War I, there was very little in the way of Dutch immigration control policy. Nor were there many incidents involving foreign workers. Under the Dutch Aliens Act of 1849, only those aliens who had enough money and were respectable could be admitted. Once admitted, aliens could not easily be expelled.[4] In 1858, the government restricted state positions to citizens. This was the sole clause prohibiting the occupation of economic positions by foreigners.[5] In 1887, all foreigners were required to register at state offices.[6] And in 1899, it became mandatory for all foreigners to register at the municipality where they were resident.[7]

Lucassen explains the very limited opposition to foreign workers by the fact that relatively few workers came to the Netherlands during that period.[8] An analysis of trends in permanent immigration shows a similar picture: immigration to the Netherlands remained relatively stable and low—ranging between 0.29 and 0.43 percent of the Dutch population during the 1877–1899 period (in comparison to 0.94 percent in 1975 and 1.13 percent in 1946).[9] The restrictions at the end of the nineteenth century did not limit the size of immigration, and did not coincide with recessions.[10] Instead, they increased the surveillance of foreigners, and were caused by fears of foreign subversion.[11]

World War I and the Bolshevik victory in Russia exacerbated these fears and generated further restrictions. In 1918, a central registration of foreigners was installed, and the government obtained powers to intern aliens if they were threatening domestic order. After the war, a visa requirement was imposed, and the Central Passport Office was established.[12] In 1920 and 1922 the 1877 registration requirement was revised, and landlords were required to keep a record of an alien's stay on their premises.[13] By the middle of the 1920s, immigration control policy moved toward the liberal pole. Visa requirements for immigrants from most European states were replaced by reciprocal treaties with those states, although the requirement for Germans was upheld until 1926. In 1930, the Dutch and German governments also agreed not to obstruct the employment of each other's nationals in their own country.[14]

But as the Dutch (and the global) economy deteriorated during the 1930s, restrictions were applied to foreign labor. The Netherlands granted visas to foreign workers only after the Director of the State Service of Unemployment Insurance and Labor Intervention had informed the consular officer that, with a view to the condition of the labor market, no objection exists to the employment of the foreigner.[15] In 1931, domestic servants were asked to produce an offer of work from an employer. After March 1933, the employer's work offer had to be approved by the local police. The law of May 16, 1934 stated that foreign workers in specific trades and industries will be subject to government permits, and that these permits would be refused if Dutch workers could be found to fill the vacancy. The number of economic sectors affected by the legislation was gradually increased until it included almost all occupations in October 1936. In 1937, a law restricted the establishment of foreign-owned businesses in particular sectors of the economy, and in 1938 a Royal Decree denied aliens with Dutch law degrees access to the bar.[16]

Between 1933 and 1938 the Netherlands also tightened its refugee policy in response to the influx of left-wing and Jewish refugees who fled from Germany after the Nazis came into power. Initially, the restrictions were mainly applied to refugees of Polish or Russian nationality and those suspected of being communists, while those immigrants who had German citizenship were exempted. In 1933, consular officials were told to carefully scrutinize applications for visitor's visas from stateless and Eastern European nationals, and most applications for visas were refused. In 1934, Dutch authorities attempted to identify aliens engaged in political activity, and a number of refugees, mostly communists, were expelled. In 1935, policy was changed in order to allow for internment of subversive aliens. In 1936, the Netherlands signed in Geneva the provisional agreement on German refugees, which stipulated that the first country where a refugee from Germany and of German nationality applied for asylum was responsible for his or her asylum application. However, Jewish refugees were not considered for refugee status. In 1937–1938 the Netherlands enacted the aforementioned restrictions on the establishment of foreign-owned businesses and on access to the bar, which particularly targeted Jewish refugees. In March and May 1938 new regulations strengthening border controls to cover all crossing points. Refugees with papers were given permits for no more than 14 days, while those without papers were only admitted if they could prove that they were in mortal and imminent danger. Finally, in December 1938 the Minister of Justice ordered the border to be closed except for those Jews whom the Dutch authorities had already given permission to enter.[17]

Dutch Immigration Policy, 1946–1972

After World War II, the Netherlands continued to view itself as primarily a country of emigration. Fears of "overpopulation" led the government to actively encourage emigration. Between 1946 and 1972 481,000 Dutch citizens emigrated. In the early postwar period, immigration was officially discouraged.[18]

In practice, however, the Netherlands started accepting large-scale immigration of several kinds. Between 250,000 and 300,000 refugees of Dutch nationality arrived from the former Netherlands East Indies and the Netherlands New Guinea between 1946 and 1962.[19] Initially, the Netherlands attempted to look for alternative places to settle some of these refugees in New Guinea or in America. But their Dutch nationality ruled out any attempt to prevent them from coming to the Netherlands. In addition, as Penninx notes, "the ties of these repatriates with groups in the Netherlands appeared sufficiently strong to turn them into political pressures in favor of an active policy of integration with ample provision of means."[20] Their relatively rapid assimilation into Dutch society was facilitated by the fact that some of the refugees were European, while others, who were of mixed Indonesian–Dutch descent (Eurasians), were culturally oriented toward the Netherlands. In addition, they belonged to the middle and upper levels of government and business, and had a relatively high degree of education.[21] In contrast, a group of 12,500 Moluccans—members of the dissolved Royal Netherlands East Indies Army and their families—who arrived in

1951, faced greater difficulties. The Moluccans were forced to migrate to the Netherlands, and hoped to return and form an independent Moluccan Republic, a hope that never materialized. In addition, they had a low level of education and lacked knowledge of the Dutch language.[22]

A second group of immigrants, of limited size in the pre-1973 period, came from the Dutch colonies of Surinam (in South America) and the Netherlands Antilleans (in the Caribbean). A third group of immigrants included political refugees, mostly from Hungary and Czechoslovakia.

In addition to the permanent immigrants and the refugees, the Netherlands also accepted hundred of thousands of migrant workers. Some of them came from neighboring European countries, their migration facilitated by the free movement of workers within the EEC/EC and the Benelux Economic Community. But the number of Dutchmen working in other member states was greater than the number of EEC/EC workers in the Netherlands during that period. The other group of migrant workers came from countries of the Mediterranean. Starting in the mid-1950s, employers recruited workers from Mediterranean countries—first from Italy, Spain, and Portugal, later in Yugoslavia and Greece, and finally also in Turkey and Morocco.[23] Other workers arrived from these countries spontaneously. Between 1960 and 1970 the government mediated and regulated recruitment though bilateral agreements signed with Italy, Spain, Portugal, Turkey, Greece, Morocco, Yugoslavia, and Tunisia. But about half of the foreign workers obtained employment without going though the official recruitment channels.[24] Labor migration reached its peak in the years 1970 and 1971, with more migrant workers entering the country between 1968 and 1971 than during the previous ten-year period. The number of foreigners from Mediterranean countries—most of them workers without their families—grew from 6,900 in 1960 to 140,200 in 1972.

Overall, the Netherlands implemented a relatively liberal immigration control policy between World War II and 1972. It signed bilateral agreements for the recruitment of labor with Mediterranean countries, and accepted immigration from former colonies. In addition, between 1956 and 1958 the Netherlands signed the Benelux Labor Treaty, the Benelux Economic Union Treaty, and the EEC Treaty, which allowed for the free movement of people between Germany, France, Italy, Belgium, Luxembourg, and the Netherlands. The 1965 Aliens Act and General Administrative Orders set rules for the admission of immigrants, created a system of work permits, and required a minimum of five years of uninterrupted residence before a foreigner could apply for a permanent residence permit. These rules initially sought to regulate rather than to decrease immigration, which was generally thought to be a temporary phenomenon. With regards to asylum seekers/refugees, the 1965 Act and the Decree on Aliens of 1966 implemented the principles of the 1951 Geneva Refugee Convention.[25]

Only in 1970 did the government publish its first serious government policy paper on migrant labor. This *Nota buitenlandse werknemers* (Note on Foreign Employees) stated that: (a) the admission quota for foreign workers has to be linked more closely to economic needs; (b) measures shall be taken to encourage return migration; and (c) the formulation of social policy with regard to migrant workers is officially delegated to subsidized organizations specially founded for this purpose. Admission standards for migrant workers became stricter: (a) employers had to recruit foreign workers through recruitment offices abroad or through Dutch consular offices; (b) they had to check at home in order to verify that there were no indigenous workers available to fill the vacancies; and (c) the government restricted the number of provisional work permits. In practice, however, the policy paper and the greater control of labor recruitment had little influence on immigration: the recruitment of foreign labor continued, reaching its peak in 1970–1971; the question of return migration was only discussed, but was not acted upon.[26]

Anti-immigrant parties gained little support between World War II and the early 1980s. The Farmers Party, which received 6 percent of the vote in 1966, exploited anti-immigrant sentiments to some degree, but they did not play a major role in the ideology of that party.[27] The Netherlands People's Union (NVU), an anti-immigration and "Greater Holland" party, was founded in 1971, but it was only able to gain a seat in some municipal councils. And a number of race riots erupted against migrant workers after 1971 (i.e. in the town of Schiedam and against Turkish migrants in Rotterdam).

Dutch Immigration Policy, 1973–1984

After 1973, Dutch labor migration policy became restrictive—mainly as a result of the economic recession, but to some degree also due to the cost of family reunion, which started during that period. In 1974, the Dutch government issued the *Memorandum in Reply to the Law on Foreign Workers,* which proposed to control the entry of foreign workers more rigorously, and to promote return to the countries of origin. The document also suggested limiting the stay of Mediterranean workers to a maximum of two years.[28] Labor recruitment was not formally stopped, but the number of new work permits issued fell sharply, and it became difficult to obtain a job without a permit (although the number of foreign workers in the Netherlands did continue to grow until 1978).[29] The main policy measure proposed by the 1974 *Memorandum* that materialized was the 1976 Law on Foreign Laborers, which prohibited employers from hiring more than 20 Mediterranean laborers. The November 9, 1978 Act on the Employment of Foreign Workers established various grounds for refusing work permits.[30] And in 1979, the government announced "the need to limit the number of foreigners employed in the country to a ceiling in line with economic conditions."[31]

During the mid-1970s, the government continued to characterize the immigration of the previous 20 years as temporary. But a series of events and processes that took place between 1973 and 1980 made it increasingly apparent that the immigrants' residence in the Netherlands had become permanent. These included: (a) the failure of government attempts to encourage return migration; (b) the immigration of family members of the former migrant workers from Mediterranean countries; (c) the increase in immigration from Surinam and the Netherlands Antilles; (d) the growing presence of immigrants in the large cities and their use of public services; and (e) the Moluccan terrorist attacks.[32]

Between 1974 and 1977 the government attempted to encourage return migration by: offering a departure bonus and special training for returning migrants; supporting the transport of the emigrants; allowing them to benefit from unemployment payments and pensions; starting a mother-tongue and culture program for children from Mediterranean countries; and stimulating development in the regions of origin, wherever possible by making use of the returning migrants and their funds. The Reintegration of Emigrant Manpower and the Promotion of Local Opportunities for Development (REMPLOD) research project suggested that measures of regional development must be a prerequisite for return migration. It generated a number of bilateral cooperative projects between the Netherlands and recruitment countries, such as Tunisia and Turkey.[33] Finally, throughout the 1970s, there was no integration policy for the Mediterranean workers and their families, comparable to that for colonial immigrants. The 1976 Law on Foreign Workers deliberately restricted the social advancement possibilities of the migrant workers. The Dutch government policy continued to state that "the Netherlands may not become a country of immigration," and it was hoped that the former migrant workers would return to their countries of origin.[34]

Overall, the attempts to encourage return migration failed. The departure bonus plan met with opposition from public opinion and was rejected by Parliament. The development programs proved to be too small-scale and expensive to have much of an impact on return migration.[35] Moreover, the former migrant workers were increasingly joined by their families. The number of foreigners from Mediterranean countries grew from 140,000 in 1972 to 196,000 in 1976, 244,000 in 1979, and 266,000 in 1980.

While the post-1973 restrictions mostly stopped the recruitment of foreign workers, immigration from two Dutch colonies—Surinam and the Netherlands Antilles—continued on a fairly large scale. Surinamese migration reached its peak in 1974 and 1975, shortly before the colony gained its independence, with almost 40,000 immigrants arriving in 1975, more than five times the number in 1970. The migration also changed in composition, from what was mostly a middle- and upper-class migration (many of them students) to lower-class and more labor-oriented migration from rural areas. In 1976, in an attempt to stop the mass flow of Surinamese, J.P. Pronk, the Dutch minister for Development Cooperation, went to Surinam to encourage the local government to join in a program of migrant return and reintegration, for which the Dutch were prepared to pay.[36] Immigration from Surinam and the Netherlands Antilles increased again in 1979–1980, when 37,000 immigrants from Surinam and 10,000 immigrants from the Netherlands Antilles arrived in the Netherlands.

This increase in immigration of various sources was particularly felt in Dutch urban areas. The number of foreign pupils in primary schools increased from a mere 10,000 in 1972 to 45,000 in 1980. In 1980, foreigners constituted 3.4 percent of the total Dutch population, and immigrants from Turkey and Morocco alone constituted almost 2 percent. The presence of the immigrants was especially felt in the large cities, where they were highly concentrated. In the mid-1980s, only 13 percent of the total population lived in the four largest cities (Amsterdam, Rotterdam, The Hague, and Utrecht), 38 percent of the foreign population lived there.[37]

Finally, Moluccan terrorism also made the Dutch public more aware of the unsettled status of these migrants. In 1970, Moluccans occupied the house of the Indonesian ambassador in the Netherlands. In 1975 they attempted to capture the queen of the Netherlands and hijacked a Dutch train. And in 1977 Moluccans hijacked another train, holding its passengers and children from a nearby school as hostages. The "Facilities Act" of 1976 awarded the Moluccans with the legal position of Dutch nationals, except that they still lacked the right to vote and could not be drafted into the army.[38]

These post-1973 developments gradually caused Dutch policymakers to recognize the *de facto* permanency of immigration. A 1978 policy document reviewed the policy pursued for 25 years with regards to the Moluccans. It acknowledged past mistakes and set new directions, which acknowledged that the Moluccans should be considered permanent immigrants. These may be regarded as a preamble to the general minorities policy that followed two years later.[39] The "Ethnic Minorities" report of the Scientific Council for Government Policy of 1979 recommended that the government "proceed on the assumption that [the immigrants'] residence in the Netherlands could be permanent." In its March 1980 reaction to the 1979 report, the government admitted that the Netherlands had become a country of immigration. The Draft Memorandum on Minorities, published in April 1981, stated the need to improve housing, education, and social welfare services to the immigrants. It also proposed granting local voting rights to foreigners who have lived in the Netherlands for a certain period, and setting up consultative councils at the national level for each ethnic minority group. The same year, the Penal Code was amended in order to strengthen anti-discrimination legislation. Finally, in 1983 the government published a "White Paper," which officially recognized that the Netherlands was *de facto* an immigration country.[40]

The growing recognition of the permanency of immigrants also contributed to the liberalization of naturalization policy. In 1984, the law on Dutch citizenship and procedures on naturalization was modified so that: (a) children born on Dutch territory and residing there since birth could acquire Dutch citizenship between the ages of 18 and 25 by declaration; (b) children of a Dutch woman (rather than only children of Dutch men) would become Dutch citizens by birth; (c) both male and female non-Dutch spouses of a Dutch national would have special rights to apply for Dutch citizenship, and (d) the children of the third generation (born to parents who themselves were born in the Netherlands) would automatically be Dutch citizens.[41]

But the growing foreign population, and the recognition that the Netherlands had become a country of immigration, also caused the government to implement stricter restrictions on new immigration. In fact, the Dutch government considered a restrictive admission policy as an important condition for the minorities policy to succeed. The 1979 Memorandum on Alien Policy expressed the need for a more restrictive immigration policy with regard to all immigrants. The new admissions policy, outlined in 1979–1980, introduced visa requirements for nationals of certain countries with a high immigration potential (Turkey, the

Maghreb countries, and Surinam).[42] It also applied the rules for family reunification more strictly, made "pseudo-marriages" for the purpose of illegal entrance more difficult, and introduced sanctions against employers of illegal immigrants.[43] In 1981, the Ministry of Justice put an end to the very liberal attitudes adopted by some municipalities toward family reunification. Permanent labor permits for persons who had worked five years in the Netherlands were abolished. And the 1981 Draft Memorandum on Minorities called for the creation of better facilities for migrants who wanted to return, although it did not force them to do so.[44]

The support for anti-immigrant parties somewhat increased between 1973 and 1983, but they still received less than 1 percent of the vote at the national level.[45] The NVU received 0.4 percent of all votes in the 1977 elections to Parliament. In 1980, the anti-immigrant Centrum Party (CP)—an offshoot of the NVU—was established. In the 1981 elections, the NVU and CP together received 0.3 percent of the vote. In the 1982 general elections, the CP, running on a fierce anti-immigration program, gained 0.8 percent of the vote and managed to obtain one of the 150 seats in the Second Chamber (Lower House) of the Parliament (the CP and NVU together received 0.9 percent of the vote). The extreme-right parties fared better in the March 1982 municipal elections, where they won between 1.7 and 2.4 percent of all votes in the cities of Amsterdam, Rotterdam, and The Hague. And in September 1983 the CP got 9 percent in the Almere municipal elections.

Dutch Immigration Policy Since 1985

Immigration to the Netherlands has changed since 1985. The last major wave of migrants from Dutch colonies or former colonies ebbed in 1981, following the visa requirement imposed on immigrants from Surinam, although immigration from Surinam, the Netherlands Antilles, and Aruba still continues. Labor recruitment from Mediterranean countries substantially declined after 1973.

Instead, post-1985 immigration to the Netherlands has been composed of several groups: (a) family reunion and family-forming migration; (b) asylum seekers, mostly from Third World and former communist countries; (c) illegal immigration; (d) labor migration; and (e) immigration of Dutch nationals, including those from the Netherlands Antilles and Aruba. The Dutch government has attempted to regulate and/or limit the immigration of these groups (with the exception of Dutch citizens and EU workers).

Family Reunion and Family Formation

According to Nicolaas and Sprangers, the term *family reunion migration* described immigrants joining their family members who had come to the Netherlands in previous years, including children who had arrived after their father and/or mother.[46] Family reunion has often been preceded by labor migration, most notably from Turkey and Morocco. The family reunification immigration of spouses of the former migrant workers was especially strong between 1975 and 1985.[47] Nevertheless, there are still comparatively large numbers of Turks and Moroccans who reunite with family members already living in the Netherlands: both groups accounted for more than 1,600 immigrants in 1998.

Asylum migrants with a residence permit also have the right to bring their partner and/or children to the Netherlands, and this accounted for a growing number of family reunion immigrants during the 1990s. In 1998, for example, the number of family reunionists from Iraq (a major source of asylum seekers) nearly equaled the numbers from Turkey or Morocco, and was much higher that those from neighboring countries such as Germany, Britain, or Belgium.

Family formation migration occurs when someone settles in the Netherlands for the purpose of marriage or cohabitation with a partner already living in the Netherlands. The family reunion migration of Turks and Moroccans, for example, was followed by an increasing family formation migration during the 1980s. In recent years, family formation as a motive to immigrate has been more important than family reunion. In 1998, 2,700 Turks and 2,800 Moroccans settled in the Netherlands for the purpose of family formation. In addition, a relatively large number of Surinamese have migrated to the Netherlands as part of family formation.[48]

The European Convention on Human Rights and the EC Treaty stipulate that anyone who has legally settled in one of the member states of the EU can claim the right to family life. This means that Dutch citizens as well as foreigners have the right to bring over non-Dutch partners and children. The Dutch government has not disputed this right. Moreover, it has applied a liberal definition of family, including partners in homosexual relationships.[49] Nevertheless, it has tried to regulate and limit migration for purposes of family formation and family reunion. After 1985, as the immigration of marriage partners increased, the government tried to limit it by introducing the requirement that persons wanting to bring over their marriage partner should have housing and a minimum income. This requirement did not apply to Dutch citizens. In 1993, the rules were tightened: they required that residents who are not citizens of a EU member state and wish to form a family should have lived legally in the Netherlands for at least three years. And they stipulated that family reunion would only be possible within three years of arrival in the Netherlands.[50]

The Dutch government has also attempted to guard against fraudulent marriages by requiring that (a) marriages involving one or more non-Dutch partners has to be approved by immigration authorities, and that (b) all family and marriage documents from "problem countries" (i.e. Ghana, Nigeria, India, Pakistan, and the Dominican Republic) have to be verified. In addition, the Netherlands planned to introduce voluntary DNA testing for applicants who want to join families in the country.[51] The new Aliens Act, which came into effect in 2001, specifies that in cases of family reunion, the applicant has to provide sufficient means for all members of his (her) family, and that Dutch nationals are no longer exempted from this requirement.[52]

In June–July 2002, the parties that were about to form the new center–right coalition government (including the anti-immigration List Pim Fortuyn) agreed to tighten immigration control policies. One aspect of the new rules was severely restricting family reunion: only children up to the age of 12 were to be allowed to join their parents in the Netherlands, and migrants who wanted their partners to join them would have to be 21 years of age and earn 130 percent of the minimum wage. Scholars, such as Han Entzinger, warned that the new rules could violate the convention on human rights.[53]

Asylum Seekers

Since 1985, the number of asylum applications to the Netherlands has substantially increased, while its composition differed from what was the case with previous waves of refugees. Between 1980 and 1984, the number of asylum applicants was only 1,300–2,600 per annum. But starting in 1985, it mounted: 5,600 immigrants applied for asylum in 1985; 13,500 in 1987; 20,300–21,600 between 1990 and 1992; and 29,300–52,600 between 1993 and 2000.[54] Between 1993 and 1997 the Netherlands coped with the second or third largest number of asylum seekers among European countries, preceded only by Germany and usually Britain (both much larger and more populated countries). Taking into account population size, the Netherlands is dealing with the second largest number of asylum seekers in the EU, preceded only by Sweden.[55] And while the main influx of refugees between 1946 and

1962 came from Dutch colonies, the post-1985 asylum seekers arrived from Asian and African countries (and for some years also from the former Yugoslavia), which did not have any cultural links with the Netherlands.[56]

The sudden arrival of a large number of Tamils in 1985 caused a change in Dutch asylum policy. As Amersfoort notes, until that time there had not been much of a special asylum policy. Asylum seekers had been temporarily lodged and given access to the general welfare security system. But after the arrival of the Tamils a formal regulation was introduced. Based on the Regulation for the Care and Accommodation of Tamils (RVVT) the asylum seekers were lodged and given a small amount of money, but were not given access to general social security, nor were they allowed to enter the labor market while waiting for the outcome of their hearings. This arrangement came to be known as the "Bed, Bread and Bath" Regulation.[57]

Between 1985 and 1987 the influx of asylum seekers continued, with growing numbers of immigrants arriving from Ghana, India, Pakistan, and Bangladesh. Consequently, the RVVT served as a blueprint for the Regulation for the Reception of Asylum Seekers (ROA), which applied to asylum seekers in general rather than being limited to the Tamils. The ROA, implemented in 1987, restricted the asylum seekers to "Bed, Bread and Bath" facilities (reception centers and ROA housing) and prevented their access to social security while they were waiting for a decision in their cases. This led to a temporary decline in the number of asylum seekers.[58]

Between 1990 and 1992 the number of asylum seekers increased again to over 20,000 per annum. This led to another attempt to streamline admittance policy, titled the New Admittance and Reception Model for Asylum Seekers (NTOM). Applications would have to be made in an Investigation Center, where it would be immediately decided whether the request stands a chance or not. People making unfounded claims would not be allowed to enter the country and would have to await their deportation in these centers. The Dutch government also extended the extraterritorial zone to an area near Schiphol Airport, and removed the Ministry of Foreign Affairs from participation in the granting of asylum to individuals.[59] In addition, the Schengen group signed a formal treaty with Poland on the return of aliens in 1991, and Benelux signed a similar treaty with Slovenia in 1992.

These new procedures did not yield the intended result, and the number of asylum seekers continued to grow to 35,400 in 1993, and 52,600 in 1994. The former Yugoslavia now accounted for the largest group of asylum seekers: 5,600 in 1992, 10,200 in 1993, and 13,400 in 1994.[60] In 1994, in response, the Dutch government implemented a series of policies aimed at streamlining the procedures for handling asylum seekers and further restricting their entrance:[61]

- A new status—Conditional Temporary Residence Status (VVTV)—was created in order to cope with the asylum applicants from the former Yugoslavia and with similar cases. According to Amersfoort, the idea behind this status was that in a period of civil war, people could not be sent back to their country of origin although they were strictly speaking not personally persecuted. They should, however, return to their home country as soon as the situation was considered to be sufficiently normalized.[62] The new status does not give access to the labor market;
- Since October 15, 1994, asylum seekers arriving by land were to report to one of two reception centers, Rijsbergen, on the Belgian border, or Zevenaar, on the German border, where Immigration and Naturalization Department (IND) officials determine their admissibility to the procedure. Asylum procedures were streamlined so that most cases could be handled within 24 hours, and difficult cases could be decided in six months. Those whose claims were found to be clearly unsubstantiated would be rapidly deported;
- A new law stated that immigrants wishing to settle in the Netherlands must apply to the Dutch embassy in their home country;
- The Dutch government started detaining rejected asylum seekers, who were waiting their deportation, in converted army barracks;
- In December 1994 and January 1995 the Parliament approved "safe third country" laws that would prevent persons from applying for asylum if they arrived from a "safe country of origin," or entered the Netherlands via a "safe third country." The list of "safe countries," which is drawn up by the Minister of Justice, consisted in 1997 of Bulgaria, Ghana, Hungary, Poland, Romania, Senegal, Slovakia, The Czech Republic, and all countries in the EU and the EEC. The criterion emulated similar criteria applied by Germany and Belgium at an earlier date;
- The Netherlands signed a protocol of cooperation with Morocco in regard to repatriation;
- The Netherlands strictly implemented the Schengen Agreement, whereby asylum seekers who travel through other member states

> before arriving in the Netherlands are deemed inadmissible to the asylum procedure. Airplanes started taking aerial photographs of suspected illegal entrants crossing Dutch borders so that the Netherlands could prove that an asylum seeker entered from Belgium or Germany and should be returned there to apply for asylum.

The series of restrictions, and particularly the introduction of the "safe country of origin" and "safe third country" criteria (plus the fact that Germany and Belgium applied similar criteria) facilitated a decrease in the number of asylum seekers from 52,600 in 1994 to 29,300 in 1995 and 22,200 in 1996.[63] During this period, the most commonly employed criterion for declining a request for asylum has been the fact that the applicant originated from a country deemed to be "safe."[64]

But these measures did not eliminate the pressures for asylum. A major source of asylum applicants since 1993 has been Iraq. In 1996, the number of asylum seekers from that country increased from 2,400 to 4,400, which led the Netherlands to conduct discussions with other countries. In October 1996, Turkey agreed to help halt the flow of refugees from northern Iraq to the Netherlands. A Dutch delegation also met with German representatives to discuss how to deal with a German crackdown on Iraqi asylum seekers that might drive them into the Netherlands. But the number of Iraqi asylum seekers continued to rise, reaching 9,600 in 1997 and 8,300 in 1998. Thus, the Dutch government announced in November 1998 that it would return more than 1,000 rejected asylum seekers to northern Iraq, northern Sudan, and Somalia, which it deemed "safe countries."[65]

The Netherlands also signed a series of bilateral agreements regarding the return of aliens. The measures include general support to the respective country of origin and specific programs to support the training, reception, accommodation, and employment of those who return. In 1995 Benelux signed a formal treaty with Romania. In 1997, the governments of the Netherlands and of Sri Lanka signed an agreement for the forcible repatriation of rejected asylum seekers.[66] The same year, the Netherlands also signed a return program with Somaliland, and protocols of return cooperation with Ethiopia and Angola. And in 1998 Benelux signed formal treaties on the return of aliens with Bulgaria and with Estonia.[67]

The renewed increase in asylum applications since 1997 (34,400 applications in 1997; 45,200 in 1998; 42,700 in 1999; and 43,900 in 2000) caused the Netherlands to adopt additional measures, including:[68]

- One of the problems the Netherlands had faced when dealing with asylum seekers was that many of them lacked identity papers. For example, Between January and October 1997, 70 percent of those seeking asylum had no papers. This lack of identification made it extremely difficult to deport rejected asylum seekers. Consequently, in November 1997, the Ministry of Justice announced a number of measures, including: placing the burden of proof on asylum seekers without documents to prove that they did not destroy their identity papers; establishing a language test to determine whether refugees claiming to be Afghanis are indeed from Afghanistan; the appointment of special staff in embassies receiving large number of queries and requests for asylum; increased use of fingerprinting as a means for checking identity; and an intensification of behind-border controls (e.g. extension of pre-boarding checks on certain flights), especially with regard to air travel.
- The share of asylum applicants under 18 rose to 16 percent in 2000, prompting Immigration Minister Ella Kalsbeek to return underage asylum seekers to safe third countries, and to return the others when they reach age 18.
- In August 1998, in contrast to the increasingly restrictive asylum policies, the Dutch Chamber of Standardization of Aliens Law agreed with UNHCR that persecution could exist in states without a central government, and that persons fleeing from such countries may be entitled to refugee status.
- In June 1999, the government decided that, beginning in January 2000, rejected asylum seekers would have four weeks to leave Dutch territory, after which they would lose all assistance and face arrest.

The 2000 Aliens Act, which replaced the 1965 Aliens Act, was adopted in December 2000 and went into effect in April 2001.[69] The Act, which aimed to simplify and shorten procedures for asylum seekers:[70]

- Created a single (temporary) refugee status, which, after a period of three years, would change into a permanent status. However, the permit could be revoked if the government decided that conditions in the home country had improved sufficiently to allow repatriation;

- Introduced new conditions for the granting of refugee status and related rights;
- Made it impossible for foreigners to apply for a permit in the Netherlands. Instead, they would have to do so at the Dutch embassy in their country of residence;
- Required that an applicant wishing to qualify for a residence permit would have to prove that he (she) has sufficient means to provide not only for him/her (as under the old laws) but also for the persons with whom he (she) would reside;
- Shortened the asylum procedure. As a consequence, it has become easier to expel unwanted foreigners;
- Made changes in the system whereby asylum seekers may enter the labor market. Three types of work permits were introduced for this category of foreigner: for a work period of indefinite length, for a fixed period, and a temporary permit. These permits granted the holders different rights. In effect, the government lifted its prohibition of asylum seekers getting work while they wait for authorities to decide on their applications.

Finally, in June 2002, the parties that were about to form the new center–right coalition government (including List Pim Fortuyn) agreed to tighten immigration control policies. The key objective was to halt the influx of asylum seekers into the Netherlands, and one of the rules planned was the creation of a new agency in order to remove foreigners whose asylum requests were rejected.[71] But the coalition collapsed soon after taking power, when the List Pim Fortuyn party disintegrated.

Illegal/Undocumented Immigrants

Like other industrialized countries, the Netherlands has also coped with illegal/undocumented immigration. Estimates with regard to the number of illegal immigrants run between 40,000 and over 100,000: A research project by the University of Utrecht published in 1998 estimated the number of undocumented migrants at around 40,000; another 1998 report estimated that there were 40,000 to 80,000 foreigners illegally present in the four biggest Dutch cities (Amsterdam, Rotterdam, Utrecht, and The Hague)—most of them from Suriname, the Netherlands Antilles, and North Africa; a third estimate put the number of illegal immigrants at about 75,000; and the government offered an estimate of over 100,000.[72] An official investigation, which took place during the first six months of 2000 in the horticultural sector in the West of the Netherlands, revealed that 10 percent of all employees were illegally employed.[73] Policymaking with regard to illegal immigration has also been influenced by highly publicized events in addition to evidence with regard to the number of illegal immigrants. For example in 2000, in the wake of the death of 58 Chinese migrants being smuggled into the United Kingdom, the police in France, Belgium, and the Netherlands stepped up their cooperation to learn about smuggling operations.[74]

The illegal immigration issue partially overlaps with that of asylum seekers (similar to the situation in Britain). Many, possibly most, asylum seekers whose requests are turned down stay in the Netherlands as illegal workers. Autonoom note that among the asylum seekers who were ordered to leave the country in 1994–1995, 3,000 were actually deported annually (under escort by border police); 2,000 have left "under supervision" (which means they have been dropped at a train station near the border with a ticket to Belgium or Germany, with no one checking if they really get on the train); and 9,000 were not found when the police checked the address they were staying at.[75] Bennekom et al. add that for many years, expulsion of aliens, who either did not apply for or had been refused admission, was not a priority in Dutch politics. The core of the policy was that return is the responsibility of the alien concerned, although in recent years, efforts to expel aliens in an active manner have been intensified.[76] In fact, the growing restrictions on labor migration and later on asylum seekers apparently contributed to the increase in illegal immigration. In addition, 60 percent of asylum seekers were found to have false or no documents, while others entered without being registered instead of actually applying for asylum.[77] For example in January 1995 Dutch police reported that it broke up a syndicate that smuggled Tamils from Sri Lanka into the Netherlands via Russia at a charge of $5,000 each. Once arrived, the Tamils applied for asylum without documents.[78] Consequently, some of the measures dealing with asylum seekers have also targeted illegal immigrants.

In some respects, Dutch policy toward illegal immigrants was relatively liberal. In 1975, the government declared a general regularization for illegal immigrants who could prove that they had resided and worked in the Netherlands for at least one year. Another small regularization took place in 1980. During the mid-1990s and up to 1998, the Dutch government permitted illegal migrants who could prove that they had held jobs in the Netherlands and paid taxes for six consecutive years to become legal immigrants. In 1998, this policy ended, although a limited amnesty remained available until December 1, 1999.[79]

Policy with regard to illegal immigration started turning more restrictive after 1985. One possible reason was that the growing restrictions on asylum seekers caused an increase in illegal immigration. Another reason was the fear that the number of migrants would rise as soon as the borders between the Netherlands and its neighbors disappeared under the Schengen Agreement. In 1989 a special commission was created to investigate what measures could be taken for more effective control over "aliens" when border controls were abolished. In its conclusions, published in 1991, the commission suggested:[80]

- Carrying out controls in a more administrative way in those institutions implementing social security regulations;
- Introducing a "restricted form" of identification requirements;
- Adopting new legislation to exclude undocumented migrants from the social security system;
- Implementing more active control inside the borders, especially in bigger cities, and allocating more manpower for the aliens police and military police. This last measure led to the formation of the MTV (Mobile Surveillance on Aliens). In addition to the 1,000 police officers already working at Schiphol Airport and at the borders, 1,200 new people were hired to conduct checks on anyone entering the Netherlands.

In 1991, it was decided to link the computerized register of population/the "Municipal Base Administration Personal Data" (GBA) together with the computerized registers of the aliens police/the "Aliens Administration System" (VAS). This link became operative in 1994. Also in 1991, it became impossible to obtain a "social-fiscal number" (i.e. the Dutch social security number) without the approval of the police. This measure restricted the ability of illegal/undocumented migrants to participate in the formal labor market. In 1992 it also became impossible to register at the local register of population without the approval of the aliens' police.[81]

Despite these various measures, the effectiveness of restrictions on illegal immigration was still relatively limited at that stage, and the highest officials in the big cities stated that their priorities do not include noncriminal illegal immigrants.[82] Amersfoort and Penninx conclude that it all made the impression of symbolic policy implementation. Amersfoort adds that external controls are hard to implement because of the great importance of tourists and visiting businessmen to the Netherlands. More rigorous internal controls were impossible because there was no standard central identification document, nor were people in normal circumstances obliged to identify themselves.[83]

Dutch policy with regard to illegal immigrants turned more restrictive in 1994:[84]

- Alien smuggling became a crime, punishable by a maximum of one year in prison;
- The Netherlands tightened its border controls. Immigration officials were stationed at the airports to identify those suspected of entering the country and then illegally overstaying their tourist visas. Such immigrants were expelled immediately;
- Dutch immigration officials began conducting pre-boarding checks at airports in countries from which many asylum seekers travel to the Netherlands;
- The Identification Law allowed Dutch police to demand identification on more occasions, and a limited set of permitted identification documents was defined;
- It became the duty of an employer, when contracting a new employee, to identify the person and to keep a copy of the identification document;
- As noted, the link between the GBA and VAS computerized registers became operative.

The next set of measures aimed at limiting illegal immigration was declared in 1996. The government announced plans to raise the prison sentence for human smuggling from one to four years, and to impose fines on airlines and other transport companies that bring foreigners without proper documentation into the country.[85] The Linkage Law (*Koppelingswet*), which was approved by the Second Chamber of the parliament in November 1996 and came into force in 1998, linked the various government and official databases in the Netherlands. The explicit purpose of that law was to link the residence status of foreigners to their entitlements such as housing, education, unemployment benefits and health insurance, and thus to facilitate immigration control.[86]

The government also started targeting the so-called white illegal immigrants, that is those illegals who paid taxes and were eligible for health insurance and other social benefits, in contrast to "black" illegals who avoided taxes by accepting under-the-table wages. According to the "six years rule," illegal immigrants who could prove that they had held jobs in the Netherlands and paid taxes for six consecutive years were supposed to receive favorable consideration in applying for residency permits. The government cracked down on those who could not prove that they paid taxes for six years, a policy that divided public opinion and resulted in two years of marches and street demonstrations over illegal immigrants' rights.[87]

In 1997 it was announced that the Netherlands would tighten enforcement in order to prevent an influx of illegal immigrants, especially from Afghanistan, Iraq, and Turkey. It would do so by establishing a special task force on alien smuggling, and by cooperating with Belgium, France, and Germany to inspect trucks entering the Netherlands that might be carrying illegal immigrants.[88] In June 1998, the Parliament passed the "loophole law," which granted border guards and immigration officials greater authority to search vehicles, question passengers, and obtain and make copies of the identity documents of persons believed to have entered the Netherlands illegally. The law also closed legal loopholes that had enabled undocumented foreigners arriving by air or ship to enter the Netherlands. Also in 1998, KLM Royal Dutch Airlines was charged with transporting 4,500 foreigners to Amsterdam Schiphol Airport without valid documents, a charge that carried a fine of 5,000 guilders per person.[89]

An official investigation, which took place in the first six months of 2000 in the horticultural sector in the West of the Netherlands, revealed that 10 percent of all employees were illegally employed. Consequently, legal measures were implemented to make it more difficult for employers previously convicted of illegal employment of foreign workers to do so again.[90] The same year, in the wake of the death of Chinese migrants being smuggled into the United Kingdom, the police in France, Belgium, and the Netherlands stepped up their cooperation with regard to smuggling operations.[91] And Dutch police conducted 30 raids on November 30, 2000 in Amsterdam against gangs that specialized in smuggling immigrants, drugs, and weapons.[92]

The new Aliens Act, which came into effect in 2001, focused mainly on asylum seekers. But it also established new rules with regard to the control and expulsion of illegal immigrants. In June 2002, the parties that were about to form the new center–right coalition government (including List Pim Fortuyn) agreed to make illegal immigration a criminal offense and to create a new agency that would force illegal immigrants back. In addition, border controls would be tightened up, as well as the rules with regard to people who do not carry a passport upon entry.[93]

Migrant Workers

Labor migration to the Netherlands was relatively limited during the 1980s and the first half of the 1990s. It then increased from approximately 9,000 in 1996 to 20,800 in 1999. This rise in the number of migrant workers was related to the growing need for labor in the Netherlands: unemployment decreased from 7.5 percent in 1994 and 6.6 percent in 1996 to 4.1 percent in 1998, 3.1 percent in 1999, 2.6 percent in 2000, and 2.4 percent in 2001—the lowest rate since 1971. In 2001, Dutch Integration Minister Roger van Boxtel urged more immigration: "The entire European population is aging, so the demand for labor is rising. The Netherlands too will need to attract more people."[94]

The increase in the number of migrant workers from non-EU sources has been especially notable: while labor migration from countries of the EU rose between 1996 and 1998 by 7 percent, the immigration of workers from non-EU countries increased by 40 percent during the same period. This trend is significant because only workers from outside the EU require work permits. The growth in the number of work permits has also been caused by an increase in the number of permits granted to asylum seekers while they wait for the authorities to decide on their applications. In particular, the number of work permits granted to Iraqi, Russian, Polish, and Afghani immigrants (many of them asylum seekers) has substantially increased from 1998 to 1999.[95]

Nicolaas and Sprangers note that most of these asylum seekers are employed as seasonal workers in agriculture, and that this situation is to a certain degree comparable with the situation of labor shortages in the 1960s, when lower-skilled workers were employed in manufacturing industries. Nevertheless, there are still several differences between the labor migration of the 1990s and that of the 1960s and early 1970s:[96]

- The number of migrant workers who came to the Netherlands in the 1990s was lower than that in the earlier period;
- While most migrant workers during the 1960s and early 1970s came from Mediterranean countries, the majority of the more recent workers came from EU and other economically developed countries. For example, of the 15,300 migrant workers who came to the Netherlands in 1998, 9,700 were from the EU, 1,100 from the United States, and approximately 500 were from Japan. In contrast, between 1968 and 1972, the number of foreign workers from nine Mediterranean countries alone grew from 64,100 to 140,200. As noted, whereas workers from EU countries do not

require a work permit in order to work in the Netherlands, labor migration from outside the EU is restricted, and a work permit is needed. Such a permit is granted only in case that recruitment from within the EU is impossible.

- In the 1990s (and contrary to the 1960s), many foreign workers migrating to the Netherlands were highly educated. They included managers, technical experts, and IT experts from the United States, India, the Republic of South Africa and so on. A third of the workers arriving in the Netherlands from outside the EU were posted there by their companies.

In addition to migrant workers from the EU and from outside the Union, the number of Dutch nationals (mainly from the Netherlands Antilles and Aruba) immigrating into the Netherlands has also increased dramatically (detailed later). Since these immigrants possessed Dutch passports, they did not need a work permit.[97]

Immigration of Dutch Nationals

A relatively substantial share of immigration to the Netherlands is composed of Dutch nationals. For example of the 122,400 immigrants who arrived in the Netherlands in 1998, 40,700 were Dutch nationals; of the 119,200 immigrants who came to the Netherlands in 1999, 40,800 were Dutch. The majority of them were former emigrants born in the Netherlands. However, others were born in the Netherlands Antilles and Aruba, and their numbers grew from 3,341 in 1995 to 10,167 in 2000. In addition, between 2,647 and 4,603 (mostly non-Dutch nationals) immigrants arrived from Surinam during the same period, the majority of them under the categories of family formation or family reunion (see table 4.1).

Immigration from the Dutch West Indies and Surinam is unlikely to reach the level of 1975, when 43,800 immigrants arrived in the Netherlands, mostly from Surinam. This is because Surinamese who were in Surinam at the moment of independence in 1975 automatically lost their Dutch citizenship. Nevertheless, immigration from the Netherlands Antilles and Aruba has fluctuated substantially: it increased to 10,167 in 2000 due to the poor economic conditions in the Caribbean. This was a relatively high number, compared, for example with a total of 13,000–15,000 asylum applicants granted in 1998 and 1999. It then decreased to 8,310 in 2001 and an estimated 5,700 in 2002, and the migration surplus (immigration minus emigration) for this group has shrunk from 54,000 to 2,000, the lowest since 1992.[98]

Table 4.1 The Netherlands: immigration and emigration by people born in the Netherlands, the Netherlands Antilles, Aruba, and Surinam, 1995–2001

	The Netherlands		*The Netherlands Antilles and Aruba*		*Surinam*	
	Immigration	*Emigration*	*Immigration*	*Emigration*	*Immigration*	*Emigration*
1995	21,396	34,848	3,341	3,056	2,647	1,122
1996	22,566	35,742	3,845	2,471	3,643	1,243
1997	22,715	33,137	4,751	2,085	3,555	1,316
1998	25,984	32,076	7,590	1,899	4,603	1,151
1999	24,974	30,833	8,813	1,959	3,205	874
2000	23,817	32,749	10,167	1,867	3,601	793
2001	23,150	34,240	8,310	2,293	3,569	783

Source: Central Bureau of Statistics, 2002a.

Anti-immigrant Parties Since 1984

Since 1984, electoral support for anti-immigrant parties fluctuated, until they achieved their greatest success in 2002. The anti-immigrant Centrum Party (CP) gained 2.5 percent of the vote, and 4–8.1 percent of the vote in some municipalities, in the 1984 European Parliament elections.[99] But it did poorly in the May 1986 general elections, receiving only 0.4 percent of the vote and losing its only seat in Parliament, mainly due to the break away of the Centrum Democrats (CD). As was the case in previous elections, the extreme-right parties (NVU, CP, and CD) fared better in the March 1986 municipal elections, where they got 2.6–4.0 percent of the vote in the larger cities of Amsterdam, Rotterdam, The Hague, and Utrecht.

In the 1989 general elections, the CD won 0.9 percent of all votes and gained a seat in Parliament. The party also gained 0.8 percent in the elections for the European Parliament of the same year. In the 1990 municipal elections, the anti-immigrant parties (CP'86 and CD) achieved 5.0–7.1 percent of the vote in the four larger cities. In the March 1994 general elections, the Central Democrats won three seats in the 150-member Second Chamber of Parliament. But in the municipal elections in March 1998, the three extreme right-wing political parties (CD, NB, and CP'86) lost nearly all their seats. In the parliamentary elections of May 1998, the CD lost their three seats.[100] In March 2002, the List Pim Fortuyn party won 36 percent of the vote in Rotterdam's city elections. Finally, in the May 15, 2002 general elections, List Pim Fortuyn received 18 percent of the vote, and became the second largest party in

Parliament, despite the murder of its leader a few days prior to the elections. The party joined the coalition government and Hilbrand Nawijn from the Pim Fortuyn List party was nominated as immigration minister. The government promised to be stricter on immigration, stating that: "A restrictive aliens policy is necessary and illegal immigration should be fought with vigor." It also announced plans to have asylum seekers pay a E7,000 deposit for compulsory Dutch language and citizenship lessons, to restrict family unification, and to better enforce employer sanctions. But, as noted, that government collapsed in October 2002, less than 100 days after taking power, when the Pim Fortuyn List party disintegrated.[101]

Factors Shaping Dutch Immigration Policy—An Analysis

The Netherlands has admitted (or coped with) immigrants of six types:

(a) Migrant workers from neighboring Western European states—during the early twentieth century and then within the framework of the EEC/EC/EU;
(b) Migrant workers from outside the EEC/EC/EU—first, during the 1960s and 1970s, most migrant workers originated from Mediterranean countries (and were followed by family reunion and marriage migration during the 1970s and 1980s). Later, during the second half of the 1990s, labor migration from various countries increased again;
(c) Immigrants and refugees from Dutch colonies and former colonies in Southeast Asia, Latin America, and the Caribbean, mainly between 1946 and 1980;
(d) Asylum seekers/refugees—Jews fleeing Germany during the 1930s and later asylum seekers from the Third World and former communist countries since the mid-1980s;
(e) Illegal/undocumented immigrants;
(f) Returning Dutch nationals who had lived abroad.

The model advanced here argues that the type of immigration—for example temporary labor migration, permanent dissimilar immigration, permanent similar immigration, refugees and illegal immigration—determines the relative influence of the various socioeconomic and foreign policy factors on immigration control policy.

Migrant workers According to hypothesis 8, labor migration policy is mainly determined by the state of the economy. It is influenced to a lesser degree by the volume of immigration and by racist/liberal ideology. During the 1930s, the Netherlands experienced high unemployment rates, and recruited few migrant workers. But by the mid-1950s, there were already sectoral labor shortages, which caused employers to recruit workers from several Mediterranean countries (starting with Italy). Between 1960 and 1971, unemployment rates were 2 percent or lower, leading the Dutch industry, with the support of the authorities, to expand the recruitment of migrant workers. Bilateral agreements were signed with Italy, Spain, Portugal, Turkey, Greece, Morocco, Yugoslavia, and Tunisia. The number of foreigners from Mediterranean countries reached 140,200 in 1972.

The 1967 recession motivated the Netherlands, like other Western European countries, to assume greater control over labor migration by linking the admission quota more closely to economic needs and by channeling the recruitment of workers through recruitment offices abroad or Dutch consular offices. But after 1968 the economy revived. Between 1969 and 1971 unemployment rated decreased again to 1.1–1.6 percent, causing the recruitment of migrant workers to reach its peak in the years 1970 and 1971. Finally, the economic recession brought an end to the foreign labor program. Unemployment increased to 2.8 percent in 1972–1973, and rose to over 5 percent during the second half of the 1970s. Following the 1973 oil crisis, a government document proposed to control the entry of foreign workers more rigorously, and the number of new work permits issued fell sharply. In 1974–1977, the Dutch government attempted to encourage foreign workers to leave the country, and in 1976–1978 it further restricted the right of employers to hire foreign workers.

The link between the state of the economy and policy toward migrant workers was explicitly made by the government. The 1970 government policy paper "Note on Foreign Employees" stated that the admission quota for foreign workers has to be linked to economic needs. The State Commission on the Population Question, which was set up in 1972 and submitted its final report in 1977, similarly linked migration from the Mediterranean area to developments in the Dutch economy, as these were foreseen by the Central Planning Office.[102]

During the 1960s, the stay of the foreign workers was viewed as *temporary*, and a topic not worthy of discussion in the Netherlands.[103] This perception of migrant temporality was further facilitated by the fact that the great majority of immigrants from the Mediterranean area were unaccompanied males.[104] Thus, according to the model, *the perception that the migrant workers were only temporary facilitated the acceptance of 140,000 immigrants of dissimilar origin*—mainly from Turkey and Morocco. The government tried to reinforce the temporary nature of labor migration by stating in its aforementioned 1970 policy paper that the admission quota for foreign workers should be linked more closely to economic needs, and that measures should be taken to encourage return migration. The paper stated that "With due respect for the human aspects, we cannot escape the conclusion that our country needs manpower and not the immigration of families."[105] Between 1974 and 1977, the government attempted to encourage return migration, thus striving again to sustain the notion of temporality and that the workers would be rotated. It offered a departure bonus, acted to stimulate development in the regions of origin, and started a mother-tongue and culture program for children from Mediterranean countries.

Throughout the period between the mid-1950 and the late 1970s, the government clung to the illusion that labor migration was temporary. For the most part, the public also accepted this view and anti-immigrant sentiment was limited. No anti-immigrant party succeeded in winning a seat in Parliament until 1982. But between 1974 and 1978 the attempts to encourage the return of migrant workers to their previous homes failed and family reunion migration increased. Only then, in 1979–1983, the government finally recognized that the former migrant workers should be considered permanent immigrants, and at the same time announced restrictions on new immigration. According to hypothesis 9, *the government's recognition of the former migrant workers as permanent immigrants should cause the importance of the volume and composition of immigration to increase in comparison to that of the economy*. And, indeed, the 1979 Memorandum on Aliens Policy stated that admissions should be "as restrictive as possible . . . even if an upswing occurred in the economy."[106] Anti-immigrant sentiments also intensified, and in 1982 the CP, running on a fierce anti-immigration program, managed to obtain a seat in Parliament.

Labor migration to the Netherlands during the 1980s and the first half of the 1990s was relatively limited. It then increased from approximately 9,000 in 1996 to 20,800 in 1999. In contrast to the labor migration of the 1960s, the majority of the more recent workers came from EU and other economically developed countries. Thus, they benefited from the free movement of workers within the EU, from the need for highly skilled workers, and from their similar ethnic composition—factors that are detailed below. In addition, the number of migrant workers from non-EU and particularly Third World and Eastern European sources has especially increased since the mid-1990s. Some of them are asylum seekers who benefited from a liberalized employment policy. But the rise in their numbers was facilitated by the growing need for labor in the Netherlands: unemployment decreased from 7.5 percent in 1994 to 2.4 percent in 2001.

Refugees and permanent immigrants from the colonies According to hypothesis 6a, considerations of foreign policy tend to facilitate the liberalization of immigration control. According to hypothesis 11, refugee policy is mainly influenced by foreign policy considerations, and to a lesser degree by the volume of immigration, the state of the economy, and so on. Foreign policy considerations clearly influenced immigration control policy with regard to refugees from the Dutch East Indies/Indonesia as well as immigrants from Surinam and the Netherlands Antilles. These refugees and immigrants were Dutch citizens, and therefore eligible to settle in the Netherlands. But foreign policy considerations (in this case colonial policy) led to the granting of Dutch citizenship, and thus also influencing immigration control policy. A 1954 attempt to "enlighten" colonial policy led the Netherlands to award residents of the colonies with Dutch nationality, which allowed them to settle freely in the Netherlands.[107]

The primacy of foreign/colonial policy considerations over the other factors (the composition of immigration and the state of economy) is evident in those cases where the former conflicted with the latter. The Netherlands accepted refugees from the Dutch East Indies/Indonesia during the early 1950s, and from Surinam between 1973–1975 despite recessions. It admitted the Moluccans and immigrants from Surinam despite the racial and cultural differences between them and the native population of the Netherlands.

Other characteristics of the immigrants and in some cases the state of the economy facilitated a liberal immigration policy, thus complementing the influence of foreign/colonial policy considerations rather than conflicting with it. First, the stay of many of these immigrants was viewed as temporary: "the immigrants were stubbornly classified as temporary residents who 'one day' would return home."[108] Only in the late 1970s, following the peak immigration of Surinamese and the hijackings by Moluccans, was the permanency of these two groups finally recognized. This presumed temporality of the immigrants helped to limit the antagonism toward the immigrants. Second, starting in the mid-1950s, an expanding economy and labor market facilitated the acceptance of the immigrants from Indonesia.[109]

The eventual restrictions on immigration from Surinam indicate that the "volume and composition of immigration" and the economic factors overcame the influence of foreign policy considerations. In fact, the influx of "Dutch nationals born in Surinam" was the main reason that the Dutch government induced Surinam to become an independent republic.[110] In effect, the restrictions were another symbol of the Netherlands' long decline from the status of a global power, similar to the case of Britain. The decreasing role of foreign policy considerations in Dutch immigration policy was also evident in organizational terms: traditionally, the Ministry of Foreign Affairs was responsibly for policy and coordination with regard to refugees.[111] But in the early 1990s, the Ministry of Foreign Affairs lost its role in the granting of asylum to individuals.

In addition to the refugees from the Dutch East Indies/Indonesia, the Netherlands has admitted a relatively small number of refugees (usually between 500 and 700 per annum) from other regions. It has made a distinction between "invited refugees"—persons whose refugee status had already been established by the UNHCR, and who were admitted to the country as such—and asylum seekers, whose numbers were limited until the mid-1980s.[112] Two types of international relations considerations have influenced the admission of "invited refugees." First, there were pressures from international organizations. Amersfoort and Penninx describe the reluctance of the Netherlands to accept immigration: "Immigration was—and is—considered to be undesirable and has at best been accepted as an unavoidable consequence of the colonial past, the recruitment of labor in the 1960s, or *international treaties with regards to refugees*."[113] After 1984, when the number of spontaneous asylum seekers started increasing, the government decide to decrease the number of "invited refugees" from 500 per annum to 250. But under pressure from the UNHCR it soon brought the number back to 500.[114]

The second case was partially linked to the Netherlands' geostrategic position and to the Cold War. During the 1950s and 1960s, the three main groups of refugees admitted were from Hungary (1956), Czechoslovakia (1968), and Portugal (1960s). Thus, in the first two instances the Netherlands followed the United States and other Western countries in favoring refugees from communist countries, although in the third case it accepted refugees from a right-wing dictatorship. In the 1970s and 1980s this has changed, as the Netherlands accepted refugees from a wide variety of countries, including Ugandans, Chileans, Uruguayans, Argentineans, Ethiopians, Eritreans, Vietnamese,

Cambodians, Surinamese, Iranians, Turkish Christians, Poles, and others.[115]

Asylum seekers Starting in 1933, the Netherlands faced an influx of left-wing and especially Jewish refugees (i.e. asylum seekers in today's terms) who fled Germany after the Nazis came into power. Initially (in accordance with hypothesis 4), fears of subversion caused the Netherlands to mainly restrict refugees holding Polish or Russian nationality and those suspected of being communists. Consular officials were told to scrutinize applications for visitor's visas from stateless and Eastern European nationals, the Dutch authorities attempted to identify aliens engaged in political activity. A number of refugees—mostly communists—were expelled, and policy was changed in order to allow for internment of subversive aliens. But the growing influx of German Jews, and opposition to them within the Netherlands, caused Dutch authorities to increasingly restrict the admission of refugees, until the border was closed to new Jewish refugees in December 1938.

In 1965 the Netherlands incorporated the principles of the 1951 Geneva Convention on Refugees into its Aliens Act. The Royal Decree of January 10, 1974 added the category of "persons entitled to asylum," also known as persons with "B" status, as opposed to persons admitted as refugees who have "A" status. It should be noted that in contrast to the case of migrant workers, the deteriorating economy did not prevent the Netherlands from further expanding its definition of asylum seekers eligible to remain in the country (at least temporarily).

Since 1985, the number of asylum seekers attempting to enter the Netherlands has substantially increased. In proportion to the size of the local population, the Netherlands is dealing with the second largest number of asylum seekers in the EU, preceded only by Sweden. The composition of migration changed in comparison to the past: while the main influx of refugees between 1946 and 1962 came from Dutch colonies, the post-1985 asylum seekers arrived from Asian and African countries (and for some years also from the former Yugoslavia), which did not have any cultural links with the Netherlands. The Dutch government responded to the increase in the number of asylum seekers, starting with the arrival of the Tamils in 1985, by implementing successive restrictions. It annulled their eligibility for welfare, required that their applications would be made in an Investigation Center, extended the extraterritorial zone to an area near Schiphol Airport, created central registers, required that applicants be made in Dutch embassies in their home countries, detained rejected asylum seekers in converted army barracks, prevented persons from applying for asylum if they arrived from a "safe country of origin" or entered the Netherlands via a "safe third country," cooperated with the countries of origin and countries of transit in an attempt to limit the influx of asylum seekers, and shortened the asylum procedures.

In accordance with hypothesis 9, the timing of the restrictions on asylum seekers better correlates with the number of applications for asylum than with the state of the economy. The analysis is somewhat blurred by the fact that (a) new restrictions were frequently declared; and (b) the 1994 peak in the number of asylum seekers coincided with the highest rate of unemployment of the 1990s. Nevertheless table 4.2 demonstrates the aforementioned correlation. In addition, official statements linked restrictive immigration control policies to specific waves of asylum seekers (i.e. from Sri Lanka and from Iraq). The government

Table 4.2 The Netherlands: unemployment rate, number of asylum seekers, and immigration control policy, 1980–2001

The period	*Unemployment rate*	*The number of asylum seekers*	*Immigration control policy with regard to asylum seekers*
1980–1984	Increasing	Small	None
1985–1990	Decreasing	Increasing (except for 1988)	Restrictions in 1985/1986 and 1987
1991–1994	Increasing	Increasing (except for 1992)	Restrictions in 1990–1992 and in 1994 (plus: Benelux and the Schengen group sign treaties with Poland and Slovenia for the return of aliens)
1995–1996	Decreasing	Decreasing (except for an increase in asylum applicants from Iraq)	Discussions with Turkey and Germany with regard to Iraq, but no legislation (plus: Benelux signs a treaty with Romania for the return of aliens)
1997–2000	Decreasing	High (increasing 1997–1998, stable afterward)	Restrictions in 1997–2000 (plus: the Netherlands signs agreements with four countries for the return of aliens; Benelux signs treaties with two more)

also noted that reception centers for asylum seekers were overflowing, forcing officials to rent hotels and boarding houses to house asylum seekers.[116]

Illegal immigration The Netherlands has also coped with illegal/ undocumented immigrants, the numbers of which range, according to various estimates, between 40,000 and over 100,000. Until recently, it implemented several regularizations, as well as permitting illegal migrants who could prove they had held jobs in the Netherlands and paid taxes for six consecutive years to become legal immigrants. But policy with regard to illegal immigration started turning more restrictive after 1985, and particularly since 1994, though a combination of external and internal controls. The former included checkups at the borders with Germany and Belgium and in Schiphol Airport; aerial photographs; establishing a special task force on alien smuggling and cooperating with Belgium, France, and Germany; defining alien smuggling as a crime and increasing the punishment for it; and placing fines on airlines transporting foreigners without valid documents. But external controls were hampered by the need to avoid interfering with the flow of tourists and businessmen into the Netherlands. Internal controls included: linking various computerized registers (population, foreigners etc.), which in practice limited the ability of illegal/undocumented migrants to enter the formal labor market and to obtain housing, education, and unemployment benefits; requiring the approval of the police in order to obtain a "social-fiscal number"; allowing the police to demand identification on more occasions and defining a limited set of permitted identification documents; and implementing legal measures against employers of illegal immigrants.

The reasons for the restrictions on illegal immigrants included: (a) evidence of their growing numbers: (b) highly publicized events—such as the death of migrants being smuggled into the United Kingdom; and (c) fears of additional illegal immigration following the opening of borders between the Netherlands and its neighbors under the Schengen and EU Agreements.

Dutch nationals and immigrants from neighboring Western European countries According to hypothesis 10a, immigration control policy with regard to permanent similar immigration tends to be more liberal than the policy with regard to permanent dissimilar immigration. This includes (a) former emigrants who had retained their citizenship; (b) descendants of former immigrants, who are viewed as "repatriates"; and (c) immigrants who share ethnic and cultural characteristics with the indigenous population. The Netherlands has applied a liberal immigration control policy toward these three groups of immigrants. In addition, until recently, they were favored over non-EU immigrants with regard to the accommodation requirements in the context of family reunion.

According to hypothesis 10b, the two factors that do, occasionally, produce restrictions on permanent similar immigration are severe depressions and doubts with regard to the degree of similarity between the immigrants and the dominant element of the receiving society. The former caused restrictions on foreign workers, including those from neighboring countries, during the 1930s, while the latter contributed to the attempt to find alternative settlement possibilities for immigrants of mixed Indonesian–Dutch descent.

Dutch citizens have constituted a substantial share of immigration to the Netherlands. For example, in 1994, citizens of the Netherlands accounted for 30 percent of all immigration to that country. Dutch nationals immigrating to the Netherlands have included three subgroups. First, there were those who were born in the Netherlands and emigrated, but retained their Dutch citizenship. Until World War II the Netherlands was primarily a country of emigration. Also since the war, a large number of Dutch citizens have emigrated, especially to the United States, Canada, Australia, New Zealand, and South Africa. Between 1946 and the mid-1980s, over half a million Dutch people emigrated to the New World. Of all the Dutch who departed for Australia, Canada, and New Zealand in the period 1980–1984, almost a third were back in the Netherlands eight years later. About 60 percent of the Dutch emigrants to the United States also returned during the same period.[117]

Second, there were the children of Dutch citizens. If at least one of the parents holds Dutch nationality, then his or her offspring and descendants also have access to Dutch nationality, at least for an extensive period.

Third, there were those immigrants, mentioned earlier, who held Dutch citizenship by virtue of having been born in a Dutch colony or former colony. The immigrants from the Dutch East Indies/Indonesia were formally defined as "repatriates," and some of them were of Dutch origin. Other immigrants from Indonesia (not including the Moluccans) were of mixed Indonesian–Dutch descent, and never set foot in the Netherlands before, although many of them were culturally oriented toward the Netherlands.[118] These immigrants might be defined as somewhere between "similar" and "dissimilar," and the Netherlands accepted them, but also looked for alternative settlement possibilities for them. In this case, the aforementioned foreign/colonial policy considerations clearly contributed to the acceptance of the immigrants.

The third category of immigrants to whom the Netherlands has applied a liberal policy are immigrants from neighboring Western European countries, that is, immigrants who share racial and cultural characteristics with the Dutch population. Prior to the 1930s, the admission of these immigrants was facilitated by three additional factors: (a) the immigrants were mostly temporary migrant workers; (b) the Netherlands signed reciprocal agreements with its neighbors, and gained from the free movement of labor; and (c) Germany was a major trade partner of the Netherlands, and "the importance of an economically resurgent Germany to the well-being of the Dutch economy dictated the free movement of people across the shared frontier."[119] Despite these factors, the great depression of the 1930s was severe enough to lead to restrictions even on West European migrant workers to the Netherlands. Since World War II, the admission of West European migrants was again facilitated by four factors: (a) for the most part, they have been migrant workers or students who have established themselves in the Netherlands temporarily; (b) European students and others who do not take part in the labor process usually have a means of existence in their home country and are required to take out health insurance. Thus the burden they impose on Dutch society is relatively light;[120] (c) some of the immigrants are highly skilled, and are viewed as beneficial to the Dutch economy; and (d) since 1956–1957, the immigration of Western European workers has been facilitated by the free movement of workers within the EEC/EC/EU and in the Benelux Economic Union. Moreover, during the early stages of the EEC, the Netherlands was mainly a country of origin in terms of intra-EEC movement of labor, which made it supportive of the free movement of labor.

The social conflict/national identity theory argues that social cleavages, social unrest, and debates over national identity explain the timing of restrictions on immigration. This theory may help explain the growing supervision of aliens, especially those suspected of threatening domestic order, between 1918 and 1922. According to Caestecker and Moore: "Crucial in the decision to control migration was a perceived need to prevent subversive aliens entering the country. [Swiss and] Dutch political elites were traumatized by revolutionary events elsewhere in Europe and saw their authority being undermined at home by political events such as . . . the threats of Troelstra, the Dutch Socialist leader, to overthrow the bourgeoisie in November 1918."[121] However, in addition to the domestic national conflict, Caestecker and Moore also point at the role of external threats and a decrease in the need for foreign labor as causes for the Dutch decision to stem immigration.

The pillarization of the Dutch political system, which according to Rowen "removed most of the tinder from Dutch politics," received official confirmation in the Pacification of 1917.[122] This contradicts, to some degree, the social conflict/national identity explanation for the 1918–1922 supervision of immigrants, but it could be argued that it facilitated the relatively liberal immigration control policy during much of the 1920s. The same could be argued with regard to the impact of the polder model: immediately after the war, the private Labor Foundation, which consists of representatives of both employers and employees (the "social partners"), was established, and five years later, in 1950, the government set up the public Social and Economic Council (SER), which encouraged ongoing consultation between employers and unions.[123] But on the other hand, the friction in Dutch society with regard to its conduct under German occupation does not seem to have had any impact on the immigration control policy of the Netherlands.

During the 1960s, the religious pillars began to crumble. The "provo" movement protested against conservatism, the Church and established norms, producing some rioting of youth and labor groups. In 1966, a public debate followed the marriage of Princess Beatrix to a German diplomat, and the same year the Farmers Party gained 6 percent of the popular vote. But neither of these developments generated restrictions on immigration. The pillarization further disintegrated around the late 1960s/1970. But while this event coincided with the 1970 policy paper calling for greater control of immigration, that paper had little influence on migration policy, and labor migration reached its peak in 1970–1971.

Restrictions on labor migration were finally implemented in 1973–1976, and on colonial migration in 1980, when, according to Voerman and Lucardie the protest voting that followed modernization and the breakdown of pillarization died down.[124] In 1982 representatives of business and trade unions signed the Wassenaar accord under which "the unions promised to deliver pay restraint, including more decentralized wage bargaining, in exchange for a new emphasis on jobs. For its part, the government undertook to sort out its fiscal mess and to lower taxes. The Wassenaar accord laid the foundations for the economic renaissance of the late 1980s and 1990s."[125] But as the employers, unions, and government reached this renewed compromise, restrictions on immigration mounted. To conclude, for the most part (with the exception of the 1918–1922 period), Dutch restrictions on immigration cannot be attributed to social conflicts or national debates in the Dutch society, and thus the social conflict/national identity theory fails to explain Dutch immigration control policy.

Surges in the percentage of workers on strike (over 1.5 percent of the employed labor force) occurred in 1913, 1918–1923, 1946–1947, and 1960. Again, the increase in the number of strikers between 1918–1923 may have contributed to the greater supervision of potentially subversive aliens. In neither of the other major cases (i.e. where over 1.5 percent of the employed labor force was on strike) did the surge in the number of strikers coincide with restrictive immigration control policy. On the contrary: the years 1913, 1946–1947, and 1960 were all periods of relatively liberal immigration policy or of stability in Dutch immigration control policy. Furthermore, as I noted in chapter 1, a problem with the argument that industrial unrest contributes to restrictions on immigration is that when large numbers of local workers are on strike, employers are rather likely to recruit foreign workers in order to break the strikes. The largest number of Dutch workers were on strike in 1960. This was also the beginning of the mass-recruiting period. As Vellinga describes: "Production capacity could not be used to its full extent and sharp tensions were created in the labor market where one wage claim followed another and the 'official' trade union movements had great problems controlling the situation. To regulate and control the situation of individual companies recruiting workers abroad, the government made recruiting contracts with eight countries in the Mediterranean area in the period 1960 to 1971."[126]

The percentage of workers on strike also increased, to a lesser degree (1–1.5 percent of the employed labor force), in 1931–1932, 1970, 1973, and 1982. The 1931–1932 increase was mostly due to the large number of unemployed workers (which influences the denominator when calculating the percentage of workers involved on strike), rather than because of a substantial number of workers striking. The 1970 and 1982 surges did not coincide, nor where they followed, by restrictions on immigration. Only the 1973 rise in the percent of the employed labor force on strike supports the aforementioned hypothesis. But overall, the hypothesis linking industrial unrest to restrictions on immigration does not offer a good explanation for Dutch immigration control policy.

CHAPTER 5

Immigration Policies of Germany

German Immigration Policy Between 1871 and World War I

Until the mid-1880s, Germany was mainly a country of emigration. Yet, after 1871 the German Empire faced a labor shortage, first in the agricultural sector of the eastern provinces of Prussia, and later in the industrial centers of the west. The labor shortage in the east was mostly ameliorated by the recruitment of Polish foreign labor from Russia and Austria. The shortage in the industry and mines of the Ruhr was met by Poles who moved from the areas annexed by Germany, and by foreign labor from various Western and Central European countries. The number of foreigners in Germany increased from 206,000 in 1871 to 1.26 million in 1910, constituting 1.9 percent of Germany's population. According to the 1910 census, about half of the foreigners were from Austria-Hungary, followed by those from the Netherlands, Russia, and Italy.[1]

Germany started restricting the usage of foreign labor in 1885. After 1872, the government of Prussia enforced a rigid policy of "Germanization" on the Poles living in the annexed territories. The government feared that the employment of "foreign" Poles would jeopardize this policy, and in 1885 it deported between 30,000 and 40,000 Poles from the eastern Prussian provinces, closed the eastern border, and prohibited further immigration of Polish foreign labor.[2] However, these deportations generated fierce protests from Prussian landowners, who faced an acute shortage of agricultural workers. A compromise was reached in 1890 between the political and economic interests, which allowed Polish migrant laborers to work in the eastern provinces of Prussia, but prevented them from taking up permanent residence. The laborers had to leave the country every year for 4.5 months during the winter (the *Karenzzeit*). The compromise also prohibited the Polish workers from moving from the agricultural and industrial areas in the east to the industrial areas in the west. The following year, the government extended the regulations to the central and western provinces of Prussia, but still limited the foreign Poles to employment in the agricultural sector. In 1907–1908, the government implemented measures that controlled immigration as well as the working and living conditions of foreign Poles in Prussia. The new regulations introduced a "compulsory domestic permit," which assisted the employers to fight breaches of contract, and gave the German Farm Workers Agency a monopoly over the recruitment of foreign labor for agriculture. However, they did not restrict the volume of immigration. Finally, in 1914, on the eve of the war, a surge in unemployment resulted in increased dismissals and deportations of foreign workers.[3]

The pre–World War I legislation with regard to foreign labor was the result of conflicts between agricultural employers on the one hand, and nationalistic circles in the government on the other hand. But as the model predicts for temporary labor migration, the timing of legislation and regulations was related to the economic cycle. The deportations of 1885 and 1914 coincided with surges in unemployment. The compromise of 1890 was reached in the early stages of a recession in industry, and at a time of high prices for agricultural products and manpower shortages in agriculture. Consequently, the compromise prevented foreign Polish workers from moving to the industrial centers in the west, but kept them coming for agricultural labor in the east.

The arrival of immigrants of dissimilar ethnic composition contributed to the pressures for restrictions on immigration. But the temporary nature of the immigration limited the impact of its volume and composition. In fact, the compromise of 1890 weakened the fears of a "Polanization" of Prussia by guaranteeing that Polish immigration would be temporary. Advocates of the "national identity" approach would argue that the timing of restrictions on Polish foreign workers was determined by a social conflict and a lack of confidence in national identity. But the policy of "Germanization" started in 1872, while the deportation of Polish workers occurred only in 1885. Similarly, restrictions on the use of the Polish language in Germany in 1899 and 1908 were not followed by restrictions on the volume of Polish immigration.

At the outbreak of World War I, Germany prevented Russian Polish agricultural workers, particularly those eligible for military service, from returning home. But the military defeats in the autumn of 1914, the prospect of a prolonged war, and the rapid expansion of the armament industry changed the focus of that policy. It led to the extension of restrictions on departure to all Polish Russian laborers. Later in the war Germany also recruited Polish, Hungarian, Belgian, and Dutch workers, mainly through the use of force.[4] Altogether, over two million foreigners were working in Germany at the end of the war.

The wartime employment of foreign workers bears greater resemblance to the recruitment of temporary workers than to permanent immigration because the foreign workers were not eligible for any social or political rights and were deported or released at the end of the war. The recruitment was generated by manpower shortages in the agricultural and industrial sectors, a result of the "war–migrant worker" link. Considerations of foreign policy also influenced immigration policy during the war: German and Austria-Hungarian proclamation of the revived Kingdom of Poland caused Germany to ease the restrictions on the change of locality and job for Polish workers in December 1916. In addition, Germany improved the treatment of Belgian workers to some degree because of protests from neutral countries, such as Spain, Switzerland, the Netherlands, and the United States.[5] Finally, the war led to the initiation of passport and visa requirements, which served as the basis for postwar restrictions on immigration.

German Immigration Policy, 1918–1945

The next phase, between 1918 and World War II, can be divided into three periods. During the Weimar Republic, the employment of foreign labor was restricted. The recruitment of foreign labor began again under Nazi rule between 1933 and 1939. Finally, the Nazis used prisoners of war and forced labor on a large scale during World War II.

The period between 1918 and 1933 was characterized (with the exception of 1921–1922) by increasing and high unemployment, particularly in the industrial centers. Consequently, policies regulated and restricted the recruitment of migrant labor, but were applied with less severity to the agricultural sector. At the end of World War I, the new government, faced with the prospect of returning soldiers and the conversion of industry to peacetime production, sent the foreigners back to their homelands as quickly as possible. The restrictions also involved the repatriation of Polish workers and the closure of the frontier to potential foreign workers.

By 1924, the number of foreign workers in Germany declined from more than two million to 174,000. The repatriation of Polish workers aimed at mitigating unemployment, which rose particularly in the industrial towns. But it generated manpower shortages in the agricultural sector, which could not be filled by transferring German workers from industry to agriculture. Thus, in 1919, the government, responding to demands from the large landowners, authorized the employment of some 50,000 Polish agricultural workers in eastern Germany. From 1920, foreign workers were admitted under the following conditions: (a) foreigners could be hired only when no domestic workers were available; (b) foreigners and Germans were paid according to equal, fixed, and agreed-upon wage scales; and (c) special committees, made up equally of management and workers, monitored the admission of foreigners.[6] In 1922, the Labor Exchange Act unified rules and controls that had been issued in individual regulations, and made the movement of foreign labor from agriculture to industry more difficult. In 1923, the Prussian interior minister issued a decree on the deportation of aliens. And in 1929, the 12-month limit of work and residence permits, which previously applied only to Poles, was expanded to all foreigners. The final ordinances restricting the employment of foreign labor were implemented in 1932 and 1933. Throughout the Weimar Republic period, foreign labor constituted less than 0.4 percent of the German population.

The Nazi regime, which came into power in 1933, expanded Germany's industrial capacity, and in particular its armament industry. The rate of unemployment decreased from 26.3 percent in 1933 to 8.3 percent in 1936 and 4.6 percent in 1937, and labor shortages developed. As a result, the illegal immigration of Polish workers, employed in the agricultural sector of eastern Germany, increased. The German government also concluded labor recruitment agreements with Poland, Italy, and several other governments. By 1939, there were an estimated 90,000 (legal) Polish, 37,000 Italians, 15,000 Yugoslavs, 12,000 Hungarian, 5,000 Bulgarians, and 4,000 Dutch workers in German agriculture as a result of such agreements.

The employment of foreign labor reached its peak during World War II, when millions of prisoners of war and people from occupied countries worked in labor camps and private industry. Recent German research indicates that 12 million non-German workers—prisoners of war, concentration camp inmates, and civilians in German-occupied areas—were required to work in German factories and other workplaces, so that, by the end of the war, non-Germans were 40 percent of the German manufacturing workforce.[7]

The timing of legislation and ordinances on temporary labor migration between 1918 and 1945 followed the economic cycle. First, the return of the soldiers and growing unemployment led the government to repatriate foreign workers and close the borders to new ones. The Labor Exchange Act also restricted the movement of foreign labor from the agricultural sector—where there was a demand for workers—to the industrial sector, where unemployment was high. Then, Germany, faced with a severe economic crisis, restricted immigration in 1923, 1929, and 1932, all of which were years of high unemployment. In contrast, labor shortages during the Nazi era—produced by the expansion of the armament industry and by mobilization—generated the recruitment of foreign labor and later to the use of prisoners of war and inmates of labor camps.

The Nazi period illustrates the weakness of the social cleavage theory. It also demonstrates that the level of dissimilar immigration had limited effect on migrant labor policy. The 1930s was a period of major social conflict in German society, and it produced a racist regime. Nevertheless, once the economy revived, the regime encouraged labor immigration. The composition of labor migration caused alarm over grave "dangers in respect to cultural policy" and with regard to the threat to the purity of the German blood. But it did not prevent Germany from signing agreements for the recruitment of foreign labor.[8]

German Immigration Policy, 1946–1960

Between 1945 and 1948, 12 million ethnic Germans were expelled from former German provinces annexed to Poland and the USSR, from other parts of Poland, and from Czechoslovakia, Hungary, Yugoslavia, and Romania to the occupation zones within Germany. By 1950, some 7.9 million expellees (*Vertriebene*) were living in West Germany—mostly in the British and American zones—and another 3.6 million in East Germany (GDR).[9] About 500,000 more Germans from the eastern provinces, who came to Germany during the war and could not return to their old homelands, were given the same legal status as those actually expelled.[10]

After 1950, the West German government decided to facilitate the immigration of the remaining ethnic German minorities living in the communist countries of Europe, officially called resettlers (*Aussiedler*). Over three million refugees migrated from East Germany to West Germany before the building of the Berlin Wall in 1961. The immigration and integration of the ethnic German immigrants was facilitated by several policies implemented by the West German government:[11]

- The West German Constitution (*Grundgesetz*) of 1949, which defined as citizens not only former citizens of Nazi and interwar Germany but also all ethnic Germans who had found refuge on German territory within the boundaries existing in 1937. Since the 1950s, an extensive interpretation included other ethnic Germans still living in Central and Eastern Europe as potential citizens;
- The Federal Law concerning Refugees and Expellees of 1953, which regulated the privileged admission and absorption of former German citizens and ethnic Germans;
- The law of 1957, which for the first time officially termed the ethnic German immigrants *Aussiedler*, and gave them the same status and access to benefits as postwar expellees. The law clarified the concept of ethnic origin, and defined ethnic Germans by descent, language, and cultural or ethnic orientation.

The Federal Republic of Germany (FRG) welcomed the ethnic German immigrants and granted them immediate citizenship upon arrival despite the size of the migration wave, relatively high unemployment (until 1954), and a severe housing shortage. Moreover, the FRG facilitated the integration of these immigrants by providing them with financial aid, as well as giving them priority in housing, free German language courses, vocational training, and a claim to transfer payments such as public pensions even for those ethnic German immigrants who did not contribute to German pension insurance.[12]

Until 1955, the government rejected demands by German farmers for organized recruitment of migrant workers. This situation changed in 1955, when the requests of German farmers for Italian workers coincided with Italian demands that these workers should be recruited under the terms of a bilateral agreement. Consequently, Germany and Italy signed an agreement for the recruitment of labor in December 1955.[13] Between 1954 and 1959, unemployment rates in Germany declined from 7–7.6 to 2.6 percent, and the number of foreign workers rose from 72,000 to 167,000. But it was still limited in comparison to the mass recruitment of migrant workers that took place during the 1960s.

The period 1946–1952 also witnessed the rise of extreme right-wing parties of the "old right-wing extremism" type. Six of them successfully gained national or regional representation, including the Economic Reconstruction Association (WAV), the German Rightist Party (DRP), the German Reich Party, the German Social Party (DSP), the Socialist

Reich Party (SRP), and the German Community (DG).[14] With a few exceptions at the regional level, none of these parties was very durable.

German Immigration Policy, 1960–1973

Between 1960 and 1973 Germany recruited foreign labor on a large scale. It signed bilateral agreements for the recruitment of labor with Greece and Spain in 1960, Turkey in 1961, Morocco in 1963 (revised in 1966), Portugal in 1964, Tunis in 1965, and Yugoslavia in 1968. The system was well organized, with German employers applying for workers at local employment offices. The latter first made a pro forma search for local workers, and then the request was sent to German offices in the countries where labor was being sought.[15]

The number of foreign workers increased from 73,000 in 1954 (0.1 percent of the population) to 2.6 million in 1973 (4.3 percent of the population), with only a temporary decline to 1–1.1 million workers during the 1967–1968 recession. Initially, the majority of migrant workers were Italians. But during the second half of the 1960s, the Yugoslavs and the Turks became the fastest growing groups of foreign workers, and by 1972 Turkey was the largest source of foreign workers to Germany. Until 1973 there were no restrictions on the recruitment of migrant workers, although during the 1967–1968 recession the government encouraged the repatriation of workers by limiting their eligibility for unemployment benefits and by refusing to extend their work permits.[16]

During the 1960–1973 period, the government passed several acts that regulated the recruitment and status of migrant workers, included the Aliens Act (the Law on Foreigners) of 1965, the Labor Promotion Act of 1969, and the Work Permits Decree of 1971. But it did not limit the size of the foreign workforce until 1973. The Aliens Act of 1965, which sought to make labor migration more flexible and controllable, was the basis for further regulations. It established the conditions for migrant residency, requiring every foreigner staying in Germany for more than three months to get a residence permit, and making it possible to grant permanent residence after five years of residency. It also gave the authorities broad discretionary powers. The Labor Promotion Act of 1969 required aliens to obtain work permits before taking employment in Germany, unless they benefited from international agreements excluding them from this duty.[17] The Work Permits Decree of 1971 set out detailed rules governing the issue of work permits, based on the state of the labor market. It allowed foreigners who had been employed for more than five years to obtain a special work permit of additional five years.[18] In 1971, the labor minister still asserted: "The extent to which foreign nationals will be required beyond the present levels of employment depends on developments in the labor market. In that respect, there can thus be no talk of the imposition of a 'ceiling' on the employment of foreign nationals."[19] In 1973, for the first time since the war, the government implemented formal restrictions on the recruitment of foreign labor. In January 1973 Chancellor Brandt stated, "we should carefully consider where the ability of our society to absorb has been exhausted, and where social common sense and responsibility dictate that the process be halted."[20] In July of that year, the fee for recruitment of foreign workers was increased, and in November 1973, a ban on the recruitment of foreign workers from outside the EEC was implemented.

Until 1973, foreign labor was generally viewed as temporary in nature. According to Mehrländer, the expectations listed in the early arrangements were that foreign workers would spend a relatively short period of time in Germany and then be replaced by others on a short-term, rotating basis.[21] In 1959, the *Frankfurter Allgemeine* stated: "in the event of unemployment in Germany, the foreign workers could be sent back home again."[22] According to the 1965 Aliens Act, an extension of the work and residence permit beyond one year was granted only if the interests of the FRG were not damaged as a result. Permanent settlement in the FRG was interpreted by the courts as a violation of this regulation. The 1965 Act also lacked any rules for family reunification. Overall, the 1965 Aliens Act and the following regulations on work permits, were "intended to make immigrant labor in the Federal Republic of Germany a maneuverable resource, easily controlled and regulated, for the solving of economic problems."[23] Between 1966 and 1967 the recession set in and the number of foreign workers declined by 25 percent, which seemed to substantiate the assumption that labor migration was a temporary phenomenon, and that the migrant workers would leave in the event of unemployment in Germany.

In practice, however, it gradually became apparent that the foreign labor phenomenon was less temporary than initially envisioned. Migrant workers were employed for longer periods, as "rotation made little sense for business and industries where experience and continuity contributed greater efficiency and productivity, and the 'revolving door' principle was never really enforced."[24] Southern European governments, German unions, migrant assistance groups, and international organizations also successfully pressured the German government to relax rules on prolonging stays and on family unification. In February 1970, the German government established, for the first time, principles for the integration of immigrant workers, later defined as "temporary integration," although it still linked the extent of immigrant employment to developments in the labor market.[25] The Work Permits Decree of 1971 created a five-year work permit that was not dependent in any way on changes in the economy and the labor market. In addition, between 1969 and 1972 the government tightened the regulations regarding immigrant housing. It also agreed that immigrant children should be fully integrated into German schools (even if they did not intend to stay in Germany for long). The Ordinance of Worker Permits of 1971 allowed foreigners employed for more than five years in Germany to obtain a special work permit. Though limited to five years, the permit was not dependent in any way on changes in the economy and labor market.[26] In 1972 immigrants received equal rights in unions. On April 22, 1972 the "Foreign Workers" Coordinating Committee in the Ministry of Labor published a statement favoring the integration of foreign workers and their families. The same year, Labor Minister Arendt stated, "The regional mobility of foreign workers lessens with increasing length of stay and the associated fact that such workers are often joined by family members and dependents . . . Somewhere a point will be reached where the drawbacks outweigh the advantages of growth."[27] But the 1973 Action Program on Employment of Foreigners reaffirmed the position that Germany was not an immigration country. That statement was repeated throughout the 1970s, and the migrant workers who arrived between World War II and 1973 were not granted citizenship.

Until the mid-1960s, the recruitment of foreign workers generated little political discussion or public involvement. In the early 1960s the press occasionally reported problems between the German population and the foreign workers. But as Herbert observes, neither reports in the press at that time, nor contemporary investigations, give any indication of the presence on a large scale of open hostility toward foreigners. A limited theoretical discussion of the issue began after 1964, and intensified during the 1967–1968 recession.[28] During the 1965 election campaign, conservative politicians criticized the employment of foreign labor in general and the foreign workers themselves.[29] In 1967, an article by the economist Föhl, which questioned the economic advantages of recruiting foreign workers, became the object of a parliamentary question raised in the *Bundestag*. Between 1966 and 1968, the National Democratic Party of Germany (NPD), an extreme-right party using xenophobic slogans, won seats in seven *Länder* parliaments. In the national election of 1969 it nearly surpassed the 5 percent barrier with 4.3 percent of the vote; but after 1972 it lost all of its seats in *Länder* parliaments.[30] Nevertheless, as Herbert indicated: "the debate on *Uberfremdung* [overforeignization], so pronounced in the Swiss context, likewise failed to play any role in the Federal Republic [in the 1960s], aside from right-wing radical groups."[31] The debate on the economic advantages of employing foreign labor resurfaced in 1970 and intensified following the 1971 Ordinance on Work Permits.

German Immigration Policy, 1974–1984: Migrant Workers and Family Reunification

The recruitment of migrant workers was banned in November 1973, causing their number to drop from 2.6 million in 1973 to 2.1 million in 1980. But instead of returning to their countries of origin, most of the migrant workers stayed in Germany and were joined by their families. In fact, the halt on labor recruitment contributed to this situation, as the migrant workers feared that if they went home they would not be allowed to return. Consequently, the foreign population temporarily declined from 6.7 percent of the total population in 1974 to 6.4 percent in 1976–1977, but increased back to 6.7 percent in 1979 and 7.2 percent in 1980. The share of foreigners employed dropped from 65 percent in 1973 (2.6 million foreign workers out of 4 million foreigners) to 47 percent in 1980 (2.1 million foreign workers out of 4.5 million foreign residents).[32]

During the second half of the 1970s and the early 1980s, successive governments would neither declare Germany a country of permanent immigration, nor forcefully repatriate millions of foreigners. As a result, these governments offered ambiguous policies such as "temporary integration," and attempted to facilitate the return of the migrant workers to their countries of origin by offering them monetary incentives. Nevertheless, policy gradually moved toward recognizing the *de facto* permanency of the former migrant workers.

In 1975 the government presented a program for immigrant employment that for the first time systematically outlined "social" aims and the idea of integration, and made the idea of "temporary integration" explicit. The same year, migrants were barred from taking up residence in certain designated urban districts where over 12 percent of the residents were foreigners. But protests from employers, court decisions that declared such measures unconstitutional, and limits placed by EEC agreements caused the lifting of restrictions on the domestic mobility of foreigners.[33] In 1976, a special commission was formed and charged with drafting comprehensive proposals for future policy. Its proposals, published in 1977, stated that the FRG was not a country of immigration, foreign workers should return after a certain length of time to their countries of origin, the halt to recruitment should be maintained, and the readiness and ability of workers to return home should be increased. However, the proposals also rejected measures based on compulsion and urged the government to intensify its programs of integration.[34] In 1978 the Office of the Commissioner for Foreigners was established. Also in 1978, the Aliens Act was amended, making it possible for foreign workers to receive an indefinite residence permit after five years and a permanent residence permit after eight years if certain conditions were met. In addition, the constitutional court, in a landmark decision known as the "Indian Case," argued that the nonrenewal of residence permits was in violation of the Basic Law.[35] The Court held that the previous routine renewals of residence permits had created a constitutionally protected "reliance interest," and that this reliance interest outweighed the no-immigration maxim of public policy. Consequently, "the Indian decision entailed a significant limitation on the government's options in foreigner policy: a policy of expulsion and forced repatriation was ruled out for constitutional reasons."[36] In 1979, the Commissioner for Foreigners, Heinz Kühn, published a memorandum on the "situation and further development of the integration of immigrant workers and their families in the FRG." The memorandum called for the recognition of *de facto* immigration while simultaneously excluding the possibility of new immigration. It also recommended enhanced efforts to integrate foreign children and youth, abolishing all segregation measures, granting youths born and raised in the FRG the legal right to naturalization, giving those youths unhindered access to jobs and job training, improving the political rights of migrants by granting them local voting rights after extended residence, and improving social assistance.[37] The same year the Coordination Committee on Foreign Workers, set up by the Federal Ministry of Labor and Social Affairs, published a list of guidelines for the "integration of second generation immigrants." The guidelines served as the basis for the cabinet's 1980 decision on the "development of immigration policy," which gave preference to the social integration of the second and third generations, although at the same time stating the need to maintain ties with the countries of origin in order to strengthen the willingness of the immigrants to return home.[38]

German policy with regard to family reunification and to the right of family members to find employment also suffered from ambiguity, and alternated between restrictive and liberal modes. Spouses and children who entered after November 1974 (the cut-off date was later changed to January 1, 1977) were no longer allowed to take employment.[39] In April 1979, policy was liberalized: subject to the priority of German workers and regardless of the date of entry, spouses were granted a work permit after four years, and children after two years, for employment in branches that suffered from severe manpower shortage (e.g. restaurants and hotels). Children who had taken part in vocational courses for at least six months could be exempted from this residence requirement. In December 1981 family reunification policy moved again toward the restrictive pole. The government decided that immigrant youths would be admitted only if they were under 16, that the immigration of children would be prohibited unless both parents lived in Germany, and that spouses would not be granted entry if they were married to persons who immigrated as children or were born in Germany.[40] Despite these fluctuations in policy, Germany mostly accepted the immigration of dependents of former migrant workers.[41]

In February 1982, the Schmidt (SPD) government stated its three "basic aims" with regard to foreigner policy: (a) "to limit effectively further migration of foreigners into the Federal Republic of Germany"; (b) "to promote the willingness of migrants to return home"; and (c) "to improve the economic and social integration and clarify the residency rights of those foreigners who have lived in the Federal Republic of Germany for many years."[42] The Christian Democratic Union (CDU) government that followed, headed by Chancellor Helmut Kohl, used tougher rhetoric, but its actual policy, for the most part, differed little from that of its predecessor. The main policy change was the November 1983 "Law to Promote the Willingness of Foreigners to Return Home," which aimed at encouraging the return of the former migrant workers to their home countries. The government offered migrant families, who were willing to give up their work and residence permits and permanently leave Germany, a departure bonus of up to DM10,500. Departing workers could also get their share of social security contributions refunded immediately upon returning home. In practice, the foreign population declined in 1984 and 1985, but then rebounded in 1986, and studies showed that most of the foreigners who returned home would have left in any event, regardless of the departure bonus.[43]

To summarize, during the 1970s and early 1980s successive German governments proposed ambiguous policies with regard to the former migrant workers and their families. They called for "temporary integration," and attempted to facilitate the return of the migrant workers to their countries of origin by offering them monetary incentives. On the one hand, Germany would not forcefully repatriate millions of foreigners. But on the other hand, it repeatedly (with the partial exception of the Kühn memorandum) declared that it is not a country of immigration. In practice, the "temporary integration" programs for the former migrant workers and their families, the weakening of the links between the migrants and their countries of origin and court decisions meant that the stay of the former migrant workers was, *de facto*, permanent.

German Immigration Policy Since 1979: Asylum Seekers, Illegal Immigration, Ethnic Germans, and Renewed Labor Migration

After 1979, Germany faced growing immigration of several types: asylum seekers, illegal immigration, ethnic Germans from Eastern Europe (particularly after 1988/1989), and migrant workers (during the 1990s). The combination of new immigration and low naturalization rates among the former migrant workers and their family members caused the foreign population in Germany to rise from 6.7 percent of the total population in 1979 to 8.4 percent in 1990 and 9.0 percent in 1997.[44]

Germany's leaders persistently declared (until 1998) that "the Federal Republic of Germany is not, nor shall it become, a country of immigration." German immigration control policy strove toward the goals announced in 1981: reducing immigration, promoting voluntary returns, and integrating the foreigners who choose to remain.[45] But in practice, immigration to Germany continued to grow, reaching over one million immigrants per annum during the early 1990s. The number of immigrants declined following the 1990–1993 restrictions on asylum seekers and ethnic Germans. But Germany remains the primary destination of immigration in Europe.

Asylum Seekers

Until 1993, Germany implemented an exceptionally liberal asylum policy. Since asylum was a constitutionally guaranteed right, applicants were also entitled to public assistance and accommodations until their applications were resolved. The policy was based on Article 16 of the 1949 Basic Law, according to which: "Persons persecuted for political reasons shall enjoy the right of asylum." It was linked to the FRG's attempt to atone for its Nazi past. Also, according to Martin, some of the framers of the 1949 Law had sought refuge outside Germany during the 1930s and 1940s, and their recollection of the difficulty of finding countries willing to accept them gave impetus to the provision dealing with asylum seekers.[46]

Germany's liberal policy (as well as economic factors and historical links with several countries of origin) made it the main destination for asylum seekers in Europe, receiving 50.8 percent of asylum applications to EU countries between 1980 and 1993.[47] The number of asylum seekers spiraled from 5,000 in the early 1970s to 438,000 in 1992. In an attempt to reduce this influx, Germany passed a series of restrictive policies in the 1980s and 1990s. In 1980, following an upsurge in asylum applications—more than half of them made by Turkish nationals—a new regulation made asylum seekers wait for one year before receiving a work permit. The waiting period was extended to two years in 1981. Also in 1980, nationals of Turkey, Afghanistan, Bangladesh, India, and Sri Lanka were required to obtain visas before traveling to Germany. The Asylum Procedure Act of 1982 authorized the federal authorities to dismiss an asylum request if it appeared to be ill-founded. The Act also permitted German local authorities to disregard applications for asylum made by individuals who had been granted refugee status by another country.[48] The same year, an amendment to the Social Welfare Act stated that applicants for asylum were entitled to no more than the bare necessities of life until their legal status was determined.[49]

The restrictive immigration policies succeeded in decreasing the number of asylum applicants from 107,818 in 1980 to 19,737 in 1983. But between 1984 and 1992 the number of asylum seekers rose again from 35,300 to 438,200. In response, German governments applied various restrictive measures:[50]

- Some of the immigrants arrived in East Berlin, where the East German authorities helped them transfer to the western sector of the city. Therefore, in 1985–1986, West Germany persuaded East Germany to block the migration of Third World "economic refugees" lacking proper papers. In return, West Germany allocated more interest-free credit to East Germany.
- In 1989, asylum applicants were prohibited from working while their cases were being considered.
- Between 1990 and 1993, Romania was one of the two major sources of asylum applicants to Germany, many of them Gypsies. In September 1992 the German government responded by announcing an agreement with Romania that was expected to lead to the deportation of thousands of Rumanians from Germany.

- Finally, in mid-1993, Germany amended its constitution and revised its asylum policy. The constitutional right to asylum was preserved, but a new law severely restricted that right. According to the law, asylum seekers who come from a country that Germany considers free of persecution are denied asylum, unless they prove that they have been singled out for persecution. This includes, for example, Romania and Bulgaria, which Germany now considered free of persecution. In addition, those who enter Germany by land are no longer entitled to claim asylum, since all neighboring countries are signatories to the Geneva Convention and thus they are regarded as "safe countries." Instead, these asylum seekers have to apply for asylum in the countries they passed through.

The reform of German asylum policy achieved its goal of decreasing the inflow of asylum seekers. The number of applications for asylum declined from a peak of 438,200 in 1992 to 322,600 in 1992, 127,000–128,000 in 1994–1995, and it continued to declined each year down to 78,800 applications for asylum in 2000.

Bosnian and Kosovar Refugees[51]

The main development in the context of asylum/refugee policy during the second half of the 1990s was the repatriation of Bosnian, Croatian, and Kosovar asylum seekers/refugees. Between 1991 and 1999 (with the exception of 1996), the former Yugoslavia was the main source of asylum seekers to Germany.[52] Due to the war and ethnic cleansing in their countries of origin, Bosnians and Croatians were given a provisional status of refugees. And they joined a substantial Yugoslav population already residing in Germany—mostly composed of former migrant workers and their families.

Following the end of "open" war in Bosnia, and the signing of the Bosnia peace plan in Paris, a debate started in Germany about the repatriation of the 320,000–350,000 Bosnian refugees.[53] There were several reasons for the attempt to repatriate the Bosnians. First, the war seemed to be ending, and while the Bosnians were granted the status of "tolerated" foreigners, they did not earn the right to permanently live in Germany. Second, the Bosnians represented a financial burden for the *Länder*: they lived in rent-free accommodations provided by local authorities, and a family of four receives about $250 per week for food and other necessities. Chancellor Kohl argued that instead of spending DM15 billion on Bosnians in Germany, it made "more sense to send them home and to spend the money on reconstruction." The cost of accommodating the refugees also produced a debate between the *Länder* and the federal government over sharing the financial burden. Third, Germany was suffering from peak unemployment (11.5 percent in 1996 and 12.7 percent in 1997). On January 24, 1996 the Christian Social Union (CSU) called for cuts in the payments to Bosnian refugees and asylum seekers in Germany in order to safeguard the Germany economy. Finally, xenophobia and even racism may have contributed to the opposition to the settlement of Bosnians, 60 percent of whom were Muslim.

On January 26, 1996 the interior ministers of Germany's 16 states met and agreed to begin to return the Bosnians in Germany to Bosnia on July 1, 1996.[54] Bosnians without families in Germany were expected to leave by June 30, 1997; other Bosnians were expected to depart by August 31, 1997. This, however, proved to be impossible due to the continuation of ethnic cleansing and the devastation in Bosnia. An estimated 60 percent of the housing in Bosnia had been destroyed or damaged. And while the Dayton agreement stated that Bosnians have the right to return to their homes, up to half of the Bosnians in Germany were Muslims from areas that were under Serbian control. In addition, the Bosnian government was demanding that young men who avoided military service pay DM1,000 to DM10,000 in fines, which also discouraged them from returning. A poll commissioned by the UNHCR found that 25 percent of the Bosnians in Germany were ready to return, but that 45 percent did not feel that conditions were right for their return. The UNHCR itself stated in February 1996 that resettlement was premature. The 16 *Länder* interior ministers met on May 3, 1996, and agreed that local safety must be guaranteed before Bosnians could be returned.

It took two years, up to 1998, until the majority of Bosnian refugees left Germany.[55] The *Länder* used various means in order to encourage their return, such as reducing the social security allowances by 20 percent and investing the funds saved in the rebuilding of houses in Bosnia, deporting some families, and initiating counseling programs and orientation visits in Bosnia. The decisions on when to return the Bosnians, and the measures used, varied among the German *Länder*.

As the repatriation of Bosnian refugees was taking place, a somewhat similar debate evolved with regard to refugees from Kosovo. There were about 150,000 Kosovo Albanians in Germany at the end of 1997, and 180,000 in mid-1999. Unlike Bosnians, the ethnic Albanians from Kosovo were not given a TPS status, and could be deported if their regular asylum applications were rejected. But similar to the Bosnian case, the civil war in Kosovo produced a debate over the feasibility of returning the Kosovars. At the same time, the asylum seekers represented a financial burden: most of the new arrivals were housed in government-operated camps that cost the government about $500 per month a person. In addition, Kosovars received $170 a month for food and $50 in cash. The fact that the Kosovo Albanians were Muslim may also have added to the opposition to their stay.

Germany and its 16 *Länder* struggled to decide what to do with rejected asylum seekers who arrived from Kosovo. This time the German federal representative for the Balkans urged the interior ministers of the 16 states to continue to deport the rejected asylum seekers to Kosovo. But several states, including Lower Saxony, North Rhine-Westphalia, Hessen, Saarland, and Brandenburg stopped deportations due to the fighting in Kosovo. Beginning in early July 1999, Kosovars were offered DM450 plus a free flight home if they voluntarily returned. And in September 1999 Interior Minister Otto Schily said that Germany was prepared to forcibly repatriate Kosovars because the situation in Kosovo had stabilized. In early 2000 the federal and state interior ministers decided that the rejected asylum seekers should return to Kosovo by the end of 2000, despite the fact that some critics argued that Kosovo was not ready for massive repatriations.

Deportations did take place, but approximately 130,000 Kosovars still resided in Germany in May 2001. Moreover, in 2001, as the economy was improving, critics of the deportations—such as Germany's Commissioner for Foreigners Marieluise Beck (Greens)—argued that it makes no sense to force Kosovars who are employed and integrated in Germany to return, and at the same time recruit green-card foreigners. The proponents of deportations pointed out that unemployment remains high and that Kosovars must rebuild their own country. But Beck pushed for a policy that would allow Kosovars who have IT skills to remain in Germany. In February 2001 it was decided that 10,000 to 20,000 Bosnians who had resided in Germany for at least six years, had been employed for at least two years and who were not dependent on welfare would be able to remain in Germany. In May of the same year federal and state interior ministers agreed that Kosovars who had lived in Germany for at least six years (as of February 15, 2001), had held a steady job for at least two years, had sufficient accommodations, were not dependent on welfare, and had not been convicted of a crime would be able to obtain two-year renewable residency permits.

Illegal Immigration

The estimated number of illegal aliens residing in Germany is in the range of 150,000 to 1.5 million, or according to other estimates between 500,000 to one million.[56] But in contrast to various other countries (notably the United States), scholars note that there has been little debate about illegal immigration to Germany. Thränhardt postulates that "part of the explanation is that asylum applications have functioned as a sort of overflow or protection mechanism for immigrants who have managed to enter the country, providing them with social assistance."[57] Martin observes: "In Germany and most other European nations, there is not much U.S. style illegal immigration of millions of persons slipping surreptitiously across borders."[58]

Nevertheless, illegal immigration has gained some prominence during the past decade. Politicians of both major parties have voiced the need to limit illegal immigration.[59] On August 14, 1997, CSU Chairman and Finance Minister Theo Waigel said that the presence of foreign workers was partly to blame for record German unemployment. He added that Germany has "the highest immigration rate in the world. We must be resolute with the return of illegal foreigners living here and also stop the flow of immigration where it is possible and justified." In November 1997, German Interior Minister Manfred Kanther (CDU) spoke of his plans to discourage illegal immigration. The following month, Kanther proposed that the names of foreigners and Germans who broke German immigration laws be marked in the central register for foreigners, so that the police and other government agencies would know more about the foreigners with whom they come into contact. He added that marking suspected foreigners in the database could hinder illegal immigration. And in April 1998 Kanther called for an EU fingerprinting system, EuroDat, which would include prints from all asylum seekers and apprehended illegal aliens. During the run-up to the September 1998 elections, the SPD promised to deport illegal immigrants who commit crime in Germany more quickly. In March 2000, Interior Minister Otto Schily (SPD) stated that Germany is at its "carrying capacity" for immigration, and that he wants to shift the mix of newcomers away from what he calls organized illegal immigration toward immigrants that Germany needs. In June 2001, Angela Merkel, who was expected to be the CDU/CSU candidate for chancellor in the 2002 elections, claimed that East Germans see the high crime rate among illegal immigrants, and that the police are doing nothing about it. And in June 2002 Interior Minister Otto Schily said that the new immigration law "makes it possible to further limit the influx of illegal immigrants."

German policy has mainly dealt with four aspects of illegal immigration: (a) the link between illegal immigration and applications for asylum; (b) the attempt to block illegal immigration along the eastern borders; (c) the illegal employment of foreigners; and (d) the attempt to repatriate Vietnamese immigrants.

The issues of *illegal immigration and asylum seekers* partially overlap in Germany, as they do in other countries (see chapters 3 and 4 about Britain and the Netherlands). This is because some asylum seekers enter the country illegally, and because asylum seekers whose applications for asylum were rejected sometimes remain in Germany illegally. For example, of the 40,000 illegal Vietnamese living in Germany, 20,000 were rejected asylum seekers.[60] Consequently, laws that restricted the number of asylum seekers sometimes also aimed at limiting the size of illegal immigration.[61] Starting in April 1994, stricter border controls have been in applied in order to prevent asylum seekers from entering Germany illegally by ferry from Norway, Sweden, and Finland. In 1997, Interior Minister Manfred Kanther indicated his intention of halting state benefits for immigrants who were not granted asylum in order to discourage illegal immigration. And in early 1998, the *Länder* of Baden-Württemberg proposed in the *Bundesrat* that foreigners who illegally arrive in Germany should not receive any assistance under the asylum law. Some observers credit the asylum law reform of 1993 with discouraging illegal immigration over the eastern border.

During the past decade, Germany has attempted to *block illegal immigration coming though its eastern borders.*[62] It did so by expanding its own border policy forces and by cooperating with Poland and with the Czech Republic. The number of German border guards positioned along the Polish and Czech borders more than tripled within three years—from 2,000 in 1993 to 5,800 in 1996. And starting in September 1, 1998, German border police could also perform random identity checks within 30 km. of German borders. As a result of these efforts, the border police apprehended (between 1993 and 2001) 20,000 to 54,000 illegal immigrants each year, together with a number of smugglers, along its eastern borders. But the actual number of illegal immigrants was apparently much higher: In 1996 the German border police estimated that it apprehend only one in five foreigners attempting illegal entry.

In addition to its own efforts, Germany also granted financial aid to its eastern neighbors in return for their cooperation in stopping illegal immigration.[63] It also linked such cooperation to the eastward enlargement of the EU. On April 5, 1995, Germany and Poland signed an accord to deal with illegal immigration. All police radio communications, telephone, and fax links were to be standardized on both sides of the border, and the cost was to be covered from the DM120 million marks in aid pledged by Bonn to Warsaw for crime-fighting measures.

On April 10, 1997, German Interior Minister Kanther and his Polish counterpart, Leszek Miller, agreed to join forces to combat cross-border crime—in particular the smuggling of illegal aliens across the Polish–German border—by establishing joint administrative departments and border patrols. In addition, Poland tightened the control over its own borders in order to make itself more attractive as a potential member of the European Union.[64] These restrictive measures probably contributed to the shift of illegal immigration from the Polish to the Czech border. But the Czech Republic has also been trying to strengthen its border controls in response to pressure from the EU.[65]

Much of the discussion with regard to illegal immigration has been in the context of *illegal employment of foreigners*. The two phenomena do not fully overlap because, as Martin notes: "European nations are fairly open to Eastern and Southern Europeans, so most unauthorized workers enter legally and become unauthorized only when they violate the terms of their entry by going to work."[66] In addition, many of the foreigners employed illegally—for example those paid below minimum wage—are citizens of EU member states, and thus eligible to move freely within the Union. Nevertheless, measures used against illegal employment also served, in practice, to lessen illegal immigration. Already in 1981, penalties of up to DM50,000 were placed on businesses that employed foreign nationals (other than EC nationals) without a work permit. In 1985 that law was strengthened: the employment of more than five migrant workers without permits became an offense punishable by imprisonment for up to one year, and in the event of a particularly serious infringement, imprisonment for up to three years.[67] During the 1990s, inspections of worksites were expanded, especially after the 1996–1997 compromise that set a minimum wage for foreign construction workers. In 1996, for example, the labor ministry conducted 147,300 inspections, and in 87,000 cases employers were suspected of employing illegal foreign workers. Dawn raids on building sites became particularly common, as government inspectors searched for illegal immigrants. In November–December 1999, some 4,600 labor and tax inspectors conducted a nationwide sweep of 5,400 construction, hotel, restaurant, and transportation businesses, looking for illegal migrants and German workers working "off the books." And in mid-2001, the labor ministry checked 1,200 slaughterhouses and found that 200 were employing illegal workers.[68]

The growing numbers of Eastern European illegal immigrants also caused the German government to establish new foreign worker programs (described later). Hönekopp observes that the main purpose of the 1990s work programs has been to convert illegal workers into legal ones.[69] Similarly, Martin argues that "Germany was reluctant to 'recreate the Berlin Wall' on its eastern borders, but was also unwilling to tolerate the widespread employment of unauthorized foreigners.[70] The compromise was to develop several foreign worker programs that permitted Eastern Europeans to work legally in Germany." And Rudolph points to the fact that 98 percent of the applications of Eastern European seasonal workers were made for specific individuals, which indicates that this was mainly a way of legalizing formerly illegal workers. Generally, Germany has been reluctant to formally legalize unauthorized foreigners.[71] But in November 2001, Labor Minister Walter Riester said that illegal in-home care workers currently in Germany might be able to legalize their status.[72]

A fourth policy initiative related to illegal migration has been the attempt to *repatriate Vietnamese immigrants*. There were about 62,000 Vietnamese in East Germany in 1989, the legacy of labor recruitment during the days of the German Democratic Republic (GDR). After German unification, Germany offered Vietnamese guestworkers a ticket home and a $2,000 departure bonus. In 1992 Germany and Vietnam also negotiated an agreement, whereby Vietnam agreed to accept the migrants back in exchange for a $130 million aid package and $65 million in risk insurance for German companies making investments in Vietnam. An estimated 50,000 Vietnamese left, but 12,000 stayed, and were later joined by new Vietnamese immigrants. On January 11, 1995, Germany announced that it would begin to forcibly repatriate some of the 40,000 Vietnamese illegally residing in the country. This group included 20,000 rejected asylum seekers, 10,000 former guestworkers in East Germany, and 10,000 illegal entrants. Under a July 1995 agreement between Hanoi and Bonn, Vietnam agreed to accept the 40,000 undocumented Vietnamese by the year 2000, and Bonn promised to pay Hanoi at least $72 million in financial aid.[73] The agreement called for the return of 2,500 Vietnamese in 1995 and 5,000 in 1996, but in practice smaller numbers left.[74]

Ethnic Germans

Until 1987, ethnic Germans living in Eastern Europe could not freely leave their home countries and migrate to the FRG. Between 1953 and 1987, an average of only 37,000 *Aussiedler* per year came to Germany, although their numbers fluctuated due to (a) periods of domestic political liberalization or crisis in the countries of origin; (b) concessions made by the communist regimes of Poland and Romania in order to improve their political relations with the FRG and to receive economic or financial aid; and (c) attempts by the political elites of these two sending countries to weaken the German ethnic minorities by allowing them to emigrate.[75]

The situation changed considerably with the abolishment of administrative travel restrictions in East-Central and Eastern Europe at the end of the 1980s, and the fall of the Iron Curtain. In 1989 thousands of East Germans migrated to Germany through Hungary and Czechoslovakia. Eventually, East Germany permitted them to travel directly by train into West Germany. Almost 800,000 East Germans moved to the FRG in 1989–1990. After German unification, the German government invested heavily in the eastern part of the country in order to limit migration to the western part, but domestic east–west migration continued on a smaller scale.[76]

The collapse of the Iron Curtain also produced a substantial increase in *Aussiedler* migration—from 42,700 in 1986 to 397,100 in 1990. Up until 1989 the main source of ethnic German migration was Poland.[77] But in 1990 over two-third were from the former USSR and Romania, and since 1991 most *Aussiedler* have migrated from the post-Soviet successor states—mainly from Kazakhstan, Russia, and Kyrgyzstan. The sharp increase in immigration, economic difficulties in Germany, and particularly doubts with regard to the German heritage of the newcomers caused Germany to restrict the migration of *Aussiedler*. In 1990 ethnic Germans were required to apply for an *Aussiedler* status and for a special entry permit at the German consulate in their country of origin. In 1992 Germany established an annual admission quota of 220,000 *Aussiedler*, and in 2000 it was reduced to 110,000. The 1992 law, implemented in January 1993, also limited the cash payments that *Aussiedler* receive upon arrival and the duration of their language training. It restricted the right of immigration to ethnic Germans living in the successor states of the Soviet Union (others have to prove that they are discriminated against because of their German origin), and provided funds for development and cultural assistance in the countries of origin in order to discourage emigration. Finally, the so-called "law concerning late consequences of World War Two" also limited the options of future applications for *Aussiedler* status to ethnic Germans born before 1993. This means that after the year 2010, when people born in 1993 reach the age of 18, this younger generation of ethnic Germans will have no independent claim to *Aussiedler* status.[78] In July 1996, Germany introduced a language test, in which potential *Aussiedler* have to prove their proficiency in German in order to prove their German identity. Between a third and a half of the applicants who have taken the test failed it, and it is very difficult to repeat the test.[79] The same year the German government also announced that it would prefer that the 500,000 ethnic Germans living in Kazakhastan remain there, but that they can migrate to Germany if they must.[80]

The restrictions applied by Germany succeeded in decreasing the number of *Aussiedler* from almost 400,000 in 1990 to 218,000–230,000 between 1991 and 1995, 135,000–178,000 in 1996–1997, and around 100,000 between 1998 and 2001. In fact, the various impediments to migration, as well as the declining numbers of ethnic Germans remaining in the former USSR and the decision of some of them not to exercise their right to emigrate, caused the number of *Aussiedler* to fall far below the quota of 220,000.

Migrant Workers

The 1973 policy change brought an end to the large-scale recruitment of foreign workers from the Middle East and Southern Europe, although German employers continued to recruit relatively small numbers of workers from EC/EU member states. Since the early 1990s, growing demand for labor in specific sectors, as well as foreign policy considerations and attempts to cope with illegal immigration, produced policy changes with regard to labor migration of three types: (a) EU workers, especially in the construction industry; (b) migrant workers from Eastern Germany; and (c) migrant workers for high-tech industry. In addition, during certain periods, asylum seekers waiting for a decision on their application were allowed to work in Germany, thus adding to the foreign labor force. Finally, foreign labor in Germany continues to include a substantial number of former migrant workers and refugees, as well as their descendents, who have resided for many years in Germany, but have not acquired German citizenship. At the end of the 1990s, the largest groups of foreign workers still originated from Turkey, Italy, the former Yugoslavia, and Greece.[81]

Migrant workers from EU member states and the conflict over their employment in the construction industry[82]

The free movement of workers among EEC member states was established in the Treaty of Rome of 1957, and was achieved, for the most part, by 1968. In practice, intra-European mobility of workers has been relatively limited. During the height of labor recruitment, between 1960 and 1973, most foreign workers in Germany arrived from outside the common market. In 1973, Italy—the main source of foreign labor within the EEC/EC—accounted for only 17 percent of the employed foreigners in Germany, while Turkey accounted for 23 percent of the employed foreigners and Yugoslavia for 21 percent. Citizens of EU member states constituted 35.1 percent of the foreign population in Germany in 1985 (Italians constituted 12.1 percent), 30.6 percent in 1990, and 25.1–25.3 percent in 1995–1999.[83]

Generally, the labor migration of EC/EU workers caused little opposition in Germany. But in the mid-1990s, the employment of EU labor—particularly from Britain, Ireland, Portugal, Spain, and Greece—in the German construction industry created conflicts between unions and employers, the workers and sections of the German public, and between several member states.[84] Following German unification, the country experienced a building boom. Many German employers favored EU construction workers over German ones because the latter cost them between two and four times as much.[85] This was because employers did not need to make German social welfare and health contributions on behalf of the EU workers, and because the workers were not covered by German laws that regulate work hours, severance pay, and minimum wages. The difference in cost caused German employers to recruit between 150,000 and 210,000 EU workers, including 80,000 to 100,000 British and Irish ones, while 140,000 to 400,000 German construction workers were unemployed.[86] The German building union estimated that there were 400,000 to 500,000 foreign construction workers in Germany, including non-EU and illegal alien workers.

Starting in 1995, German construction worker unions responded to this situation by arguing that foreign workers on German construction sites should receive the same wages and benefits as German workers from the first day of employment. On June 15, 1995, 6,000 German construction workers in Berlin protested the employment of foreign workers at wages less than the prevailing German wages. On March 22, 1996, some 12,000 workers demonstrated in Munich. Six thousand workers demonstrated in Magdeburg on March 23, and 20,000 workers demonstrated on March 13, 1997. In addition, British construction workers in Berlin were attacked by neo-Nazi gangs.

In response to the June 1995 protest by the construction workers, the German cabinet approved on September 1, 1995 a proposal to require foreign firms sending workers to Germany to pay those foreign workers at least the minimum wage negotiated between German unions and employers. On November 30, the *Bundestag* approved a resolution that would permit the government to require foreign construction workers to be paid at least the German minimum construction wage from their first day of work in Germany. The resolution was to remain in force for two years and apply to workers employed directly in construction, but not to those in related trades such as electricians and painters. However, the equal pay law was not to go into effect until a wage commission composed of employer and union representatives agreed on a minimum wage for foreign workers. And the employers were reluctant to approve such a measure because they feared it would open the door to a minimum wage in Germany. Based on the government's proposal, collective bargaining took place between the German construction union (IG Bau) and the employers in the construction industry. In April 1996 a compromise was reached, according to which EU workers sent by their employers to Germany would be paid a minimum wage of DM18.60 per hour in what had been West Germany and DM17.11 in what had been East Germany. But the general employers association refused to accept the agreement because employers in the metal and textile industries feared that the construction *Entsendegesetz* might set a precedent for their industries. Consequently, in mid-June 1996, the German construction employers association withdrew from the umbrella German employers' association to protest the latter's failure to approve a minimum wage for all workers on construction sites in Germany. On August 23, 1996, the IG Bau union and the two leading construction employer associations agreed to request a lower minimum hourly wage of DM17 for West Germany, and DM15.64 for East Germany. In November 1996 the German employers and construction unions agreed on the aforementioned minimum wage for all construction workers for the period January–August, 1997. The minimum wage was later revised, increased to DM18.50 an hour in the West and DM16.26 in the East starting in September 1, 1999.

It should be noted that the compromise did not completely prevent German employers from favoring foreign workers over German ones. First, minimum wages for German workers under union contract are higher than those paid to foreign workers and the former are also entitled to additional benefits. Second, government sweeps of construction sites have revealed that many employers employ the foreign workers illegally, paying them less than the minimum wage.

Migrant workers from Eastern Europe

Another group of foreign workers, whose numbers have grown since German unification, has arrived from Eastern Europe. In the late 1980s and during the 1990s, a demand for labor in certain sectors, an increase in illegal immigration from Eastern Europe and foreign policy considerations led Germany to establish new foreign worker programs.[87] In contrast to the guestworker programs of the 1960s, those of the 1990s–early 2000s: (a) have regulated the recruitment of workers from Eastern Europe; (b) have included fewer workers; (c) most of the foreigners have been employed for less than a full year; (d) the programs have included various measures intended to encourage the workers to return to their countries of origin and prevent their stay from turning permanent; and (e) the workers have been channeled to very specific sectors of the labor market. Five foreign worker programs have been established (see table 5.1):[88]

- Project-tied workers, where German firms subcontract with foreign firms and the foreigners are admitted for a maximum two years. There are no firm-specific quotas on the number of subcontracted foreign workers who can be employed. But there are industry-by-industry ceilings and a countrywide quota, which was 10,000 in 1992, then reduced to 50,000. The average number of project-tied foreign workers in Germany surged from 6,600 at the

Table 5.1 East European program workers in Germany, 1991–1999

Program	*Project-tied workers*[1]	*Seasonal workers*[2,3]	*Border commuters*[1]	*New guest workers/work-and-study*[2]	*Nurses*[4]	*Total*
1991	51,770	90,000	7,000	2,234		151,004
1992	93,592	212,000	12,400	5,057	1,455	324,504
1993	67,270	164,377	11,200	5,772	506	249,124
1994	39,070	140,656	8,000	5,529	412	193,667
1995	47,565/ 49,400	176,590/ 192,000	8,500	5,478	367	238,500
1996	45,800	220,900				
1997	38,500	226,000				
1998	33,000	201,600				
1999	40,000	223,400				

Notes:

[1] Persons employed; yearly average based on monthly figures.
[2] Job placements.
[3] Annual employment volume equivalent might be a fourth or fifth of the mentioned figures.
[4] Persons employed; estimated cumulative figures.

Source: Hönekopp (1997:169), based on Central Placement Unit and Headquarter of Federal Employment Services, statistics on border commuters, for the years 1991–1995. SOPEMI (2000:187 and 2001:170) for the years 1995–1999.

beginning of 1990 to 94,000 in 1992. Later, as the countrywide quota was decreased, it declined to 33,000–48,000 in 1994–1999. Contracting companies have to make sure that subcontractors pay standard wages, and no work permits are granted in regions where the unemployment rate is more than 30 percent above the average.

- Seasonal foreign workers can work up to three months per year in Germany if indigenous workers are not available to fill the vacant jobs. They are mostly employed in agriculture (farming and the processing of farm products), restaurants, and construction. Their numbers increased from 90,000 in 1991 to 212,000 in 1992, then fluctuated between 141,000 and 221,000 in 1993–1999. But most stayed only a few months, so they only contributed the equivalent of approximately 30,000–55,000 fulltime workers to the German labor force during that period.[89]
- Polish and Czech residents living within 30 miles of the German border can work in Germany. Daily cross-border commuting is encouraged, but frontier workers are permitted to remain overnight in Germany for up to two days each week.
- New guestworker or work-and-study programs, which permit 6,000–10,000 young East Europeans to work and study in Germany for up to eighteen months.[90]
- Nurses from the former Yugoslavia are permitted to work in Germany. In addition, policy has recently been liberalized with regard to Eastern European caregivers in private German homes.

It should be noted that despite this proliferation of migrant worker programs, workers from Eastern Europe still constitute a small share of foreign labor in Germany. Their percentage of the total number of foreign employees increased from 3.2 percent in 1989 to 7.8 percent in 1993 and 7.4 percent in 1994.[91] But they are still outnumbered by other major groups of migrant workers, and they constituted only 0.7 percent of the total employees in 1994.[92] The aforementioned numbers do, however, underestimate East European employment because (a) they do not include illegal immigration; (b) they do not show the contribution of ethic Germans from Eastern Europe, some of whom came for economic reasons; and (c) the legally employed Eastern European workers are concentrated in certain sectors—agriculture and construction—where their percentage is higher.[93]

The demand for labor in certain sectors, the increase in illegal immigration, and foreign policy considerations contributed to the establishment of the new foreign worker programs. But the employment of

Eastern European workers also produced some opposition in Germany and in the EU, and debates on whether the foreign workers could be replaced by German workers and asylum seekers:

- In July 1997, the EU concluded that because Germany's agreements with Eastern European countries were bilateral, they discriminated against workers from other countries and violated the EU freedom to provide services provisions. On October 2, 1997, it was announced that the EU would force Germany to reduce the number of non-EU seasonal workers permitted to work in Germany. Some observers speculated that the German government welcomed the EU decision, since it enabled the government to stop recruitment for an increasingly controversial program.[94]
- Commissioners for Foreigners in several German states, who urged state governments to make it easier for asylum applicants to get work permits, argued that work permits would make it less necessary to import seasonal workers from Poland and other Eastern European countries.[95]
- The German government has been attempting to get unemployed Germans to do seasonal farm work, such as harvesting asparagus in May and June. In Brandenburg, for example, farmers had to have at least 15 percent German workers before receiving permission to import Polish asparagus harvesters.[96] Germany has also supported the implementation of a transition period before nationals of Eastern European states joining the EU could obtain the right to seek work anywhere in the EU on an equal basis with local workers.[97]
- In November 2000, Labor Minister Walter Riester announced that beginning January 1, 2002, it would become easier for Eastern Europeans willing to care for the elderly and the infirm in private German homes to receive three-year work and residence permits. Riester also proposed that East Europeans be given a new version of "green cards" to enable old and disabled people in private homes to employ them as caregivers. But the German Association of Private Nurses complained that there were 40,000 jobless German caregivers, and said that if caregivers received appropriate wages there would be no shortage of workers in this field.[98]

Green card: migrant workers in the high-tech industry

The high-tech information technology (IT) industry is characterized by high surplus value, and is viewed by many countries as the key to success in today's competitive global economy. Given the lack of sufficient domestic highly skilled labor (at least until the recent downturn in the industry), many countries have opted for highly skilled migrant workers.

In February 2000, the industrial association BITKOM asked the German government to allow German employers to hire up to 30,000 foreign professionals from outside the EU in order to help fill vacant jobs for computer programmers and engineers. Chancellor Gerhard Schroeder responded that his government supported what he called a U.S.-style "green card" program that would allow high-tech specialists to work in Germany for up to five years, without their families. The details of the plan, announced in mid-March 2000, called for 20,000 temporary work visas to be issued to non-EU foreign computer professionals over the next three years. After the first 10,000 foreigners were in Germany, the government would review the labor market to determine if another 10,000 are needed. The visas would be valid for up to five years, but extensions of the permit would be permitted. The non-EU foreigners would have to have a university degree in an IT field (85 percent) or to have been promised an annual salary of E51,000 a year by their German employer (15 percent).

According to the original plan, the foreign workers could not bring their families with them. Later it was elaborated that family members could accompany the foreign workers to Germany, but that if they wanted to work, they would have to secure work permits of their own. Then it was announced that family members would have to wait two years in order to work in Germany. In mid-2001, the German government—concerned over the smaller-than-expected number of permits issued, considered permitting the spouses of green card holders to work upon arrival in Germany. Further, according to the original plan, the foreigners could change employers in Germany. However, the states of Bavaria and Hesse announced that foreigner computer specialists would receive "blue cards" that would link the duration of their residence permits to their work contracts. The work permit would expire if the foreigner lost his job.[99]

The decision to initiate a green card program inspired a debate over its advantages and disadvantages. Initially, this debate focused on the economic aspects of the program, where the proponents of the plan included the Federal Minister of Education and Research, the Minister of the Economy, the German Industrial Association, employers in Baden-Wüerttemberg, and the biotech and health care industries. The opponents of the program included the Labor Minister and the unions. Later, some politicians from the CDU/CSU—FDP opposition attempted to turn the topic into a partisan debate by linking the program to broader immigration policy issues such as family reunification, asylum seekers, and deportations.[100]

The proponents of the green card plan, such as the Minister of Education and Research, pointed at the small number of computer science students who graduate each year, and warned that IT companies may move abroad because of the shortage of highly skilled personnel. The economy minister and Chancellor Gerhard Schroeder illustrated the job-multiplying aspects of green cards in the IT industry. And Chancellor Schroeder argued that Germany had to compete with other countries for the best people—such as non-EU foreign computer professionals—in order to succeed in the global economy. The opponents of the plan, such as the labor minister, maintained that with four million unemployed people, including 31,000 unemployed IT workers, Germany cannot open its job market to foreign workers. The unions and some specialists noted that IT companies want to hire only recent graduates who are familiar with the latest software and are willing to work long hours. Others suggested that instead of recruiting foreign computer programmers, Germany should (a) train additional computer and engineering students in order to reverse the slide in their numbers; (a) reduce the demand for programmers by encouraging German companies to move some of their routine programming operations abroad; and (c) employers should reduce overtime so that they could employ more workers. Finally, politicians from the CDU/CSU-FDP opposition argued that the green card program should not stand alone, but rather be part of comprehensive immigration legislation that lays out "clear rules" on family unification, more restrictions on asylum and faster deportation.[101]

Germany began issuing the green card visas on August 1, 2000. The visas were issued at a slower pace than originally expected, but by October 31, 2001—15 months later—Germany announced that the first 10,000 green cards had been distributed, and that another 10,000 five-year work permits would be available for 2001–2002.[102] By January 2003, about 13,600 green cards were issued. The leading country of origin was India, followed by Russia, Romania, and the former Yugoslavia. Germany announced that the green card program would end July 31, 2003, thereafter foreign IT specialists would only be able to enter Germany by seeking ordinary visas.[103] The green card program also set the stage for the 2002 immigration law, which allows up to 50,000 skilled and professional foreigners to enter Germany each year (see later).

Following the initiation of the green card program for high-tech specialists other German industries also asked to be included in a similar program. They included employers in the biotech and health care industries, the German Industrial Association, employers in Baden-Württemberg, the German hotel association, and the Federation of German Employers. In addition, following complaints from German universities, the ruling coalition proposed legislation that would permit foreign students who had graduated from German universities to remain in the country for more than one year instead of 90 days. This change was included in the 2002 immigration law.[104]

The right of asylum seekers to work

Asylum seekers may wait a long period for a decision on their application. If they are allowed to work, they become a *de facto* part of the foreign labor force. Policy with regard to the right of such asylum seekers to work in Germany has fluctuated over time. On the one had, policymakers were worried that granting these asylum seekers the right to work would encourage additional migrants to seek asylum in Germany. On the other hand, asylum seekers (waiting for a decision on their application) who did not work became a burden on the German taxpayer, which created public antagonism toward them.

In 1980, following an upsurge in asylum applications, a new regulation made asylum seekers wait for one year before receiving a work permit. The waiting period was extended to two years in 1981. In 1989 asylum applicants were prohibited from working while their cases were being considered. This ban was canceled in 1991, leaving each state to decide how long an asylum applicant must wait before being issued a work permit.[105] In May 1997, asylum applicants were prohibited from working, regardless of how long they waited for a decision or appeal on their application. But Commissioners for Foreigners in several states urged state governments to make it easier for asylum applicants to get work permits, arguing that work permits would reduce welfare spending and resentment toward foreigners while making it less necessary to import seasonal workers from Poland and other Eastern European countries. In 2000 policy was liberalized: starting in January 1, 2001, asylum applicants could work after staying for one year in Germany, as long as there was no German or permanent resident available to fill a job. War refugees were allowed to work immediately upon their arrival in Germany. The new policy was expected to enable 300,000 foreigners to work. Finally, according to the 2002 immigration law asylum seekers would be granted TPS status for a maximum of three years and allowed to work in Germany.[106]

Kurds in Germany and Deportation Policy[107]

The Kurds are between 20 and 30 percent of the two million Turks living in Germany. During the 1990s, Kurds in Germany were involved in protests against Turkish treatment of the Kurds and, in some cases, in favor of an independent Kurdish state. For example, on June 26, 1994, an estimated 50,000 Kurds demonstrated peacefully in Frankfurt against the Turkish government's treatment of Kurds. Between March 9 and 16, 1996, Turkish Kurds demonstrated in northwestern Germany, but some of these demonstrations turned violent as demonstrators clashed with police who tried to remove banned banners of the Kurdistan Workers' Party (PKK). Kurds were again involved in violent protests in February 1999. And in May 2001, about 35,000 Kurds demonstrated in Dusseldorf, calling for more autonomy in Turkey and for the release of the PKK's imprisoned leader Abdullah Ocalan. The PKK, which seeks an independent state in southeastern Turkey, northeastern Iraq, and western Iran, was estimated to have between 3,000 and 11,000 members in Germany. It has been involved in violent activities, such as firebombing Turkish establishments in Germany in 1994, and it reportedly made "revenge" death threats against German Chancellor Kohl and Foreign Minister Klaus Kinkel in 1996.

Kurdish involvement in violent activities led Germany to implement restrictive measures, which also influenced its immigration policy. In November 1993 the PKK was banned in Germany. In 1994, Chancellor Kohl called for the expulsion of Kurds who took part in highway blockades and violent demonstrations against Turkey. Rudolf Scharping, the SPD candidate for chancellor, backed the expulsion of Kurds convicted of violent offenses. Germany deported Kurds involved in violence and rejected Kurdish asylum seekers. But such deportations were temporarily halted due to Turkey's imprisonment of PKK members, including those deported from Germany. Following the violent demonstrations of March 1996, the governing CDU/CSU decided to expel foreigners involved in illegal demonstrations by redefining participation in a banned demonstration to be a severe violation of public order, which leads to automatic expulsion. This policy change was approved by the *Bundestag* in November 1996. But the deportation policy was challenged in court. In March 1999, Germany's supreme administrative court held that leaders of the PKK had no immediate right to asylum in Germany, but that they also could not be deported as long as there was a risk that they would be executed or tortured in Turkey.

In the late 1990s, Kurdish activities in Germany was linked to the question of dual citizenship. Opponents of dual citizenship used the violent protests by Kurds in February 1999 in order to argue that Germany should not permit dual nationality, since it would not allow for the deportation of Kurds who commit crimes during violent demonstrations. The CDU/CSU argued against the dual nationality reform that it would lead to divided loyalties, slow integration, violence, and terrorism. But the supporters of dual nationality—such as Cem Ozdem, the first ethnic Turk elected to the *Bundestag*—presented an opposite view, arguing that it is the "sense of alienation among ethnic Turks [that] is creating conditions for a potential social explosion in Germany," including criminal activities and Islamic radicalism.[108]

Citizenship Policy[109]

Until 2000, German citizenship law was based on the principle of *jus sanguinis*. The country's 1913 citizenship law made citizenship dependent on blood or descent rather than place of birth.[110] There have been two major types of naturalization in Germany.[111] Ethnic Germans (*Aussiedler*) have had the right to German citizenship. Other foreigners could only become German citizens based on rigorous demands. They had to reside in Germany for at least 15 years at the discretion of the German authorities. Their applications could be rejected if they committed a felony, had less than six years of schooling, were not employed or employable, had received welfare payments, did not have adequate living quarters, did not have a sufficient knowledge of the German language, or if German local authorities deemed naturalization to be "not in the interest of the German state." They had to pay a substantial fee for naturalization. And they had to renounce their allegiance to their native country.[112] Children of foreigners were not accorded German citizenship by virtue of German birth.

These rigorous demands caused Germany to have among the lowest naturalization rates in Europe (not including the ethnic Germans). In 1998, for example, only 1 percent of the foreign population in Germany had become naturalized, in comparison to 1.5 percent in the Netherlands, 2.5 percent in Austria, 3.5 percent in the United Kingdom, and 4.5 percent in Sweden.[113] Overall, less than 5 percent of the major groups of foreigners in Germany (Turks, Croatians, and Italians) became naturalized Germans. And of the seven million foreigners residing in Germany, fewer than 20,000 a year became naturalized during the 1980s.[114] As a result, a large minority with no political rights was created, which encompassed 7–8.4 percent of Germany's population.

In 1990 the *Bundestag* passed a new Aliens Act that replaced the one of 1965 and liberalized Germany's citizenship policy to some extent. Foreigners between the ages of 16 and 23 who had lived legally for at least eight years in Germany, had attended school for at least six years, and who had not been convicted of a felony, were granted the right to become naturalized Germans upon the payment of a reduced fee. They no longer had to prove that they were not collecting social assistance payments, that they had adequate living quarters, and that they had acquired a knowledge of the German language and customs. Those 23 and older had to prove that they had resided in Germany for at least 15 years, had not been convicted of a felony, and had not been collecting social assistance.[115] In 1993 the fee for naturalization of other foreigners was also lowered. But for most foreigners, naturalization remained difficult. In addition, the requirement to renounce their allegiance to their native country caused many foreigners to avoid German naturalization. According to a 1994 poll, 62 percent of the Turks in Germany wanted German citizenship, but they did not want to give up their Turkish citizenship, which would mean forfeiting any claim to property in Turkey.[116] A few nations, including Turkey, also require the completion of military service before a young man can give up his citizenship.[117]

With the exception of the 1990–1993 liberalization, the Kohl governments (1982–1998) made few changes in Germany's citizenship policy. Repeatedly, the CDU/CSU declared that Germany is not a county of immigration, and that the liberalization of citizenship policy would send the wrong message and open the floodgates to further migration to Germany.[118]

Various political players, including Cornelia Schmalz-Jacobsen (the Commissioner for Foreigners), the FDP, the SPD, the president of the Republic, the president of the *Bundestag*, and some young members of the CDU pressured the government to make naturalization easier by permitting dual citizenship and reducing the required period of residence in Germany. Schmalz-Jacobsen introduced a package of such measures in February 1994, but her proposals were rejected by the Kohl government. After five Turks were killed in a Solingen arson fire in 1993, Kohl promised to make naturalization easier, but he then backed off for fear of anti-foreigner violence.[119] On March 27, 1998, the *Bundestag* rejected a SPD-backed proposal to liberalize Germany's citizenship laws.

In October 1998, the new SPD–Green government announced its first major policy initiative, which was reforming Germany's 1913 naturalization law. Declaring that Germany is "a country of immigration," the new government proposed to ease naturalization requirements and to permit dual nationality.[120] The proposal was introduced on January 13, 1999, a revised proposal was unveiled on March 11, 1999, the law was passed in May 1999, and was implemented on January 1, 2000. The main themes of the reform in the citizenship law were:[121]

- Children born in Germany to parents without German citizenship who were in Germany legally for at least eight years would have the right to dual nationality. Between the ages of 18 and 23, these people with dual nationality would have to choose whether to become exclusively German or lose their German nationality, unless the dual national could not be released from his non-German citizenship.
- Adults electing to become naturalized Germans were expected to give up their old nationality, but this regulation was to be "administered flexibly," especially for foreigners who had lived in Germany for at least 30 years or are at least 60 years old.
- The minimum time that a foreigner must live in Germany before applying for naturalization was reduced from 15 to 8 years.
- Foreigners married to Germans for at least two years and who have lived in Germany for three years, could also apply to become German citizens.
- In order to become Germans, foreigners would have to pass a German test, show they are not on welfare, and sign a statement saying they respect Germany's constitution. Foreigners who have been sentenced to prison terms of nine months or more in Germany would not be eligible for naturalization.

The reform in the citizenship law, in particular allowing for dual citizenship, was opposed by the CDU/CSU. It should be noted that the final version of the law was somewhat less liberal than the original version due to pressures from the Right and a compromise proposal by the FDP. In addition, the reform mainly benefited children born in Germany to parents without German citizenship, and to a much lesser degree foreigners who migrated to Germany. Germany's citizenship law has gradually moved from *jus sanguinis* toward *jus soli*, but its immigration control and citizenship policies still favor ethnic Germans over other immigrants.

Toward a New Immigration System

For years, policymakers have declared that Germany is not a country of immigration. But in practice, Germany became the main country of destination in Europe, and one of the largest in the world. During the past two decades, policymakers have also faced conflicting pressures with regard to immigration control policy. On the one hand, there has been a demand for immigrants in specific sectors, and it is needed in order to augment Germany's declining population and labor force. Employers have asked for the recruitment of migrant workers, particularly in the high-tech industry (as stated earlier). Social scientists have highlighted Germany's low birth rate and aging population.[122] They warned that if current trends continue, Germany's population would fall from 82 million to 59 million by 2050. The DIW Economics Research Institute in Berlin suggested that 340,000 to 680,000 immigrants per year are needed in order to prevent this "demographic implosion." The Federal Association of German Industry (BDI) estimated that Germany should accept 350,000 to 450,000 immigrants a year in order to maintain its social security system in its present form.[123] Even the Confederation of German Trade Unions (DGB) adopted a position paper in 1993 that urges the German government to recognize that "Germany will certainly need migrants" but that immigration must "be structured and organized" by using annual quotas.[124]

On the other hand, pressures mounted to restrict the immigration of asylum seekers, family unification, and ethnic Germans whose German heritage was in doubt. These pressures produced the 1992–1993 compromise, by which the immigration of asylum seekers and *Aussiedler* was limited. But right-wing politicians and sections of the population continued asking for restrictions on asylum seekers and on family reunification.

Finally, Germany also had to cope with the unsettled status of millions of former migrant workers, asylum seekers, and their family members, some of whom have resided in Germany for over two decades, but who have not become naturalized citizens.

These conflicting pressures created a debate, which intensified during the second half of the 1990s, on the need for a new immigration system. The major parties as well as interest groups debated whether Germany is a country of immigration, whether it needs an immigration system modeled on either the U.S. or Canadian systems, whether a point system would be used, whether it would include a migrant worker program, and which groups should be included in such a system. The outcome of this prolonged debate was an immigration law, which gave Germany its first-ever regulated immigration system.

The immigration law, signed on June 20, 2002, is as follows:[125]

(a) The law allows up to 50,000 skilled and professional foreigners to enter Germany each year. Highly qualified foreigners would be able to obtain permanent permits upon arrival. Students and less skilled workers would initially get temporary permits, which could be made permanent if they scored enough points. An applicant for a permanent permit would be awarded points for being young, completing school, and knowing German.
(b) The law tightens asylum procedures. Asylum seekers would be granted TPS status for a maximum of three years and allowed to work in Germany. Their right to stay in Germany would then be judged on the basis of the foreign ministry's assessment of conditions in their country of origin. Rejected asylum seekers would not be allowed to apply for an immigrant work-and-residence permit. The government would be able to detain asylum applicants and restrict their access to welfare payments more easily.
(c) The law grants refugee status to foreigners fleeing non-state and sexually specific forms of persecution.
(d) The law streamlines deportation procedures.
(e) The law encourages newcomers to integrate. All foreigners would have a right to participate in German language and culture courses. Those in Germany for less than six years who fail a German proficiency test would be required to participate in such courses or face difficulties renewing their residence permits.
(f) The law combines the agencies that issue residence and employment permits and reduces the number of combined permits from five to two—temporary and permanent.
(g) The law enables foreigners graduating from German universities to receive one-year residence and work permits after graduation.
(h) The law converts the present Federal Office for the Recognition of Refugees into a Federal Office for Migration and Refugees.

The new immigration law was passed by the SPD–Greens coalition, and opposed by the CDU/CSU. The latter, which governed the country throughout most of the post-1980 period, declared until recently that Germany is not a country of immigration. It also argued that with four million unemployed, Germany should not launch a new immigration policy that would increase admissions, and that the law would completely change German society within a few years. Finally, the party warned of the cost of the proposed new integration classes. The CDU/CSU proposed "four clear conditions" for a revised immigration law: strict limits on the number of immigrants, limitations on access to the social security system by immigrants and political asylum applicants, guarantees that immigrants would be well qualified and in demand in the German economy, and measures to ensure the integration of resident foreigners. After the law passed, the CDU/CSU challenged it in the Federal Constitutional Court, where it was blocked based on the way it was enacted.[126] But the SPD–Green government reintroduced the migration law in the *Bundesrat* in early 2003.[127]

In practice, however, the 2002 immigration law does already represent a partial convergence between the stands of Germany's major parties. Senior CDU/CSU politicians have given up the party's traditional stand on immigration, including Saarland Premier Peter Mueller, who chaired a CDU committee on immigration and said: "Germany is a nation of immigration . . . We need more people to immigrate so Germany will not suffer a decline in living standards."[128] The Law incorporates the proposals of a multiparty commission, appointed by Interior Minister Otto Schily (SPD) and headed by Rita Suessmuth (CDU). And the law includes changes previously supported by the CDU, such as giving preference to skilled labor based on a point system and tightening asylum procedures.

The Impact of the September 11 Terrorist Attacks on German Policies[129]

Following the September 11, 2001 terrorist attacks on the United States, and the revelation that several of the hijackers studied, lived, and raised money in Germany, privacy laws were relaxed and immigration control somewhat strengthened. In the immediate aftermath of the attacks, German legislators started debating restrictions on the freedom of movement, requiring fingerprints in identity cards and passports, and removing some of the protection for religious groups. In September-November 2001, the *Bundestag* enacted an antiterrorist legislative package, which removed the constitutional protection of extremist organizations that were also avowedly religious. The laws enabled the government to act against radical Islamic organizations, and an Islamic group known as the "Caliph State," suspected of having links with Al Qaeda, was banned. In the context of immigration control, the antiterrorism laws expanded the Central Register for Foreigners to include data on visa applicants and non-Germans entering Germany. Interior Minister Otto Schilly proposed that a formal check with domestic intelligence agencies would be conducted before granting residence or immigration visas. He also called for European-wide changes, including centralized registration centers in EU countries, greater standardization, and more access to visa data and legal clarification in issues surrounding profiling. Finally, the reaction to the terror acts also caused a postponement of the liberal reform in Germany's immigration system, enactment of which was postponed from the fall of 2001 to June 2002.

Anti-Immigrant Parties

The surge in immigration and economic difficulties facilitated the emergence of anti-immigrant parties[130] and initiatives. Until the mid-1980s, extreme-right anti-immigrant parties failed at the polls: the NPD received less than 0.5 percent of the votes in the 1976, 1980, and 1983 *Bundestag* elections. It did somewhat better in the 1984 European Parliament elections, where it gained 0.8 percent of the votes. During the 1979 and 1982 regional elections the maximum combined vote for extreme-right parties at any one regional election was 0.6–0.7 percent. In addition, *Ausländerstopp* initiatives were also promoted in Keil and in Hessen in 1982 and 1983.

The breakthrough for the extreme-right occurred in October 1986, when the Republican Party, which campaigned against asylum seekers, gained 3 percent of the vote in the Bavarian *Landtag* elections. In the September 1987 election in Bremen, the DVU achieved 3.4 percent across the whole electorate, with 5.4 percent in Bremerhaven. In addition, the NPD got 0.6 percent in the 1987 *Bundestag* elections and 0.8 percent in the Rhineland-Palatinate elections. And in 1988 the NPD and the Republican Party combined for 1.8 percent in the Schleswig-Holstein elections and 3.1 in the Baden-Württemberg elections.

The extreme-right parties—the NPD, DVU, and the Republican Party—did even better between 1989 and 1993. In 1989 the Republican Party won 7.5 percent in the elections to the Berlin House of Deputies. In June of the same year, the party gained 7.1 percent of the vote for the European Parliament, and the DVU won an additional 1.6 percent. The NPD received 6.6 percent of the vote in the Frankfurt municipal elections. In the 1990 *Länder* elections the Republican Party gained 4.9 percent of the vote in Bavaria, 3.4 percent in the Saarland, and 3.1 in Berlin. It also received 5.4 percent in the Bavarian municipal elections. In 1991 the Republicans fared relatively poorly in *Länder* elections, gaining between 1.2–2 percent of the vote in Hesse, Rhineland-Palatinate, Hamburg, and Bremen, but the DVU got 6.3 percent in Bremen. The Republican Party reached its peak during the following two years, receiving 10.9 percent in the 1992 Baden-Württemberg elections and 9.3 percent in the 1993 Frankfurt elections. The DVU also gained 6.3 percent in the 1995 Schleswig-Holstein elections.

The extreme-right parties declined in 1994–1995, but rebounded in the 1996 and 1997 regional elections, receiving a maximum combined vote of 9.1 and 6.8 percent respectively. In 1998 the DVU had its greatest success, gaining over 12 percent of the vote in the Sachsen-Anhalt elections. However, according to Arzheimer, the Sachen-Anhalt result could be explained by low turnout and low levels of knowledge on what kind of party the DVU actually was.[131] The extreme-right parties got a maximum combined vote of 6 percent in the 1999 regional elections, but only 1.7 percent in the 1999 elections for the European Parliament, and 1 percent in the 2000 regional elections.

Factors Shaping German Immigration Policy: An Analysis

German immigration control policy has dealt with immigrants of five types:

- Permanent immigration of ethnic Germans from Eastern Europe, especially between 1945 and 1961, and since 1988/1989.
- Migration of Poles during the late nineteenth and early twentieth century.
- Migrant workers from Southern Europe, Yugoslavia, and the Middle East between 1955 and 1973, from other EEC/EC/EU member states since the Treaty of Rome, and from Eastern Europe during the 1990s.
- Asylum seekers from Eastern Europe and the Third World, particularly since 1979/1980.
- Illegal/undocumented migrants.

In accordance with the model advanced here, ethnic Germans encountered no restrictions, even during economic downturns, as long as they were viewed as immigrants of similar ethnic origin. Only when economic difficulties combined with doubts regarding the degree of similarity between the immigrants and the local population—that is the degree to which the immigrants were genuine Germans—did Germany limit their immigration, demanding evidence of their German background. A conflict between social and economic considerations caused Germany to implement policies that ensured the temporary status of Polish immigrants during the early twentieth century. The migration of foreign workers, as long as it was perceived to be temporary, was mostly influenced by the state of the economy, and to a limited degree by the composition of immigration. Germany accepted asylum seekers in order to atone for its Nazi past. But an influx of asylum seekers of dissimilar ethnic and cultural composition, and (to a lesser degree) an economic recession, led it to restrict the immigration of asylum seekers.

Migrant workers German labor migration policy has been primarily influenced by *the state of the economy*. Germany restricted labor migration, and in some cases deported migrant workers, during economic downturns in 1885, 1914, 1918–23, 1929, 1932, and 1973. It also encouraged the departure of migrant labor during the recession of 1967–1968. And it recruited or forcefully employed foreign workers during manpower shortages, including much of the 1890–1913, 1937–1945, and 1955–1972 periods. The link between the state of the economy and labor migration policy was particularly evident after World War II. During the early postwar period, Germany experienced relatively high unemployment rates and also accepted millions of German refugees from the East. In 1955 unemployment declined to 5 percent, and labor shortages in agriculture caused German farmers to pressure the government for foreign workers. The demand for labor further increased during the early 1960s, as unemployment dropped below 1 percent, and the construction of the Berlin Wall prevented immigration from the GDR. During the 1960s, Germany signed labor recruitment agreements with various Southern European and Middle Eastern countries, and German policymakers emphasized the economic advantages of recruiting foreign workers. The departure of foreign labor was encouraged during the recession of 1967–1968, but once the recession ended, a new labor exchange agreement was signed with Yugoslavia, and the pace of foreign labor recruitment increased. The ban on the recruitment of foreign workers was instituted in November 1973, following the energy crisis, as the unemployment rate started rising.

During the 1990s, Germany implemented two types of migrant worker programs. One was the recruitment of Eastern European foreign workers, mostly employed in agriculture, restaurants, hotels, construction, and health care. The second was the recruitment of highly skilled workers—mainly from India and Eastern Europe—to work in the IT industry. The implementation of migrant worker programs when the unemployment rate was relatively high (7.2–12.7 percent of the labor force) would seem to contradict the hypothesis linking the state of the economy to migrant worker policy. Four factors explain this phenomenon:

- The new programs mostly included sectors in which the demand for labor surpassed the supply because of (a) a sudden expansion in the demand for labor (e.g. in construction following German unification); (b) German workers were unwilling to work in these jobs for the prevailing wages; [132] or (c) German labor could not answer the demand for particular skills (e.g. in the IT industry). In the latter case, the German Ministry of Education and Research projected openings for 60,000 IT workers a year, but only 10,000 computer science students graduated each year.[133] Martin observes, ". . . there has been a shift in the rationale for temporary foreign worker programs. Instead of recruiting foreign workers to deal with macro or widespread labor shortages, most programs today are justified as a way to deal with micro labor shortages, e.g. in agriculture or construction, or to channel into legal programs otherwise illegal migrants."[134]
- The number of migrant workers involved in these programs has been relatively small. While East European foreign workers have numbered between 150,000 and 280,000 per annum, most of them have been seasonal workers, who could work up to three months per year in Germany. Thus, the employment of (legal) East European workers in annual terms has been much smaller, and they constituted less than 11 percent of the total foreign workforce.[135]
- Foreign policy considerations (described later) contributed to the recruitment of Eastern European foreign workers.
- The fluctuations in the labor market do correlate, to some degree, with policy toward foreign workers. In 1997, when unemployment reached its peak, the EU announced that it would force Germany to reduce the number of non-EU seasonal workers permitted to work in Germany. Some observers speculated that the German government welcomed the EU decision, since it enabled the government to stop recruitment for an increasingly controversial program. In 2000–2001, as unemployment declined, policy regarding high-tech and home care sectors was liberalized.

In addition, German policy on migrant workers from EU member-states has not correlated precisely with the state of the economy, because these workers have enjoyed the free movement of labor within the EC/EU. Nevertheless, the shift toward the free movement of labor within the Union was originally facilitated by economic prosperity in Germany and in Europe in general, and Germany promoted the free movement of labor during that period. In contrast, Germany attempted to discourage the free movement of labor in the EU during the 1970s economic recession.[136]

The volume and composition of immigration did not significantly affect labor migration policy because Germans believed that the stay of the migrants was temporary. Labor migration of dissimilar origin did not cause Germany to halt immigration between 1890 and 1913, during the second half of the 1930s, or during the 1960s. There are some indications that the composition of immigration influenced labor migration policy. However, in most cases there are alternative explanations for the policies, and the influence of the composition of immigration on labor migration policy seems marginal in comparison to that of the economy:

- Labor migration of dissimilar composition led to policies that attempted to reinforce its temporary nature. This was most evident in the 1890 *Karenzzeit* compromise, and to some degree in 1965 and during the 1970s and 1980s.[137] However, it could be argued that in most of these cases it was the growing permanency of immigration, rather than temporary labor migration, that produced the restrictive policies.
- The order of signing agreements for the recruitment of labor fits the degree of cultural similarity between the immigrants and the local population. The first agreements (between 1955 and 1960) were established with Italy, Spain, and Greece. Only later were agreements signed with Turkey, Tunis, Morocco, and Yugoslavia (between 1961 and 1968). It should be noted, however, that the agreement with Portugal was only signed in 1964. In addition, geographical proximity and political ties may also explain the order of the agreements.
- Some conservative politicians were already using antiforeign slogans during the 1965–1966 campaign—prior to the 1967 and 1973 economic recession.[138]
- Chancellor Brandt's statement in January 1973 referred to the absorption ability of German society.

It is reasonable to assume that had the mass recruitment continued beyond 1973, with its permanent nature becoming more and more apparent, that restrictions on labor migration would have passed regardless of the state of the economy. The 1971 Work Permits ordinance already signified an initial shift from temporary to permanent migration. And some scholars argue that the growing permanency of the migrant workers already had an impact on German immigration policy in 1973. According to Martin:

> By 1973 it was clear that many of the temporary guests had become more or less permanent residents, and that most Germans were opposed to the unanticipated settlement of Turks and Yugoslavs in Germany. The German government reacted by restricting immigration. First the government announced a tripling of the employer-paid recruitment fee in February 1973 . . . The government used the October 1973 oil embargo to announce a ban on the further recruitment of guestworkers. The November 1973 recruitment ban was justified in terms of the OPEC oil embargo which allegedly threatened to provoke an economic recession and rising unemployment throughout the industrial countries, making additional migrants unnecessary. However, German employers whose requests for new migrants were thus blocked thought that the government had simply found a convenient excuse in to halt the immigration that was troubling German voters.[139]

Other scholars do not agree with this assessment, arguing that labor migration was mostly thought of as a temporary phenomenon, and that the recession was the main reason for halting labor recruitment. This was also the official government justification for the change in policy. In any case, even according to the former interpretation, it was the growing permanency of the immigrants—that is their shift from temporary migrant workers to semipermanent ones—that caused the volume and composition of immigration to substantially influence immigration control policy.

According to hypotheses 3 and 8, *wars* facilitate the establishment of migrant worker programs in what was termed the "war–migrant labor link." During both world wars, Germany experienced labor shortages and employed foreign workers, most of them through the use of force. The wide usage of forced labor can be attributed to Germany's totalitarian regime.

According to hypothesis 8, *foreign policy considerations* rarely cause the establishment of migrant worker programs, but they influence the character of those programs: from which countries the workers will be recruited, and sometimes the nature of their employment. The impact of foreign policy considerations is facilitated by the fact that labor recruitment contracts are usually signed between the country of origin and the country of destination, or between companies and individuals with the approval of the respective governments.

In the German case, foreign policy considerations indeed influenced both the treatment of migrant workers and the countries from which they were recruited. During World War I, Germany somewhat improved the treatment of Polish and Belgian workers because of protests by other countries. During the 1960s, pressures from Southern European governments, international organizations, and various domestic groups (employers, unions, and migrant assistance organizations) caused the German government to relax the rules on prolonging the migrants stay and on family unification. And in 1977, Germany removed restrictions on the movement of foreign workers into highly congested urban areas because of the pending EC membership of Greece, Spain, and Portugal. Historical links and foreign relations between Germany and Turkey as well as between Germany and Yugoslavia contributed to labor recruitment agreements between these countries, turning the Turks and the Yugoslavs into the two largest groups of foreign workers in the FRG. Thränhardt links the 1968 recruitment treaty with Yugoslavia to the restoration of diplomatic relations in the first steps of the *Ostpolitik*.[140] He adds that the delicate neutral position of communist Yugoslavia and the fragility of her internal cohesion were of central importance for Germany, and thus German politicians again and again assured Yugoslavia that the FRG would not send back Yugoslavs against their will. With regard to Turkey, Thränhardt notes that the recruitment of Turkish workers was facilitated by the fact that Turkey was considered European being NATO's southeastern stronghold, a member of the Council of Europe and associated with the EEC since 1964. Later, the 1972 bilateral treaty with Turkey, as well as the Treaty of Association negotiated between the EEC and Turkey in 1980, prevented the CDU government that came into power in 1982 from fulfilling its promise of returning the migrants to their countries of origin.[141] At the same time, Germany ignored Turkish protests, terminating the recruitment of migrant workers in 1973. And German politicians, such as Edmund Stoiber, opposed the admission of Turkey to the EU in order to prevent large-scale Turkish immigration to Germany.[142]

Foreign policy considerations also facilitated the establishment of foreign worker programs that have allowed Eastern Europeans to work in Germany since the early 1990s. Hönekopp notes that one of the reasons for the creation of these programs was to assist East European countries by supplementing their labor markets and providing income transfers for economic development.[143] Martin adds that for foreign policy reasons, Germany was reluctant to "recreate the Berlin Wall" on its eastern border in order to stop illegal immigration from the east, and thus it developed the foreign worker programs.[144] These programs were also the product of other factors, including a demand for labor in certain sectors and an increase in illegal immigration from Eastern Europe. But the fact that Eastern European workers were favored over other non-EU ones, and that Germany preferred to legalize the formerly illegal workers, was influenced by foreign policy considerations.

Asylum seekers In contrast to labor migration, policy regarding asylum seekers was mostly influenced by Germany's attempt to atone for its Nazi past and by the volume of dissimilar immigration. Article 16 of the 1949 Basic Law guaranteed the right of asylum to persons persecuted for political reasons. But an influx of asylum seekers of dissimilar ethnic and cultural composition—about half of those applying for asylum in EU countries—caused Germany to amend its constitution and pass a law that severely restricted the right to asylum. Foreign policy considerations (e.g. emending Germany's image) may have contributed to the country's initial liberal asylum policy. But between 1989 and 1993 some 95 percent of the asylum seekers were judged to be economic rather than political refugees, and their claims for asylum were rejected.[145] Thus, in accordance with the model, they constituted regular immigrants of dissimilar composition, and the surge in their numbers led to restrictive immigration control policies.

The 1980 upsurge in asylum applications—mostly from Turkey, Pakistan, India, Afghanistan, Ethiopia, Bangladesh, Sri Lanka, Ghana, and Vietnam—caused Germany to require nationals of Turkey, Afghanistan, Bangladesh, India, and Sri Lanka to obtain visas. It also led to regulations that made asylum seekers wait for one year (and later two years) before receiving a work permit, to restrictions on the social benefits granted to asylum applicants, and to the Asylum Procedure Act of 1982, which authorized the federal authorities to dismiss an asylum request if it appeared to be ill-founded. The 1984–1993 influx of asylum seekers—mostly from Yugoslavia, Romania, Turkey, Poland, Bulgaria, and Iran—led to agreements with countries of origin (e.g. Romania) and transfer (e.g. East Germany) in an attempt to limit immigration. Eventually, the upsurge in the number of asylum seekers generated the 1993 amendment to the German constitution, which severely restricted the right to asylum.

The influx of asylum seekers—potentially permanent immigrants of dissimilar composition—produced much more antagonism than did the temporary migration of migrant workers or the permanent migration of ethnic Germans. Rudolph notes that during the late 1980s and early 1990s, the most heated public debates in Germany concerning migration focused on asylum seekers.[146] In 1993, mounting public pressure led to an amendment to the German constitution, which restricted the chances of successful applications for asylum. In comparison, the public mostly ignored the large-scale migration of *Aussiedler* and especially the recruitment of new migrant workers from Central and Eastern Europe.

The sharp rise in the number of asylum seekers between 1988 and 1993 also generated support for extreme-right anti-immigrant parties and a wave of attacks against foreigners, which in turn caused the major parties to support restrictions on immigration. The restrictions applied to asylum seekers in 1993 brought about a decline in the number of immigrants and in the support for extremist parties. The major parties usually used relatively subtle expressions in comparison to those of the extreme-right parties. But during the 1980 election campaign, less-prominent politicians of the CDU/CSU referred to the "over-flooding" of foreigners. And during the 1981–1982 debate in the *Bundestag*, the Right accused the SPD government of remaining passive in the face of floods of "*Asylantenflut*."[147]

In addition to the impact of the influx of asylum seekers, the economic difficulties Germany faced also influenced asylum policy to some degree. States and local governments paid an average $10,000 per year to house, feed, and clothe each asylum applicant during the two to four years that were often required to process a claim.[148] In a country faced with unemployment rates of 7–9 percent, and coping with the tremendous task of integrating the former GDR into Germany's market system, such expenses generated antagonism toward the applicants, and support for restrictions. For example, in April 1994, SDP candidate Rudolf Scharping warned that unemployment and the large number of foreigners in the country could lead to a xenophobic backlash in an economic downturn.[149] The economic difficulties particularly contributed to the opposition to immigration in the eastern part of the country, where far fewer immigrants resided than in the western part. The DVU won its biggest electoral triumph in the 1998 elections for the Eastern German *Länder* of Sachsen-Anhalt, where only 1.8 percent of the population was foreign, but unemployment reached 24 percent. However, overall, the influence of the state of the economy (measured according to the rate of unemployment) on German immigration control policy and on the support for extreme-right parties was less consistent than that of the number of applications for asylum.

The size and possibly the composition of immigration, the financial burden it entailed, the state of the economy, and foreign policy all seem to have influenced policy toward Bosnian and Kosovar asylum seekers during the 1990s. International obligations led Germany to accept 320,000–350,000 Bosnian asylum seekers on a temporary basis. But the end of the war, the considerable financial burden for the *Länder*, and high unemployment contributed to the decision to repatriate the Bosnians. While I found no direct evidence, it is plausible that the composition of immigration also facilitated the decision to return the Bosnians (60 percent of whom were Muslim), and to withhold TPS status from the Kosovo Albanians. The influence of the state of the economy is evident in both cases: Germany decided to repatriate Bosnians and Kosovars during 1996–1999, when unemployment was high. But when unemployment declined in 2000–2001, Germany's Commissioner for Foreigners argued that it makes no sense to force Kosovars who are employed and integrated in Germany to return, and at the same time recruit green card foreigners. Consequently, Bosnians and Kosovars who had resided in Germany at least six years, had been employed for at least two years, and who had families that did not receive welfare, were allowed to stay in Germany.

Permanent immigration of ethnic Germans According to hypothesis 10a, immigration control policy with regard to permanent similar immigration tends to be more liberal than the policy with regard to permanent dissimilar immigration. According to hypothesis 10b, neither large-scale immigration nor mild recessions are sufficient to produce restrictions on permanent immigration of similar composition. Doubts with regard to the degree of similarity between the immigrants and the dominant element of the receiving society, or, at times, severe depressions, are necessary in order to generate such restrictions.

Germany's leaders repeatedly declared (until 1998) that Germany is not a country of (permanent) immigration. Permanent immigration of non-Germans, except for political refugees and family reunification, was practically impossible until the reform of the immigration system in 2002. Moreover, since the late 1970s/early 1980s the latter two groups were also subject to restrictions. In contrast, Germany has favored the migration of ethnic German, and *Aussiedler* migration has far outnumbered all other types of immigration since World War II. Between 1950 and 1960, Germany readily accepted and integrated millions of ethnic Germans from Eastern Europe, despite a severe housing shortage and relatively high unemployment rates up to 1954.[150] Between 1961 and 1986 it continued to accept tens of thousands ethnic German immigrants per annum, their numbers only limited by emigration restrictions implemented by the communist regimes. Based on Germany's 1949 Basic Law, the Federal Law concerning Refugees and Expellees of 1953, and the law of 1957, ethnic Germans who migrated from the East were granted German citizenship and integration assistance upon their arrival. The ethnic Germans could apply for *Aussiedler* status during a short-term visit to the FRG, or even after illegal entry. And they were awarded various benefits—housing, language course, vocational training, and transfer payments—in order to facilitate their integration.

Foreign policy considerations further facilitated the reception of *Aussiedler*. According to Münz, the fact that until 1989 all ethnic Germans of Central and Eastern Europe lived under communist rule was used as an additional argument in their favor. Large parts of the West German public interpreted the *Aussiedlers'* decisions to emigrate both as a response to political and social discrimination at home and as a clear profession of being German and belief in the political system of the FRG.[151]

Between 1987 and 2001, during and following the collapse of the Iron Curtain, Germany accepted an additional 2.9 million ethnic Germans from the East (as well as 861,000 immigrants from the GDR between 1987 and 1990), despite relatively high unemployment rates. Initially, these migrants were welcomed. But during the 1990s, Germany limited their immigration by: setting a quota of 220,000 persons per annum (later reduced to 110,000); requiring them to apply for *Aussiedler* status in their country of origin rather than in Germany; introducing a language test, which half of the applicants have failed; implementing cumbersome administrative procedures; and attempting to improve the economic, social, and political situation of ethnic German minorities in their East European countries of origin. The law of 1992 also limited the options of future applications for *Aussiedler* status, with the implication that after the year 2010 ethnic Germans would have no independent claim to such status, though some of them would still be able to immigrate within the framework of family unification.

The main reason for these restrictions was doubts with regard to the German heritage of the immigrants (i.e. whether they were "sufficiently German") and to their ability to integrate. Newspapers headlined stories of Eastern Europeans wanting to migrate to Germany buying or forging documents to prove their German heritage. Public opinion polls showed that a majority of the respondents thought that the *Aussiedler* were no longer real Germans, and that their migration was economically motivated.[152] Unemployment rates of the ethnic German migrants that were often as high as those of foreign guestworkers led some Germans to consider ethnic Germans as hard-to-integrate foreigners. The failure to speak German, as well as perceptions that ethnic German youth are responsible for a disproportionate amount of crime, has reportedly led many Germans to turn against ethnic Germans, calling them Russians despite the fact that they receive German passports upon arrival in Germany. And studies found that the percentage of "real ethnic Germans" among new arrivals has been decreasing, down to 26 percent in 2000.[153] Thus, the immigration of the *Aussiedler* has been limited through the use of a language test and other means of proving their German identity rather than according to economic or skill-based criteria.

In addition to the doubts with regard to the German heritage of the immigrants, economic difficulties in Germany (the high cost of integrating the former GDR and unemployment rates of 7.2–12.7 percent), the fact that the immigrants were no longer persecuted by the countries of origin, and the decline of anticommunist foreign policy considerations also contributed to the restrictions on *Aussiedler* immigration. For example, in February and March 1996, during the election campaign in the states of Baden-Wüerttemberg, Rhineland-Palatinate, and Schleswig-Holstein, SPD Chairman Oskar Lafontaine and other politicians argued that the *Aussiedler* were bound to "immigrate into unemployment" and to become a burden for the pension system and the taxpayers. According to Lafontaine, "a million people have come as job-seekers and it's about time to stop this influx, otherwise we'll have 100,000 more unemployed at the end of the year." He also argued that endangered asylum seekers had a greater moral claim to immigrate than ethnic Germans who were no longer in imminent danger.[154] However, it should be noted that the attempt of SPD leaders to link unemployment with the need to restrict *Aussiedler* migration did not help them gain support from the electorate. The debate with regard to the *Aussiedler* ended when the Social Democrats suffered heavy losses in the elections in all three states. Dieter Spori, the SPD candidate for Baden-Württemberg, who had campaigned against the immigration of ethnic Germans from the former Soviet Union, said he would no longer play a leadership role in the SPD. In contrast, Lafontaine said he did not believe his party's losses in the three states were due to opposition to ethnic German immigration.

Despite the aforementioned restrictions, ethnic Germans have benefited from a privileged status even after 1987. Germany accepted almost three million *Aussiedler* during this period, and most of these immigrants would not have been accepted if not for their ethnic origin, that is based on a refugee status or on required skills. *Aussiedler* also get German language instruction, are eligible for pensions, and become German citizens upon request. So while doubts with regard to the German heritage of the immigrants and other factors have contributed to a more restrictive immigration control policy toward them, these factors did not eliminate the preference for permanent immigration of similar ethnic composition.

Fear of radicalism and terrorism The fear of imported radicalism and terrorism influenced German immigration control policy in two cases. First, Kurdish involvement in violent demonstrations against Turkey, and the activities of the PKK, led Germany to deport Kurds and to reject the applications for asylum of Kurds involved in such activities. Second, following the September 11, 2001 terrorist attacks on the United States and the revelation that several of the hijackers studied, lived, and raised money in Germany, the *Bundestag* enacted an antiterrorist legislative package. The government acted against radical Islamic organizations, and the Central Register for Foreigners was expanded to include data on visa applicants and non-Germans entering Germany. In addition, the relatively liberal reform of the immigration system was delayed from the fall of 2001 to mid-2002. But overall, the impact of the fear of imported radicalism and terrorism on Germany's overall immigration control policy was smaller than that of other factors.

Strikes According to Martin, "A wave of wildcat strikes that [1973] summer, which involved a significant number of migrant workers, convinced the government that foreign worker recruitment must be stopped."[155] However, an exploration of the German strikes over the past century does not reveal a correlation between the number of workers on strike and the tendency to adopt restrictive immigration policies. The peaks of strikes since 1899 were in 1905, 1917–1925, 1928, and 1955. Relatively large numbers of workers were also on strike in 1906, 1910–1912, 1927, 1971, 1978, 1984, and 1992. Of these years, only the post–World War I period and 1992 were characterized by restrictive immigration policies. In both cases, alternative factors account for the restrictions: unemployment explains the post–World War I restrictions on labor migration, and an influx of asylum seekers caused the 1992–1993 reform of asylum policy.

Social conflicts Finally, among the countries studied in this book, Germany offers the strongest support for the influence of social conflicts on immigration control policy, although even in this case it is difficult to assess the influence of such conflicts. The 1871 unification produced the heightened nationalism of the late nineteenth century, which contributed to restrictions on Polish immigration. But the peaks of nationalism did not exactly correlate with the timing of restrictions on the recruitment of foreign labor: the policy of "Germanization" started in 1872 while the deportation of Polish workers occurred only in 1885. Similarly, restrictions on the use of the Polish language in Germany in 1899 and 1908 were not followed by restrictions on the size of Polish immigration. The 1918–1923 revolution and instability did coincide with restrictive immigration policies, but the 1930s emergence of the Nazi regime led to liberalization of labor migration policies.

The social cleavage theory fails to explain German foreign labor policy during the 1946–1973 period. The social unrest of 1968 was followed by intensified recruitment of migrant workers.

Several authors assert that the reunification of Germany was responsible for the rise of extreme-right parties and for restrictive immigration policies. But there are three problems with this argument. First, German unification should have solved the problem of self-identity, rather than caused or exacerbated it. Indeed, according to Westle and Niedermayer, the decline of the Republican Party in the 1990 *Länder* elections was partly caused by Germany's reunification, which deprived it of one of its main issues. Second, the rise of extreme-right parties in Germany started in 1986, four years prior to reunification. And third, extreme-right parties emerged in other European countries during the same time period, indicating that the causes for their rise were not particular to Germany. A more plausible argument links German reunification to restrictions on immigration in an indirect way. While unification initially caused an economic boom, it then generated growing expenses for the former West Germany. It also caused disappointment in the former East Germany due to high levels of unemployment, which resulted in attacks on foreigners and support for antiimmigrant parties in that region. Unification and the fall of the Soviet block also caused an inflow of immigrants of German origin form the East, which in turn led to restrictions on such immigration, especially since their German heritage was in doubt.[156]

CHAPTER 6

Global Patterns in Immigration Control Policy

One of the most fascinating aspects of immigration control policy is the fact that the policies of the major receiving countries have been extraordinary similar for over a century. What explains these similarities? What explains their differences between the immigration policies? And why do some countries prefer permanent immigration, while others prefer migrant workers?

This chapter starts with a description of similarities among the immigration policies of the major receiving countries. It then examines six alternative explanations for these similarities, and argues that it is the interdependence between the socioeconomic and foreign policy factors that leads to most of the similarities in the immigration control policies of the various countries. The chapter concludes by presenting structural factors that cause the cross-national differences between immigration policies.

Global Similarities in Immigration Control Policy

The immigration control policies of the major receiving countries have been extraordinarily similar with regard to their content and timing. Often, similar policies were inaugurated in a variety of countries within a period of one or two years:

- Between the 1770s and the 1870s, immigration was practically unrestricted in most receiving countries, and some of them lacked the capacity to control immigration. Britain, the United States, Canada (Nova Scotia), Switzerland, and France regulated immigration in the

1790s. Britain and the United States regulated immigration, or attempted to do so, in the late 1840s.

- During the 1870s–1880s, Canada, Germany, New Zealand, the United States, and several Australian states restricted Chinese and/or other labor migration.
- Between 1890 and World War I, Australia, Canada, and the United States restricted Japanese immigration; Britain, Canada and the United States attempted to block Eastern European/impoverished immigration; and Canada, France, and Germany regulated (although not necessarily restricted) temporary labor migration. These restrictions and attempted restrictions intensified from 1894 to 1897, and from 1905 to 1908.[1] In contrast, no major restrictions were imposed from 1898 to 1904 and from 1909 to 1913, with the exception of the 1901 Immigration Restriction Act and the Pacific Island Laborers Act in Australia, which corresponded to state acts passed earlier, and an Order in Council of 1910 in Canada.
- World War I had a dual impact on immigration control policy. On the one hand, receiving countries limited permanent immigration and restricted former immigrants.[2] On the other hand, the receiving countries expanded the recruitment of migrant labor.[3]
- Between 1919 and 1924, Australia, Britain, Canada, Germany, the Netherlands, Switzerland, and the United States severely restricted immigration.[4]
- Between 1925 and mid-1928, the major receiving countries passed little immigration legislation.[5]
- Between 1929 and 1935, Australia, Canada, France, Germany, Switzerland, and the United States restricted immigration and/or stopped recruiting migrant worker.[6]
- Between 1936 and 1938, major receiving countries did not adopt new immigration control policies, but rather continued to apply restrictions imposed earlier. Several countries even implemented more liberal policies.[7]
- World War II, like World War I, had a dual impact on immigration control policy. On the one hand, receiving countries expanded the recruitment of foreign labor. On the other hand, the receiving countries strengthened their controls on permanent immigration, and some of them interned aliens from enemy countries.[8]
- Between 1945 and 1972, with the exception of 1966–1968, Western European countries first accepted permanent immigrants (mainly from their colonies or former colonies) or refugees, then recruited large numbers of migrant workers.[9] The countries of

permanent immigration—Australia, Canada, the United States, and New Zealand, but not Britain—eliminated discriminatory policies against Asian, African, and Eastern and Southern European immigration. Between 1966–1968, Western European countries limited the recruitment of migrant workers, and strengthened their control over private recruitment. But later, between 1969–1972, these measures were overlooked, and labor migration reached its peak.

- Between 1972 and 1974, Western European countries halted or sharply curtailed migrant labor recruitment.[10] During the second half of the 1970s, these same countries encouraged former migrant workers to return to their home countries by offering them financial incentives, but to no avail. Australia also decreased its immigrant intake between 1971–1975. In contrast, between 1975 and 1980, Australia, the United States, and Canada accepted large numbers of Indo-Chinese refugees, the United States took in Cuban refugees, and the Netherlands admitted immigrants from Surinam and the Dutch Antilles. Also during the 1970s, the United States, Canada, France, the Netherlands, and Sweden attempted to reduce illegal immigration.
- Since 1979 and particularly since 1985, the countries of destination attempted to halt illegal immigration and to reduce the number of immigrants granted asylum. The measures applied included stricter controls at the borders, penalties on employers of illegal immigrants, incarceration of illegal immigrants in camps and sometimes their deportation, as well as a reform of the asylum processing procedures.[11]
- During the past three decades, Australia, Britain, Canada, Germany, the United States, and other countries also created point-systems or new categories that gave preference to immigrant investors, entrepreneurs, and those with required skills.[12] Also during the 1990s, there has been a renewed tendency to accept migrant workers, but this time on a more limited and sectoral basis (e.g. in the agricultural and high-tech sectors).

Explanations for the Similarities in Immigration Control Policies

There are six possible explanations for the similarities in immigration control policies of the major receiving countries:

- A global hegemon that forces or persuades various countries to act in unison.

- Global or regional migration regimes and organizations.
- Interdependence between the immigration control policies of various countries.
- Emulation of immigration control policies of one country by other countries (as well as the possible existence of an epistemic community in the field of immigration control policy).
- The world system approach.
- Interdependence between the socioeconomic and foreign policy factors that lead to immigration control policies.

I argue that it is the last factor that explains most of the similarity among the immigration control policies of the major receiving countries.

Hegemony and International Regimes

Hegemonic stability theory and regime theory fail to explain the similarities among the immigration control policies of the major receiving countries. Nor do they explain multilateral cooperation with regard to international labor mobility in regional organizations.[13] To summarize:

(a) Multilateral cooperation does not exist with regard to the acceptance of permanent immigrants (with the exception of refugees);[14]
(b) Multilateral cooperation on the movement of labor is mostly regional rather than interregional, and thus it effects only a small fraction of international migration;
(c) Multilateral cooperation on the free movement of labor (e.g. in regional integration schemes) is not a collective good, and thus it does not warrant a regime or a hegemon in order to solve a collective-action problem;
(d) Multilateral cooperation on the free movement of labor is mostly regional—in Europe and Africa—and does not involve the American hegemon;
(e) Most international migration cooperation did not exist prior to World War II, and thus it cannot explain the similarity among the immigration control policies during that period.

Of the policies described here, international regimes may shed light on refugee policies, and on policies dealing with immigration into the EU since the 1980s. Bargaining models, such as the one presented in

Meyers, can explain multilateral cooperation on the movement of labor within regional integration schemes.[15] But neither of the aforementioned theories explains most of the similarities among the immigration control policies of the major receiving countries during the past century.

Interdependence Between Immigration Control Policies

Interdependence between the immigration control policies of various countries—notably between Canada, the United States, and Australia—explains a few similarities between these policies. In particular, restrictions on immigration in one country have produced migratory pressures in other countries, which in response also restricted immigration. Canada restricted Chinese immigration in 1885 "to protect Canada against the backwash of the U.S. [Chinese exclusion] legislation of 1882."[16] During the turn of the century, "as the United States of America began to introduce qualitative tests, the Canadian Government felt constrained to do likewise."[17] The 1921 and 1924 Quota Acts in the United States produced a surge in immigration to Australia from Southern Europe. This, in turn, led Australia to establish administrative quotas on immigration from Southern Europe. The McCarran-Walter Immigration Act of 1952 halted West Indian emigration to the United States, which contributed to the rise in West Indian immigration to Britain, and eventually led to the 1962 restrictions on New Commonwealth immigration.[18] The tightening of the rules governing entry to Germany in 1992–1993 caused an increase in the number of asylum applications to the Netherlands, which led the Dutch to restrict their asylum policy in imitation of the German policy.[19]

However, the evidence for interdependence between the immigration control policies of various countries is limited. This is quite apart from the fact that such a process requires some time: first, country A restricts immigration; second, the immigrants start converging to country B; and third, only when a substantial number of immigrants have arrived in country B does it respond by restricting immigration. This prolonged process does not fit, for instance, the almost simultaneous restrictions on immigrants in 1914 or on migrant workers in 1973. So interdependence between immigration control policies only marginally contributes to the aforementioned similarity.

Emulation of Immigration Control Policies

The emulation of immigration control policies also explains several similarities among these policies. For example, in 1994–1995, the

Netherlands prevented persons from applying for asylum if they had arrived from a "safe country of origin," or entered the Netherlands via a "safe third country." The Dutch government indicated that the new policy emulates similar criteria applied by Germany at an earlier date.[20] Emulation of immigration control policies has been especially common with regard to skill-based selection systems. The Australian Structured Selection Assessment System (SSAS), introduced in 1973, the Numerically Weighted Multi-Factor Assessment System (NUMAS) points-system, introduced in 1979 and its modifications were influenced by Canada's points-system of 1967.[21] The U.S. 1990 Immigration Act gave preference to skilled labor, professionals, and investors, partially imitating Australia's and Canada's points-systems. It was suggested that Britain try to attract needed skills by following the lead of the United States and Canada, and Britain created a new entrepreneurial business immigration category in 1994.

One reason immigration control policies are emulated might be the existence of an epistemic community. According to Peter Haas:

> An epistemic community is a network of professionals with recognised expertise and competence in a particular domain and an authoritative claim to policy-relevant knowledge within that domain or issue-area . . . . Members of transnational epistemic communities can influence state interests by directly identifying them for decision makers or by illuminating the salient dimensions of the issue from which the decision makers may then deduce their interests. The decision-makers in one state may, in turn, influence the interests and behavior of other states, thereby increasing the likelihood of convergent state behavior and international policy co-ordination, informed by the causal beliefs and policy preferences of the epistemic community.[22]

It is plausible that immigration control policy professionals in various countries share a set of normative and causal beliefs. For example, Dr. Peter Wilenski, a close advisor of Australia's Prime Minister Gough Whitlam and his Principal Private Secretary from 1972 to 1974, spent some time in Canada. He was particularly interested in Canada's manpower and immigration control policies, and thought that they might be a useful model for Australia's SSAS system, which was then in the planning stage. Later, Professor Jerzy Zubrzycki, the Chairman of the Social Patterns Committee of the Immigration Advisory Council, studied Canadian selection procedures and took part in discussions concerned with the preparation of Canada's Green Paper on Immigration control policy. His findings influenced the decision to replace the

Australia's SSAS system with the NUMAS points-system.[23] Immigration policy experts also meet and exchange ideas at professional conferences and at multinational forums such as those organized by the International Organization for Migration (IOM), the OECD, and the International Center for Migration Policy Development (ICMPD).

But again, the evidence for the influence of emulation of immigration control policies, and for the impact of an epistemic community, is limited. In addition, it has yet to be proved that the views of professionals determine immigration control policy, *as distinct from fundamental socioeconomic and foreign policy factors that are brought to bear through political channels*. For example, the Australian Population and Immigration Council produced the Green Paper of 1977, which led to major changes in immigration control policy, including an increase in the immigration intake. But in fact, Michael MacKeller, the minister of immigration who reconstituted the Council, had already suggested such an increase in 1976. In 1980, the NUMAS points-system was revised because of adverse public reaction to that system. Thus, in my opinion, professionals do not determine the *basic trends* in immigration control policy. The influence of professionals is greater with regard to technical aspects of immigration control policy, such as skill-based selection systems and mechanisms to prevent illegal immigration.[24]

World System Theory

The world system theory appears to be a good explanation for similarities in immigration control policies.[25] After all, it views all actors within the context of an overarching global structure. Immanuel Wallerstein's world system theory analyzes the emergence of capitalism, and traces its development into a world capitalistic system that contains a core, a periphery, and a semi-periphery. The core historically has engaged in the most advanced economic activities; the periphery has provided raw materials to fuel the core's economic expansion; and the semi-periphery is involved in a mix of production activities, some associated with the core and others with the periphery. The world system theory also emphasizes the importance of long economic cycles. Drawing upon Kondratieff's long cycles, Wallerstein adds a set of secular trends, which include physical expansion, commodification, and mechanization. Major changes in the system occur when these secular trends meet their natural limits and a major cyclical economic downturn occurs.

Based on the work of Wallerstein, various theorists, including Ewa Morawska, Saskia Sassen, Alizabeth McLean Petras, and Alejandro Portes and John Walton, have linked the origins of international migration to the structure of the world market.[26] They argue that the penetration of capitalist economic relations into peripheral, noncapitalistic societies creates a mobile population that is prone to migrate from the periphery to the core in Western Europe, North America, Oceania, and Japan. This basic migratory process is augmented by the existence of ideological and material ties created by prior colonization.[27] According to Sassen, significant levels of direct foreign investment also promote emigration to the core.[28]

There are various difficulties with the world system theory, as well as with the dependency theory on which it built. Critiques of the two theories question the causal relationships between economic and social backwardness and dependency presented by these theories; their excessive reliance on economics; their theoretical rigidity; and their inability to account for Third World countries that have been relatively successful from an economic standpoint.[29] But the major drawback of the world system approach in the context of this essay is its focus on the origins of migration rather than on the causes for immigration control policy. The reason for that is the theory's concentration on the global economic structure and on classes that transcend the confines of the state. Indeed, Brubaker criticizes the world system approach for focusing on political economy, while neglecting specifically social and political structures.[30] And Zolberg rejects Wallerstein's view of the world system as devoid of any overarching political structure, and of states as mere instrumentations of the capitalist dynamic.[31]

Adherents of the world system theory, who do analyze the receiving side, follow the standard Marxist approach. Portes and Walton, following Castells argue that:[32]

> In general, the function of migrant labor has not been—as conventional economics suggests—to increase the supply of labor, but rather to increase the supply of *cheap* labor . . . the role of immigrants has frequently been to counteract the organizational efforts of domestic workers and to substitute the latter in areas where labor costs have become high . . . In general, the weaker the legal standing of immigrant workers, the more employers can make use of political threats, including deportation, to obtain compliance.

But the Marxist analysis of immigration control policy has its own problems, which are mentioned in chapter 1: (a) it fails to explain policy on immigration of dissimilar ethnic origin; (b) the exclusive focus of the Marxist approach on the economic motive lessens its ability to explain refugee policies and other permanent immigration control policies that are influenced by foreign policy considerations and by wars; and

(c) Marxist writers refer to the "state apparatus of capital," and equate capital's and the state's stands on immigration. But they mostly fail to indicate exactly how capital makes the state adopt its preferred policies.

The main contribution of the world system approach, in my opinion, is its highlighting global economic cycles. When we combine these with Castells's Marxist analysis of the link between fluctuations in the economy and immigration control policy (something that the world system approach itself does not do), we arrive at an explanation for similarities in the immigration control policies of various receiving countries. This is demonstrated in the model that follows.

Interdependence Between Socioeconomic and Foreign Policy Factors

I argue that the main reason for the similarities among the immigration control policies of the major receiving countries is the international interdependence between the socioeconomic and foreign policy factors that produce these policies. The state of the economy, the volume of dissimilar immigration, wars, foreign policy considerations, and ideological considerations shape immigration control policies of individual states. Global trends in each of these factors—including the global economic cycle, shared migratory pressures, alliances that produce common considerations of foreign policy, wars that receiving countries are involved in or influenced by, and global ideological cycles—produce the similarities among immigration control policies. Based on the hypotheses presented in chapter 1.

Hypothesis 1 At the state level: recessions cause countries to accept fewer immigrants (i.e. to restrict immigration), while economic prosperity causes them to accept more immigrants (i.e. to liberalize immigration control policy).

At the global level: global economic downturns cause various receiving countries to accept fewer immigrants, while economic prosperity causes them to accept more immigrants.

Hypothesis 2 At the state level: large-scale immigration of dissimilar racial or ethnic composition contributes to restrictions on immigration (in terms of size and composition of immigration).

At the global level: common migratory pressures cause various receiving countries, which share a common racial and ethnic preference system, to restrict immigration.

Hypotheses 3–4 At the state level: wars facilitate the establishment of migrant worker programs and lead to restrictions on permanent dissimilar immigration.

At the global level: wars in which the various receiving countries are involved cause them to establish migrant worker programs and to restrict permanent dissimilar immigration.

Hypothesis 6 At the state level: receiving countries tend to accept immigrants from specific countries in order to advance foreign policy goals, such as improving military and trade relations with allies, demonstrating opposition to adversaries, gaining international respectability, and sustaining political links that evolved in the past.

At the global level: common foreign policy considerations, such as anticommunist and anti-Soviet ideological commitment, cause various receiving countries to accept immigrants from those specific countries.

Hypothesis 7 At the state level: racist attitudes facilitate restrictions on permanent immigration of dissimilar composition, while liberal attitudes promote the liberalization of immigration control policies.

At the global level: international racist trends facilitate restrictions on immigration, while international liberal trends promote the liberalization of immigration in various receiving countries.

Hypothesis 8[33] A neomercantilist economic ideology facilitates restrictive trade and immigration control policies, while an economic liberal approach promotes the liberalization of immigration and trade policies.

Global Economic Cycles

According to hypothesis 1, global economic downturns cause various receiving countries to accept fewer immigrants, while economic prosperity causes them to accept more immigrants. The unemployment rates of various receiving countries have changed simultaneously: most of them were hit by economic recessions between 1873 and 1897 (especially in 1873–1878, 1883–1886, and 1891–1897), in 1907–1908, 1914, 1919–1924 (especially between 1921 and 1923), 1929–1939 (especially between 1929 and 1935), 1966–1968, and after 1972/1973 (with unemployment rates further increasing in the 1980s). These global economic recessions simultaneously contributed to restrictions and/or attempts to impose restrictions on immigration to the United States, Germany, Canada, and the Australian state of Queensland in 1885;

in the United States, Britain, Australia, Canada, and Sweden between 1891 and 1897—in particular between 1894 and 1897; in the United States, Canada, Australia, Sweden, Germany, and France in 1907–1908; in the United States, Australia, Britain, Canada, the Netherlands, Germany, and Switzerland between 1919 and 1924; in the United States, Canada, Germany, France, Switzerland, and Australia between 1929 and 1935; in Sweden, Germany, France, and Britain during the 1966–1968 recession; and in most Western European countries in 1972–1974, during the 1980s and in the first half of the 1990s. In contrast, most of the receiving countries recruited foreign labor, expanded permanent migration, or at least avoided restrictions during global economic upswings between 1898 and 1902, between 1925 and 1928 and between World War II and 1973 (with the exception of 1966–1968). And the growing demand for workers in high-tech industries caused many countries to encourage the immigration of such workers during the 1990s and early 2000s. Policymakers in various receiving countries explicitly linked the state of the economy to immigration control policies: they emphasized the deteriorating economy as the cause for restrictions on immigration; they passed laws that linked the number of migrant workers, and sometimes also that of permanent immigrants, to the state of the economy; and they prohibited the entry of immigrants who might become "a public charge."

Shared Migratory Pressures

Migratory pressures are the second global trend causing the immigration control policies of the major receiving countries to resemble one another. The majority of the population in most of the receiving countries dealt with in this study is Caucasian and Christian; in about half of them, it is predominantly Protestant. Culture-based theories see racism as a spontaneous response to what is strange and unfamiliar.[34] Thus, Western European immigrants were favored over immigrants from Africa, Asia, and Eastern Europe. Politicians in various receiving countries explicitly said so. In the United States, Senator Henry Cabot Lodge asserted that the literacy test would bear "most heavily on Italians, Russians, Poles, Hungarians, Greeks, and Asians, only lightly on the English-speaking peoples, Germans, Scandinavians, and French." In Britain, members of parliament and memoranda portrayed the "displaced persons" (European refugees) in racist terms. Miles and Kay describe how "DPs became internally differentiated along a North-South divide. The most favorable judgements were reserved for the Balts from the 'North' . . . By contrast, DPs from south-east Europe were often referred to as 'simple peasant types,' unversed in the ways of a complex industrial culture and more 'racially distinct,' forming part of an ill-defined but inferior 'Slav race.' Consequently, there was a racialised bias towards the recruitment of Balts."[35]

Because of this racial and ethnic preference system, migratory pressures from Asia, Africa, and Eastern Europe produced coincidental restrictions on immigration. A surge in Chinese migration during the 1850s–1880s led to restrictions on such immigration to the United States (1875 and 1882), Australia (1877, 1880–1881, 1885, and 1888), New Zealand and Canada (1885). An increase in Japanese immigration was followed by restrictions on such immigration to the United States, Canada, and Australia (1905–1908). Russian Jews fleeing pogroms encountered opposition and restrictions in Britain (1894, 1898, and 1905), in the United States (1892–1898, 1912–1917, 1921, and 1924), in France, and probably in Sweden (1907–1918). Jews escaping Nazi Germany during the 1930s met opposition and sometimes restrictions in the United States, Britain, France, Sweden, and the Netherlands. In mid-1970s and 1980s, there appeared massive new flows of refugees in both Asia and Africa, attributable to conflicts that engulfed entire regions and to the explosion of long-standing ethnic confrontations.[36] An influx of Asian immigrants (from India, Pakistan, Bangladesh, Sri Lanka, and Turkey) during the 1980s produced restrictions on such immigration in Britain (1985–1986), Germany (1980, 1985), and Switzerland (1984). And the rise in applications for asylum from the

Table 6.1 Countries of origin of asylum seekers per selected European destination country in 1999

Receiving country	*First country of origin*	*Percentage*	*Second country of origin*	*Percentage*
Austria	Yugoslavia, FR	34	Iran	17
Belgium	Yugoslavia, FR	13	Romania	5
Denmark	Iraq	28	Slovakia	15
Finland	Slovakia	49	Poland	10
France	China	17	Yugoslavia, FR	8
Germany	Yugoslavia, FR	33	Turkey	10
Netherlands	Afghanistan	11	Iraq	9
Spain	Algeria	16	Romania	12
Sweden	Iraq	32	Yugoslavia, FR	16
Switzerland	Yugoslavia, FR	64	Iraq	4
UK	Yugoslavia, FR	20	Somalia	11

Source: UNHCR statistics 2000, provisional figures, in Muus (2001:36).

Third World and the former communist countries fostered restrictions on asylum seekers in all of the receiving countries. For example, as table 6.1 demonstrates, in 1999, Yugoslavia was the first or second country of origin for asylum seekers (in percentages) for Austria, Belgium, France, Germany, Sweden, Switzerland, and the United Kingdom. Iraq, too, was the first or second country of origin for asylum seekers (in percentages) for Denmark, the Netherlands, Sweden, and Switzerland.

Common migratory pressures associated with external threats, especially with imported radicalism, also produced similar immigration control policies. For example, fears of French radicals led to the enactment of the Alien and Sedition Act and two naturalization acts in the United States during the 1790s, the 1792/93 Aliens Act in Britain, the 1798 and 1799 Laws on the Rights of Citizenship and Freedom of Establishment in Switzerland, and the 1794 Nova Scotia Act in Canada. Fears of German radicals produced the 1848 Aliens Removal Act in Britain and contributed to the xenophobia of the 1850s in the United States.

Wars

The third international phenomenon producing similarities among immigration control policies of major receiving countries is their joint participation in wars. On the one hand, wartime labor shortages lead the receiving countries to recruit foreign workers. During World War I, the United States, France, and Germany expanded the use of foreign labor (voluntary in the United States and France, forced in Germany). During World War II, the United States, Britain, and France established or expanded the recruitment of foreign labor, the United States also employed German prisoners of war, and Nazi Germany exploited forced labor.

On the other hand, wars produce social conformity and an association of immigrants with foreign threats, which generate restrictions on permanent immigration. World War I led to restrictions on immigration and/or to the introduction of passport and visa requirements in the United States (1917, 1918), Britain (1914), France (1917), Sweden (1914, 1917, 1918), Switzerland (1916, 1917), Germany (1914), and the Netherlands (1918). Many of these acts shared similar elements, such as granting the executive the authority to control immigration and deport aliens.[37] Some wartime restrictions also had a long-lasting impact on immigration control policy because they were converted into ordinary laws after the war, usually during recessions.[38]

The mistrust of foreigners also led to restrictions on former immigrants from enemy countries. During World War I, many American localities prohibited the sale of German-language newspapers and the teaching of German, Britain interned German residents, Australia interned German and Austrian residents, and German place names were changed by law in Southern Australia. During World War II, the United States excluded persons of Japanese origin from the West Coast and detained them in relocation centers, Australia interned enemy aliens, Britain interned Jewish refugees from Europe, and French decrees restricted the liberties of aliens.

Alliances and Common Foreign Policy Considerations

The fourth cause for similarities among the immigration control policies of major receiving countries are alliances that produce common foreign policy considerations. During the Cold War, many Western democracies favored refugees from communist countries in order to demonstrate their anticommunist and anti-Soviet ideological commitment. The United States welcomed large numbers of refugees from communist regimes in Eastern Europe, the Soviet Union, Cuba, China, and Southeast Asia. Britain accepted Poles, Hungarians, and Vietnamese. Australia admitted Eastern European and Vietnamese refugees. Canada accepted Hungarians, Czechoslovakians, and Indochinese (Vietnamese, Laotians, and Cambodians). The Netherlands and even Switzerland welcomed Hungarian and Czech refugees. The acceptance of refugees from communist countries in Eastern Europe and later from South East Asia fostered the breakdown of the quota system in the United States and Australia. Eventually, the collapse of communism in Eastern Europe led the receiving countries to reject asylum seekers from former (and even current) communist countries. For instance, Sweden announced it would refuse to accept asylum seekers from East Germany, Poland and Bulgaria in 1990; and the United States limited Cuban immigration in 1994.

The British Commonwealth also facilitated, to some degree, the similarities among refugee policies. In 1972, when President Idi Amin of Uganda announced that all Asians holding British citizenship must leave the country, both Britain and Canada accepted a large number of Ugandan Asian refugees for permanent settlement. However, Australia declined official requests from Britain, and admitted only several hundred refugees.

But while foreign policy considerations that are shared by various countries contribute to similarities among their immigration control policies, particular foreign policy considerations cause these policies to diverge.

This phenomenon, further explored in the last part of this chapter, especially characterized colonial and ex-colonial powers, which accepted dissimilar immigrants from their colonies and former colonies in order to maintain their international standing and their political and cultural ties with the countries of origin. Decolonization and the decreased importance of links with former colonies have weakened this tendency.

Ideological Cycles

Finally, ideological cycles of two types may contribute to the similarity among the immigration control policies of major receiving countries: the cycle between racism and liberalism, and the cycle between economic openness and protectionism. However, the extent to which these ideological cycles have an independent influence over immigration control policies, one distinct from that of the economic cycle, migratory pressures, and foreign policy considerations, remains an open question.

The first ideological cycle is between racism and liberalism, that is between opposing attitudes with regard to equality and minority rights. Racist theories and terminology were prevalent in various receiving countries during the first decades of this century, and facilitated the passage of restrictions on dissimilar immigration, based on ethnic selection criteria. The war against the Fascist powers, the impact of the Holocaust, and the civil rights movements of the 1960s–1970s delegitimized the use of overt racist terminology and policies, and helped abolish ethnic-based quotas. Racist attitudes revived, to some extent, in Europe during the 1980s. However, this recent surge in racism has primarily been the product of an increase in dissimilar immigration and of the growing permanency of former migrant workers.

Prior to World War II, racism and theories of "social Darwinism" thrived not only in Germany, but also in other receiving countries to varying degrees. In the United States, for example, The Ku Klux Klan reached its peak in the first half of the 1920s. Madison Grant's racist book *The Passing of the Great Race*, was published in 1916, and Jack London wrote about Southern and Eastern Europeans swamping the blond, master race in America.[39] The "Nordic theory" and "Scientific racism" gained ground during the 1920s, with books such as Charles W. Gould's *America, A Family Matter*, Clinton Stoddard Burr's *America's Race Heritage*; and Ellsworth Huntington's *The Character of Races*.[40] These racist theories and literature legitimized restrictions on immigration from Asia and Eastern and Southern Europe, especially in the United States, Australia, and Canada.

The war against the Fascist powers and the impact of the Holocaust delegitimized the use of overt racist terminology and policies, and helped abolish the ethnic quotas in the United States, Australia, Canada, and New Zealand. By the early 1950s, most American Congressional proponents of the national origins system avoided explicitly racist arguments, while Senator Lehman, an opponent of the system, argued that it is "strikingly similar to the basic racial philosophy officially espoused so unfortunately and with such tragic consequences in Nazi Germany a few short years ago."[41] Tobin describes a similar change in Australian terminology and immigration control policies. As a result, between 1943 and 1974, the United States, Australia, Canada, and New Zealand gradually phased out their racial and ethnic selection criteria for immigration.[42] In the 1940s and 1950s, they abolished the more blatantly racist laws, while leaving numerical quotas and administrative means that still had the same effect. In the United States this process included the repeal of the Chinese Exclusion Act in 1943, the admission of Filipinos and Indians in 1946 and of citizens of Siam in 1948, and the acceptance of large number of Eastern European refugees. The 1952 McCarran-Walter Act eliminated the formal racial basis for restrictions, while informally retaining them in the form of a quota. Australia, too, accepted large numbers of Eastern European refugees and Southern European immigrants, and relaxed the citizenship laws for non-Europeans. Canada abolished its Chinese Exclusion Act in 1947, and removed most country of origin and racial restrictions in 1962. By the early 1970s, the four countries eliminated most of the remaining discriminatory measures. The United States passed the Immigration and Naturalization Act of 1965, which abolished the national origins quota system. The same year, the major Australian parties removed the "white Australia policy" from their platforms, and in 1972 a comprehensive reform annulled the racial and nationality criteria for immigration to Australia. Canada revised its immigration regulations in 1967, applying the same standards to prospective immigrants from all areas of the world.[43] The final stage in the process was facilitated by the 1960s civil rights movement in the United States, which strengthened the concepts of equality and minority rights, and influenced other countries. In the United States, President Kennedy authored the book *A Nation of Immigrants*, which stood in sharp contrast to the racist literature of half a century earlier. As Reimers notes, "Bigotry and even vague defences of national origins quotas for immigration, so easily enacted by lopsided majorities in 1952, were simply not publicly acceptable in the mid-1960s."[44] Australian Aboriginals were enfranchised in 1962, and in

1973 Prime Minster Gough Whitlam stated that: "Just as we have embarked on a determined campaign to restore the Australian aborigines to their rightful place in Australian society, so we have an obligation to remove methodically from Australia's laws and practices all racially discriminatory provisions, and from international activities any hint or suggestion that we favor policies, decrees or resolutions that seek to differentiate between peoples on the basis of their skin."[45]

World War II also delegitimized the use of overt racist terminology and policies in Europe, as the opponents of discriminatory immigration control policies equated them with Nazi racist philosophy. For example, in Britain, when Powell and several other Conservative candidates presented anti-immigration stands prior to the 1970 elections, these stands were denounced by a Labor minister as being similar to race policies pursued by the Nazis in Germany.[46] In Germany, during a parliamentary debate on asylum seekers, Herta Daubler-Gmelin from the SPD referred to Kohl as a "*schreibtischtater*," a word normally used to describe bureaucrats in the Nazi Government who administered mass murder from behind their desks.[47]

However, it is difficult to determine whether the cycle between racism and liberalism has an independent influence over immigration control policies, or whether it is a mere reflection of the other socioeconomic factors. First, the ideological cycle might reflect or be the outcome of the economic cycle. Racism tends to spread during hard times, when people look for a scapegoat for their economic troubles; it tends to contract during prosperity, such as the 1960s. Second, the ideological cycle between racism and liberalism might be the product of changing migratory pressures. An upswing in racism is sometimes the product of an increase in dissimilar immigration, as was the case in Europe during the 1980s, and possibly in the United States during the 1910s and 1920s. The increase in dissimilar immigration also explains the aforementioned British discriminatory immigration control policies. Third, ideological trends might reflect changes in foreign policy considerations. In particular, the emergence of East Asian economic and military powers, and the decolonization process that produced a large Afro-Asian bloc in the United Nations, have facilitated the abolition of race-based restrictions since World War II. Finally, the ideological cycle might only influence the form but not the substance of immigration control policy. Policymakers who come under domestic pressures to restrict immigration of dissimilar origin find ways to do so without using overt racist terminology. In Britain, growing domestic opposition to immigration and the decline of the Empire (which weakened the influence of foreign policy considerations) led the government to adopt the concept of "patriality" in order to give preference to Old Commonwealth white immigrants over New Commonwealth colored immigrants, thereby avoiding the overt use of a race-based quota.

The second ideological cycle that might influence immigration control policies is the one between economic openness (i.e. the economic liberal approach) and protectionism (i.e. neomercantilism). There is an ideological affinity between advocating the free movement of goods and that of people. Moreover, at first glance it seems that the two types of policies have coincided: (a) in the mid-nineteenth century, Western Europe moved toward free trade, and immigration was practically unrestricted; (b) between 1880 and 1914, there was a partial return to protectionism in trade, and the rate of growth of international commerce slowed somewhat between 1873 and 1896; it accelerated again in the two decades before World War I. During the same period, many receiving countries restricted the immigration of specific groups, but most immigration remained unchecked and even expanded; (c) in the interwar period, countries severely restricted both imports and immigration; (d) between 1945 and the early 1970s, the Dillon and Kennedy GATT rounds and the Bretton Woods monetary system helped expand international trade. During the same period, the receiving countries implemented large-scale migrant labor recruitment programs, increased permanent immigration, and eliminated racial barriers to immigration; (e) since the early 1970s, Western countries have used non-tariff-barriers (NTBs) and voluntary export restrictions (VERs) to limit imports, while removing barriers to trade within regions (the EC, NAFTA, etc.). The same countries have also ended migrant labor programs, attempted to halt illegal immigration and to reduce the number of immigrants granted asylum, and, at the same time, eliminated barriers to the free movement of people within the EC.

But there are four difficulties with this proposed association of trade and immigration control policies. First, trade and immigration are to some degree substitutes, that is, an increase in trade between labor-intensive and capital-intensive countries decreases the need for labor migration from the former to the latter.[48] Thus, liberal trade policies may eliminate the need for liberal policies on migrant workers. Second, labor is a factor of production, and thus a neomercantilist ideology might support immigration. Third, the empirical link between the two policies is only partial and sometimes misleading. For example, in 1860s–1870s, when Western European countries moved toward free trade, some of them were mainly countries of emigration rather than immigration. The major country of immigration—the United States—accepted immigrants but restricted imports.[49] In 1905, Britain—the champion of free trade—restricted immigration. In the 1980s and 1990s, GATT, GATS, and other international agreements have removed barriers to international trade, but most types of interregional immigration have been restricted. The partial divergence between trade and immigration control policies is evident in the American case (see table 6.2).

Table 6.2 A comparison of U.S. trade and immigration control policies

Years	*Trade policy*	*Immigration control policy*
1816–1832	Restrictive: tariff acts of 1816, 1828, and 1832	Liberal
1833–1860	Liberal: tariff reductions in 1833, 1846 (Walker Act), and 1857 (General Tariff Act)	Liberal
1861–1881	Restrictive: tariff act of 1861 (Morill Act) and "temporary" wartime tariffs that continued after the Civil War	Liberal: 1864 Contract Labor Act, recruitment in Europe, minor restrictions start in 1875
1882–1893	Restrictive: 1883 General Tariff Act	Restrictions on Chinese (1882) and contract labor (1885), but no restrictions on Eastern and Southern European immigration
1894–1896	Liberal: a moderately liberalizing tariff act under President Cleveland	Failed attempts to restrict Eastern and Southern European immigration by means of a literacy test
1897–1912	Restrictive: 1897 Dingley Tariff Act, 1909 Payne-Aldrich Tariff Act	Failed attempts to restrict Eastern and Southern European immigration; restrictions on Japanese immigration; however, peak immigration
1913–1920	Liberal: 1913 Underwood Tariff Act	Restrictive: 1917 and 1918 immigration acts, including a literacy test
1920s–1930s	Very restrictive: 1921 Fordney-McCumber and 1930 Smoot-Hawley Tariff Acts	Very restrictive: 1921 and 1924 Quota Acts; restrictions on Mexican and Filipino immigration
1945–1960s	Liberalization	Liberalization
1970s–1990s	Trade conflicts, especially with Japan; VERs and NTBs; on the other hand—NAFTA and GATT liberalize trade	Restrictions on illegal immigration and asylum seekers; 1990 Act expands legal immigration; no free movement of people in NAFTA and no global migration regime

The fourth difficulty with the ideological cycle argument is that it might reflect the economic cycle. That is, prosperity facilitates liberal trade and immigration control policies, and recessions produce restrictive trade and immigration control policies, thus generating a spurious congruence between the two types of policies.[50] According to this interpretation, a prosperous global economy led to liberal immigration and trade policies during the mid-nineteenth century; a global recession led to restrictions on immigration and trade between the world wars; a revived economy produced liberalization of both types of policies between World War II and the early 1970s; and the 1973 recession generated restrictions on immigration and the use of NTBs in trade.

Explanations for the Differences in Immigration Policies

I demonstrated how global trends in the socioeconomic and foreign policy spheres produce the similarities among immigration policies of various countries at any given period, and most of the variation in immigration policy over time. In contrast, the structural factors of each country and its preference for permanent immigration or temporary labor migration, both of which are relatively stable, produce the differences between immigration policies at any given time.

Three domestic structural factors produce the differences between immigration policies of various receiving countries. The first is the economic structure. Most countries experience similar economic trends, in what is known as the global economic cycle (or global business cycle). But the variation in economic structures and economic policies between various countries causes their economic performance to diverge, and consequently, their immigration policies as well. For example, after World War I, most European countries experienced economic hardship, and consequently they halted labor migration. But France diverged from that global economic cycle, experiencing economic growth for another decade, which led it to expand its recruitment of foreign labor. After World War II, Britain and Sweden had low unemployment rates, and thus they preceded other European countries in recruiting migrant workers.[51]

The second structural factor producing differences in immigration policies is the geopolitical position of each country. For example, Australia concluded after World War II that its geographical isolation and small population made it especially vulnerable to an Asian invasion. As a result, it shifted toward a drastic pro-immigration policy, accepting more immigrants per capita than almost any other country. Neutral

Sweden took in refugees from Chile, Turkey, Lebanon, Iran, and Ethiopia in addition to those from the Baltic republics, Hungary, and Poland.[52] Changes in the international standing of various countries also produce differences between their immigration policies. The U.S. rise to global hegemony caused it to accept a substantial number of refugees from communist regimes. In contrast, I argue that the declining aspirations of Britain and France caused them to accept fewer colonial immigrants. Until the 1960s, Britain and France still clung to their status as world powers. Thus, they took part in the Suez operation, the Algerian War, and the war in Indo-China (in the latter two only France). In the late 1940s, they also declared that nationals of their overseas territories (in the case of France) and Commonwealth (in the case of Britain) had the status of citizens and thus were eligible to freely emigrate to the mother country. Later, as it became clear that Britain and France were no longer world powers, domestic pressures overcame foreign policy considerations. Thus, Britain restricted New Commonwealth immigration in 1962, although it still admitted a small number of Indian refugees from Uganda in 1968 and Greek Cypriots in 1974.[53] Similarly, France regulated Algerian emigration.

The third set of structural factors producing differences in immigration policies is the population density and foreign policy considerations of each country, which shape its preference for permanent immigration or temporary labor migration, and consequently the degree to which various socioeconomic factors influence its immigration policy.

I demonstrated in chapters 2–5 that policies on different types of immigrants are influenced by the socioeconomic and foreign policy factors to various degrees. In particular, I argued that temporary labor migration policy is influenced mostly by the economic factor and by the "war–migrant labor link," but only to a limited degree by the other factors. In contrast, permanent immigration policy is influenced by the various socioeconomic and foreign policy factors, but the impact of the economic factor is not as pronounced as with labor migration policy. The countries of continental European favored temporary labor migration over permanent immigration (at least until 1972–1974), while Britain, Australia, Canada, and the United States preferred permanent immigration.[54] Consequently, the two groups of countries were influenced by the socioeconomic factors to varying degrees. In 1905 and 1962–1965, the global economy was doing relatively well, which caused the countries of continental European to recruit migrant workers. In contrast, large-scale permanent migration of dissimilar origin in the early 1900s (Russian Jews) and during the late 1950s and early 1960s

(New Commonwealth) led Britain to restrict immigration. During the economic recession of the 1980s, Western European countries restricted labor migration. In contrast, permanent immigration countries, including Australia, Canada, and the United States, restricted illegal immigration and attempted to reduce applications for asylum, but sometimes increased permanent immigration quotas.

Why then do some receiving countries favor permanent immigration, while others prefer temporary labor migration? The "national identity" approach partially answers this question. This approach explains variations in immigration and citizenship policies between countries of destination on the basis of their different conceptions of national identity or different characteristics (see chapter 1). Three such distinctions, which partially overlap, are (a) between settler societies, which accept large-scale permanent immigration, and ethnic states, which tend to reject such immigration; (b) between homogeneous and heterogeneous countries; and (c) between countries whose citizenship laws tend toward *jus sanguinis* and those countries whose citizenship laws tend toward *jus soli*.[55] For example, heterogeneous (multiracial and multiethnic) societies are more likely to accept dissimilar immigrants than homogeneous societies—a good example of the latter being Japan, which strictly restricts immigration.[56]

In contrast, I argue that all countries favor permanent immigration that is ethnically and culturally similar to their own population over permanent dissimilar immigration, although this preference has become less overt since World War II. For instance, the United States and Australia favored Western European immigrants at least until the mid-1960s. The heterogeneity of the society by itself does not necessarily mean that the majority group will support dissimilar permanent immigration. On the contrary, the existence of a substantial black population in the United States and Britain, especially when it lacked political power, contributed to restrictions on black immigration. And the aforementioned distinctions do not explain what made countries multiracial or multiethnic in the first place. They do, however, help to explain why some countries accepted dissimilar permanent immigration, while others (e.g. Japan) admitted only or mainly dissimilar temporary migrant workers.

A simpler answer lies, I believe, in the *interests* of the receiving countries, especially in the need for more people in sparsely populated countries versus the rejection of permanent immigration by densely populated countries, and in the influence of specific foreign policy interests. These factors are also among the reasons why countries became multiracial or multiethnic in the first place. Countries with large reservoirs of fertile land facilitated permanent immigration in order to settle these lands and defend their long borders. These countries also preferred permanent similar immigration, but during periods of economic prosperity and acute need for manpower they tended to settle for permanent immigration of dissimilar composition. Later, as these countries industrialized, and only a small fraction of the population remained in agriculture, the aforementioned considerations became less important. But the sparsely settled land, and the influence of immigrant pressure groups (created during the previous period), helped sustain the support for permanent immigration. In contrast, densely populated countries—faced with overburdened infrastructure—have preferred temporary migrant workers, mostly young males, who are expected to return to their countries of origin at the end of their contracts. Thus, the preference for permanent dissimilar immigration over temporary dissimilar labor migration correlates with low ratios of population-to-land. The United States, Canada, Argentina, and Australia, all of which are huge countries with a relatively low ratio of population-to-land, have encouraged large-scale permanent immigration. According to LeMay, "The population density [in the U.S.] in 1790 was only 4.5 persons per square mile. There was an obvious need for labor to build the cities, clear the farms on the frontier . . . Additional population was desired to strengthen the country's defenses against Indians and to avoid coming under control of the European colonial powers."[57] The demand for immigrants was especially intense in the lightly populated Western and Southern United States after the Civil War, when virtually every state appointed agents or boards of immigration and sought to lure new settlers from overseas.[58] Similarly, Australia encouraged permanent immigration after it found in World War II "how difficult it would be to defend a vast continent with a population base of only 7.5 million."[59] The opening paragraph of the 1977 Green Paper of the Australian Population and Immigration Council states, "Australians, in good times and bad, have held to the belief that Australia is a land of great promise and potential. Traditionally, they have believed that such a vast area of the world's surface . . . must continue to prosper and its population expand." According to the National Population Inquiry Report of 1975, Queensland and Western Australia, both of which had impressive resources and small populations, emphasized the need for more people, while support for slowing growth was strongest in New South Wales and Victoria, the two most populous states.[60]

Western Europe countries, on the other hand, encouraged temporary (dissimilar) labor migration, with the stated assumption that these workers would return to their countries of origin. The Netherlands had a particular obsession with population density, and thus classified immigrants (migrant workers and even migration of families from certain colonies) as temporary residents who "one day" would return home.[61] Japan, another densely populated country, has adhered to a restrictive permanent immigration policy. At the same time, it has recruited temporary migrant workers (sometimes in the guise of trainees), mainly from Asian countries, and workers of Japanese descent from Latin America.

Table 6.3 demonstrates the positive correlation between the population-to-land ratio on the one hand, and the preference for temporary *dissimilar* immigration over permanent one on the other hand. Crowded countries, such as Germany, Israel, and France, have also accepted permanent immigration of *similar* composition despite their high ratio of population-to-land.[62] Exceptions to this correlation between the population-to-land ratio and the immigration preference were caused by foreign policy considerations, which are dealt with later.

The second factor influencing the choice between permanent immigration and temporary dissimilar labor migration is foreign policy considerations. Colonial and ex-colonial powers have accepted permanent dissimilar immigrants from their colonies and former colonies in

Table 6.3 The choice between temporary and permanent dissimilar immigration according to population-to-land ratios*

	Preference for temporary dissimilar labor migration over permanent one	*Preference for permanent dissimilar immigration over temporary one*
High ratio of population to land	Japan (326.1) Germany (245.4) France (102.4) Switzerland (161.2) The Netherlands 1964–1973 (356.4) Luxembourg (140.9) Israel (210.1)	Exceptions: Britain (mainly 1954–1962) (232.9)[63] The Netherlands between 1946–1963 (356.4)[64]
Low ratio of population to land	U.S. 1953–1961[65]	U.S. (26.5) Canada (2.6) Australia (2.1) Argentina (11.5)

* The population-to-land ratios in brackets are in terms of population/square kilometer, and are based on 1989 data. Between 1973 and the late 1980s Western European states rejected both permanent and temporary immigration. During that period, they mostly accepted family members of former migrant workers and some asylum seekers.

order to maintain their international standing and their political and cultural ties with the countries of origin.[66] For example, Britain accepted New Commonwealth permanent immigration; France admitted immigration from its African and Caribbean colonies and protectorates; the Netherlands accepted permanent immigrants from the former Netherlands East Indies, Surinam, and the Dutch Antilles; and the United States and France have been relatively open to Vietnamese immigrants because of their past involvement in Vietnam.[67] Consequently, as long as these powers admitted substantial permanent dissimilar immigration (despite their high population density), they could recruit fewer migrant workers. Countries that lost their colonies at an earlier stage, such as Germany and Japan, or that did not have colonies in the first place, such as Switzerland and Luxembourg, opted for temporary labor migration in order to fulfill their manpower needs.

CHAPTER 7

Summary and Conclusions

Immigration has a tremendous impact on the demography, culture, economy, and politics of a state. It is the key demographic factor responsible for population growth in most Western societies, and the cause of cultural conflicts and of a transformation from relatively homogenous to multicultural societies. Immigration has also contributed to the rise of extreme-right anti-immigrant parties in most EU member states and to attempts to achieve a common EU migration and asylum policy. Both U.S. and European policymakers have defined immigration as one of the biggest domestic challenges and political issues facing their nations.

Immigration policy is the crucial element determining immigration patterns. Given the large number of people who would like to emigrate to the industrialized countries for economic or political reasons, and the strictly limited opportunities to do so, it is immigration control policy that mainly determines the scope of global migration (including, it could be argued, illegal migration).[1] Therefore, I explored the factors influencing immigration control policy. I first reviewed the main approaches to racism and immigration control policy: theories that focus on the economic competition between the native born and the immigrants; theories that highlight the cultural discord between the two groups; and studies that deal with the impact of international relations and multilateral agreements on immigration control policy. Each of these contributes to our understanding of immigration policy, and each of them suffers from various weaknesses. But the greatest weakness of most of the literature on immigration control policy is that it rarely relates to any theoretical approach. Numerous studies explore the immigration policies of individual receiving countries. But these studies are (a) empirically oriented and lack a general theory, and (b) they mostly examine the policy of a single country during a limited period or, in a few cases, are volumes in which each country is analyzed independently.

This book offered a theory of the socioeconomic and foreign policy factors shaping immigration control policy. The theory explained how governments decide on the number of immigrants they will accept; whether to differentiate between various ethnic groups; whether to accept refugees and on what basis; and whether to favor permanent immigration over migrant workers. It combined certain elements from all three approaches to immigration control policy, while rejecting others (i.e. the influence of social conflicts and industrial unrest). But most importantly, it attempted to present a set of socioeconomic and foreign policy factors that determine immigration control policy, and to demonstrate the relative importance of each factor under various circumstances. The main arguments of the study are:

First, immigration control policy is determined by an interaction between: (a) *socioeconomic and foreign policy factors*—the volume and composition of immigration, the state of the economy, wars and external threats, considerations of foreign policy, and general racist/liberal attitudes; and (b) *the type of immigration*—temporary labor migration, permanent dissimilar immigration, permanent similar immigration, and refugees.[2]

Second, immigration control policies of various countries are determined by the same set of socioeconomic and political factors. The study rejected the notion that the immigration control policy of each country is unique, mostly shaped by its history, its conceptions of citizenship and nationality, and by debates over national identity and social conflicts within it. Changes in immigration control policy over time, and some of the differences between immigration policies of various countries, are explained by variations in the aforementioned set of socioeconomic and political factors: changes in the state of the economy, the volume of dissimilar immigration, considerations of foreign policy, and so on. Countries do differ with regard to certain structural factors, including their population density, geopolitical position, and economic structure. And these structural factors influence the socioeconomic and foreign policy factors, and the type of immigration each country accepts. But their influence, too, conforms to predictable causal mechanisms.

Third, and following the previous point, the study emphasized the extraordinary similarity that has existed among the immigration control policies of the major Western receiving countries for over a century.

After rejecting alternative explanations, it argued that these similarities are mostly explained by the interdependence between the socioeconomic and foreign policy factors that lead to immigration control policies.

Fourth, the type of immigration—temporary labor migration, permanent dissimilar immigration, permanent similar immigration, refugees, and illegal immigration—determines the relative influence of the various socioeconomic and foreign policy factors on immigration control policy (see hypotheses 8–11 later).

Fifth, the type of the receiving society—settler societies versus ethnic states—mainly influences immigration control policy in an indirect fashion, through the type of immigration.

The fourth and fifth arguments offer a partially different interpretation of immigration control policy than does much of the literature. The literature tends to differentiate between the processes leading to immigration control policy in settler societies from those in ethnic/European states. In contrast, I argue that it is the type of immigration accepted by the country that mostly determines the influence of the socioeconomic factors on immigration control policy. Thus, the socioeconomic factors leading to labor migration policy in settler societies *resemble* those leading to labor migration policy in ethnic states. The socioeconomic factors leading to labor migration policy in any society *differ* from those leading to permanent immigration policy in the same society.

The type of receiving society does indirectly influence immigration control policy because settler societies have favored permanent migration, while the European/ethnic societies have opted for labor migration. The reasons for these preferences were, in my opinion, the structural differences between the two types of countries: the sparsely populated United States, Canada, and Australia required permanent immigrants for economic and security reasons, while the densely populated European states, when faced with a shortage of labor, preferred temporary labor migration. Geopolitical positions have also influenced the preference for certain types of immigrants: countries with colonies and/or leadership aspirations—such as the United States, Britain, and France—gave preference to permanent immigration from certain countries of origin.

The Socioeconomic and Foreign Policy Factors Shaping Immigration Policy

Immigration policies of various countries are determined by the following set of socioeconomic factors (the rationale for each of these hypotheses is detailed in chapter 1):

Hypothesis 1 Recessions cause countries to accept fewer immigrants (i.e. to restrict immigration), while economic prosperity causes them to accept more immigrants (i.e. to liberalize immigration control policy).

The four countries examined here, and particularly those that favored labor migration over the permanent kind, restricted immigration during recessions and encouraged it during prosperity. The Netherlands and Germany, which went through similar economic cycles, adopted similar immigration control policies in regard to migrant workers. Both countries restricted the recruitment of migrant workers during the great depression. Both recruited migrant workers during the 1960s and early 1970s as Western Europe was going through the post–World War II economic boom. Both were motivated to assume greater control on labor migration during the 1967–1968 mild recession, but did not implement these plans and allowed for peak recruitment of foreign workers, as the economy revived. Both countries restricted labor migration and attempted to encourage return migration following the 1973 oil crisis. And both increased the recruitment of migrant workers during the 1990s.

Similarly, the United States restricted migration during recessions: between 1882–1885, 1891–1897, 1907–1908, in 1921, 1924, and during the great depression. It encouraged migration when the economy revived and unemployment decreased: following the Civil War, between 1898 and 1906 and after World War II. The state of the economy has had less of an influence on U.S. policies since World War II, as the impact of foreign policy considerations, liberal ideology, and pressures from ethnic groups increased. But attempts were made to restrict immigration when the local economy became sluggish—for instance in California during the early 1990s.

In Britain, which mostly admitted permanent immigration, the link between the state of the economy and immigration control policy was the weakest. But a labor shortage rates did facilitate the liberal immigration policy toward New Commonwealth immigrants during the 1950s. And higher rates of unemployment may have contributed to the passage of several restrictions, including the 1905 Aliens Immigration Act and those of the 1980s and the early 1990s. Several studies (e.g. Foot and Money) also link the state of the economy with opposition to immigration at the local level.[3] The state of the economy at the national level has had greater influence on British labor migration policy: labor shortages caused Britain to establish the European Volunteer Workers program in 1947. A declining economy led Britain to issue fewer work permits to non-EU workers during the 1970s and 1980s. And labor shortages have produced foreign worker schemes—particularly in the farming, nursing, and high-tech sectors—since 1996.

Hypothesis 2 Large-scale immigration of dissimilar racial/ethnic/ cultural composition contributes to restrictions on immigration (in terms of size and composition of immigration).

All four countries favored immigration of similar composition over that of dissimilar composition, and restricted large-scale permanent immigration of dissimilar composition (including asylum seekers). Russian Jews fleeing pogroms encountered opposition and restrictions during the turn of the previous century. The Netherlands and the United States also discouraged the immigration of German Jews after 1933. During the 1980s, an influx of Asian immigrants (from India, Pakistan, Bangladesh, Sri Lanka, and Turkey/Iraq) led to restrictions in the three European countries. And the United States (as well as Canada, Australia, and New Zealand) placed restrictions on Chinese immigration during the 1870s and 1880s, Japanese immigration between 1905–1908, and Southern and Eastern European immigration during the 1920s.

Hypothesis 3–5 Wars have a dual impact on immigration policy. On the one hand, they facilitate the establishment of migrant worker programs, in what was termed here the "war–migrant labor link." On the other hand, wars, external threats, and domestic threats linked to external sources cause the receiving societies to associate dissimilar immigrants with external threats, to restrict immigration of dissimilar composition, and sometimes to encourage permanent immigration of similar composition.

As noted in chapter 6, the United States and Germany (as well as France) expanded the use of foreign labor (voluntary in the United States and France, forced in Germany) during World War I. During World War II, the United States and Britain established or expanded the recruitment of foreign labor, the United States employed German prisoners of war, and Nazi Germany exploited forced labor. The United States also encouraged labor migration through the Contract Labor Act of 1864 during the Civil War, and expanded the Bracero program during the Korean War.

On the other hand, World War I led to restrictions on immigration and/or to the introduction of passport and visa requirements in the

United States (1917, 1918), Britain (1914), Germany (1914) and the Netherlands (1918), as well as in other countries. The countries of destination also confined former immigrants from enemy countries, or discriminated against them, during both world wars. The United States, for example evacuated Americans of Japanese ancestry from the West Coast, and detained them in relocation centers during World War II. The association of immigrants with external threats, and particularly with imported radicalism, also produced restrictions, although these restrictions were relatively minor. Fears of French radicals led to the enactment of the alien and sedition acts in the United States and in Britain during the 1790s. Fears of German radicals produced the 1848 Aliens Removal Act in Britain and contributed to the xenophobia of the 1850s in the United States. Iraqis and Palestinians were interned in Britain during the Gulf War. The United States tightened the screening of immigrants—especially those coming from the Middle East to the United States—after the 1993 World Trade Center bombing and the September 11, 2001 terror attacks. Germany also acted against radical Islamic organizations and expanded the Central Register for Foreigners following the September 11, 2001 terrorist attacks on the United States. And Kurdish involvement in violent demonstrations against Turkey, as well as the activities of the PKK, led Germany to deport Kurds and to reject the applications for asylum of Kurds involved in such activities.

Hypothesis 6a Considerations of foreign policy tend to facilitate the liberalization of immigration policy (in terms of size and composition of immigration).

Receiving countries tend to accept immigrants from specific countries in order to advance foreign policy goals, such as improving military and trade relations with allies, demonstrating opposition to adversaries, gaining international respectability, and sustaining political links that evolved in the past (usually during their colonial era). For example the United States avoided for certain periods restrictions on Chinese, Japanese, and Mexican immigration in order to maintain trade and good relations with these countries. In the 1970s, Australia recognized the growing importance of its relationship with Asian countries, and consequently it liberalized its policies toward Asian immigration.

The impact of foreign policy considerations on immigration policies is particularly strong *in countries that seek leadership status.* For example Britain avoided restrictions on New Commonwealth immigration until 1961, despite growing domestic demands for restrictions, because of opposition from West Indian politicians and its fear that such restrictions would undermine Britain's leadership role in the Commonwealth. Britain's loss of world power status, marked by the 1947 withdrawal of support from Greece and Turkey, the decolonization process, and the 1956 Suez operation, weakened its commitment to free immigration. The U.S. rise to global power status led it to admit refugees from various communist countries. This represented a significant liberalization of immigration control policy, because most pre-1965 refugees came from Eastern European countries, which were allocated very small quotas according to the national-origins system. Eventually, the collapse of communism in Eastern Europe caused the United States to withdraw its preference for immigration from such countries. Cuban immigration was limited in 1994, although Cubans are still given preferential treatment over immigrants from other countries under the so-called wet-foot, dry-foot policy.[4]

Hypothesis 7 General racist attitudes facilitate restrictions on permanent immigration of dissimilar composition, while general liberal attitudes promote the liberalization of immigration control policies.

Racist theories and terminology were prevalent in various Western societies prior to World War II, and facilitated the passage of restrictions on dissimilar immigration, based on ethnic selection criteria. The war against the Fascist powers, the impact of the Holocaust, and the civil rights movements of the 1960s–1970s (as well as foreign policy considerations) delegitimized the use of overt racist terminology and policies, and led to the abolition of ethnically explicit selection criteria (see chapter 6). The influence of the racist/liberal attitudes is limited for several reasons, which are described in chapter 1.

The Type of Immigration and the Influence of the Socioeconomic and Foreign Policy Factors

A major theme of the book is that the type of immigration determines the relative influence of the socioeconomic and foreign policy factors on immigration control policy.

Hypothesis 8 Labor migration policy is mainly determined by the state of the economy. It is also influenced by the "war–migrant labor link" and by foreign policy considerations (regarding the character of the program). Labor migration policy is influenced to a lesser degree by the volume and composition of immigration and by racist/liberal ideology.

The state of the economy, and particularly that of the labor market (measured here according to the rate of unemployment), consistently influenced labor migration policy. In all four countries explored, recessions caused countries to accept fewer migrant workers, while economic prosperity caused them to accept more migrant workers (see hypothesis 1 earlier). Wars also facilitated the establishment of migrant worker programs in what was termed "the war–migrant labor link" (see hypothesis 3).

In contrast, labor migration policy was influenced to a lesser degree by the volume and composition of immigration. Western European countries recruited millions of migrant workers from Southern Europe, North Africa, Turkey, and Yugoslavia during the 1960s and early 1970s. Both the Netherlands and Germany signed bilateral agreements with Spain, Portugal, Italy, Turkey, Greece, Morocco, Yugoslavia, and Tunisia. But despite the influx of large numbers of immigrants, most of them of dissimilar ethnic and cultural background, there was limited public opposition to their arrival, and in contrast to the 1980s and 1990s, it did not become a major political issue. The reason was that the stay of these migrants was perceived to be temporary—both by the government and by the public. They were termed "guestworkers," and policymakers in both countries repeatedly stated that their country is not a country of immigration. This perception of migrant temporality was further facilitated by the fact that the great majority of immigrants from the Mediterranean area were unaccompanied males. Thus, they were not expected to have a lasting effect on the ethnic, cultural, and political character of the receiving societies.

By the late 1960s/early 1970s, there was already some evidence that many of the guestworkers in Western Europe were becoming permanent residents, which generated opposition to immigration and attacks on the migrants. Some scholars (e.g. Bernard Kayser) attribute the 1973 curbs to settlement and integration problems, and argue that the oil crisis and the threat of a recession were excuses for policy changes that were coming anyway. Similarly, Martin (1975: 202) notes that the November 1973 recruitment ban in Germany was officially justified in terms of the OPEC oil embargo, but that German employers thought that the government had simply found a convenient alibi to halt the immigration that was troubling German voters. Other scholars attribute the 1973 restrictions to the social unrest of 1968. However, between 1969 and 1972, the need for foreign labor overcame those early signs of permanency. This was especially true in countries like Germany, which succeeded in decreasing the number of migrant workers during the 1967–1968 recession, thus sustaining the assumption that the migrants' stay was temporary. Consequently, the recruitment of migrant workers reached its peak during the 1969–1972 period. The 1973 economic recession caused the governments to halt recruitment, assuming that the migrant workers would return to their countries of origin. Only in the late 1970s, after attempts to encourage repatriation failed, and the migrant workers were joined by their family members, did it become evident that they were likely to stay permanently in Western Europe. This, in turn, produced growing antagonism toward dissimilar immigration (including the former migrant workers and new asylum seekers), the emergence of immigration as a hotly debated political issue, and stricter immigration controls that were increasingly influenced by the size and composition of immigration.

Not only did the (presumed) temporary nature of the migrant worker programs help in limiting the debate about them, but the governments of the countries of destination explicitly sought to substantiate this temporary status, thus preventing the composition of immigration from becoming a major issue. In Germany, a compromise was reached in 1890 between the conservatives/national elements and the landowners, which allowed for the importation of Polish workers, but prevented them from taking up permanent residence. The laborers had to leave the country every year for 4.5 months during the winter (the *Karenzzeit*). According to the German 1965 Law on Foreigners, an extension of the work and residence permit was granted only if the interests of the Federal Republic were not damaged, and permanent settlement in the Federal Republic was interpreted by the courts as a violation of this regulation. In the Netherlands, the 1970 government policy paper "Note on Foreign Employees" stated that measures should be taken to encourage return migration and that "our country needs manpower and not the immigration of families." And during the mid-1970s, both the Netherlands and Germany attempted to encourage return migration, thus striving again to sustain the notion of temporality and that the workers would be rotated. In all of these cases, government policies were clearly influenced by economic considerations, that is, the attempt to link the number of migrant workers to the economic needs of the country, and to prevent the arrival of family members who were not economically beneficial. But at least in some cases—such as the 1890 compromise in Germany—they were also aimed at preventing the growth of a minority group, thereby keeping the composition of immigration out of the public debate.

The ratio between labor migration and permanent immigration (not including refugees) has been smaller in the United States and Britain than in Germany and the Netherlands. But here, too, labor migration policy was hardly influenced by the composition of immigration. The main opposition to the European Volunteer Workers (EVWs) in Britain, to the contract laborers recruited by U.S. employers between 1864 and 1885, to the Mexican migrant workers between 1917–1922, and to the Bracero migrant workers between 1942 and 1964 came from the unions. It focused on the economic competition posed by the migrant workers rather than on the composition of immigration. And in neither of these cases was the recruitment of migrant workers a major political issue among the parties or the public.

Since the composition of immigration did not substantially influence labor migration policy, nor did the general racist/liberal attitudes. Programs that assisted in recruiting migrant workers of dissimilar composition existed both before and after World War II, and were not influenced by the war against the Fascist powers or by the Holocaust. Nor were they liberalized due to the civil rights movements of the 1960s–1970s. In fact, the Bracero program in the United States was terminated in 1964, and the European migrant worker programs were halted around 1973, the same period the civil rights movement reached its peak.

Foreign policy considerations rarely cause the establishment of migrant worker programs, but they influence the character of those programs: from which countries the workers will be recruited, and sometimes the nature of their employment. In the United States, the Bracero program was initiated in response to pressures from southwestern farmers, and was abolished mainly due to pressures from the unions. But the United States acceded to most of Mexico's demands, including guarantees of nondiscrimination, adequate housing and employment for at least three-fourths of the contract period. In a later stage, Mexico and the State Department became prime supporters of the program. In Germany, too, foreign policy considerations influenced the treatment of migrant workers and the countries from which they were recruited. During World War I, Germany somewhat improved the treatment of Polish and Belgian workers because of protests by other countries. During the 1960s, pressures from employers caused the German government to allow for the recruitment of labor. But foreign relations between Germany and Turkey as well as between Germany and Yugoslavia contributed to labor recruitment agreements between these countries, turning the Turks and the Yugoslavs into the two largest groups of foreign workers in the FRG. During the 1990s, foreign policy considerations played an even greater role, facilitating the establishment of foreign worker programs that allowed Eastern Europeans to work in Germany.

Hypothesis 9 Immigration control policy with regard to permanent immigration of dissimilar composition is influence by all five factors, in the following order of importance: the volume and composition of immigration, the state of the economy, racist/liberal general attitudes, wars and external threats, and considerations of foreign policy. The racist/liberal general attitudes influence the selection of immigrants, and consequently the numbers accepted.

In contrast to labor migration, permanent migrants settle in the country of destination, compete for social services, and influence the ethnic and political character of the receiving society. Their impact is especially notable when they are of a different racial, ethnic, or cultural background than the native population. Consequently, immigration control policy with regard to permanent dissimilar immigration is influenced first and foremost by the volume and composition of immigration. In the United States, surges in immigration of dissimilar composition led to restrictions on Chinese immigration in 1875 and 1882; Japanese immigration in 1907; and attempts to restrict Greek-Orthodox, Catholic, and Jewish immigration from Eastern and Southern Europe, which culminated in the literacy test act of 1917 and the national origins quota acts of 1921 and 1924.[5] In Britain, the surge in Russian Jewish immigration after 1880 led to the 1905 Aliens Immigration Act. The arrival of almost 500,000 New Commonwealth immigrants between 1955 and 1962, especially in 1961–1962, led to the 1962 Commonwealth Immigrants Act. The 1968 flow of Indian refugees from Kenya led to the Commonwealth Immigrants Act of 1968. The arrival of a small number of Asians from Malawi in 1976 contributed to a more restrictive attitude by the Labor government and the Conservative Party. And the influx of asylum seekers and illegal immigrants since the mid-1980s led to visa requirements for citizens of Sri Lanka, Ghana, Nigeria, India, Bangladesh, Pakistan, the former Yugoslavia, and Slovakia, as well as to laws and regulations aimed at limiting the two types of immigration. The Netherlands also attempted to restrict the influx of Third World asylum seekers and illegal migrants since the 1980s. In each of the aforementioned cases, policymakers explicitly linked the upsurge in immigration and sometimes the composition of that immigration to the restrictions.

Germany's leaders repeatedly declared (until 1998) that Germany is not a country of (permanent) immigration. And permanent immigration of non-Germans, except for political refugees and family reunification, was practically impossible until the reform of the immigration system in 2002. Consequently, the main non-German permanent (or semipermanent) immigration was that of asylum seekers and family unification. German asylum policy was initially influenced by the attempt to atone for its Nazi past, and later by the volume of dissimilar immigration. The 1980 upsurge in asylum applications led to regulations that made asylum seekers wait for one year (and later two years) before receiving a work permit, to restrictions on the social benefits granted to asylum applicants, and to the Asylum Procedure Act of 1982, which authorized the federal authorities to dismiss an asylum request if it appeared to be ill-founded. The 1984–1993 influx of asylum seekers—mostly from Yugoslavia, Romania, Turkey, Poland, Bulgaria, and Iran—led to agreements with countries of origin (e.g. Romania) and transfer (e.g. East Germany), and eventually to the 1993 amendment to the German constitution, which severely restricts the right to asylum.

Unlike the volume and composition of immigration, the state of the economy has had limited impact on policies toward permanent immigration in Britain, Germany, and the Netherlands. In Britain, most restrictions on immigration did not coincide with economic recessions: the restrictions of 1792, 1914, 1961–1962, 1965, 1968, and 1971 were passed during periods of relatively low unemployment. But as noted, a labor shortage did facilitate the liberal immigration policy toward New Commonwealth immigrants during the 1950s, and higher rates of unemployment may have contributed to the passage of several restrictions, including the 1905 Aliens Immigration Act and those of the 1980s and early 1990s. In the Netherlands, the timing of the restrictions on asylum seekers correlates more closely with the number of applications for asylum than with the state of the economy (see table 4.2). But increasing or high unemployment rates did coincide with, and may have contributed to, some restrictions on asylum seekers (e.g. in the 1930s and between 1991 and 1994). In Germany, the influx of asylum seekers was the main cause of restrictions, but economic difficulties (i.e. the cost of German reunification) also contributed to restrictions on asylum seekers. And in 2000–2001, when the economy improved, Bosnians and Kosovars who had resided in Germany at least six years, had been employed for at least two years, and who had families that did not receive welfare, were allowed to stay in Germany. However, overall, the influence of the state of the economy (measured according to the rate of unemployment) on German asylum policy was less consistent than that of the number of applications for asylum.

In countries where permanent immigrants, rather than temporary migrant workers, are the main source of foreign labor—that is in settler societies—the state of the economy also substantially influences control policy in regard to immigration of dissimilar composition. The United States restricted permanent migration during recessions and encouraged it when the economy revived (see hypothesis 1 earlier), although this link has weakened since World War II. Australian postwar immigration control policy (which is not analyzed in this book) was also closely linked to the level of employment.

In some cases, where countries accepted permanent immigration for foreign policy or historical reasons (i.e. Britain with regard to New Commonwealth immigrants during the 1950s–1960s and the Netherlands with regard to refugees from the Dutch East Indies/Indonesia between 1946 and 1963), employers supported admitting these migrants, particularly during labor shortages. But the influence of the state of the economy on such immigration policy was not consistent: immigrants/refugees were accepted during recessions and sometimes rejected when unemployment was low. The influence of the economy was secondary to that of foreign policy considerations.

Hypothesis 10a Immigration control policy with regard to permanent similar immigration (former emigrants, descendants of former immigrants, and immigrants who share ethnic and cultural characteristics with the indigenous population) tends to be more liberal than with regard to permanent dissimilar immigration.

Immigrants of similar ethnic and cultural background face less animosity from that population than do dissimilar immigrants. As a result, the volume of immigration, moderate changes in the state of the economy, general racist/liberal attitudes and considerations of foreign policy have little impact on such immigration policy. In the United States, the opponents of Chinese, Japanese, and Eastern and Southern European immigration did not promote restrictions on Western European immigration during the late nineteenth and early twentieth century. The literacy test and the quota acts were specifically aimed at discriminating against the former while allowing the latter to immigrate to the United States. The support for Western European immigration continued even during the recessions of 1882–1885, 1891–1897, 1907–1908, 1921, and 1924, when other types of immigration were restricted. Nor did increases in immigration from Western Europe (e.g. after the Civil War) produce attempts to restrict it.[6] In Britain, immigration of whites from the "old Commonwealth" (i.e. Australia, Canada, New Zealand) was not restricted—without regard to the state of the economy and the volume of immigration. The concept of "patriality" was introduced in 1968–1971 in order to control colored immigration from the Commonwealth while allowing unrestricted access to most white Commonwealth citizens of British descent. In the Netherlands, European refugees from Indonesia were especially welcomed, and actively integrated into Dutch society, despite a recession during the first half of the 1950s. Finally, Germany welcomed millions of refugees of German origin after World War II, despite a housing shortage and high rates of unemployment until the late 1950s.

According to *hypothesis 10b*, three factors that do, occasionally, influence policy with regard to permanent similar immigration are:

(a) Wars and external threats, which sometimes cause countries that feel demographically inferior to their potential enemies to encourage permanent immigration of similar origin (hypothesis 5). Two examples for this process were post–World War II France and Australia.

(b) Severe depressions, which contribute to restrictions even on permanent immigration of similar origin. During the Great Depression, most countries restricted immigration, especially of the impoverished, even if the immigrants were of similar ethnic and cultural background. Israel also attempted to restrict Jewish immigration during the severe recession of the 1950s. And high unemployment rates contributed to the opposition toward *Aussiedler* immigration during the late 1980s and 1990s (in addition to the doubts regarding their German origins).

(c) Doubts with regard to the degree of similarity between the immigrants and the dominant element of receiving society contribute to restrictions on such permanent immigration. Doubts regarding the German origins of some *Aussiedler* led to language tests and restrictions on their immigration during the 1990s.[7]

Hypothesis 11 Refugee policy is influenced the most by foreign policy considerations. It is influenced to a lesser degree by the volume of immigration, the state of the economy, wars and external treats, and by racist/liberal general attitudes.

The influence of foreign policy considerations on refugee policy (and immigration policy in general) was demonstrated in hypothesis 6. Receiving countries have accepted refugees in order to:

(a) Demonstrate their opposition to the regimes of the countries of origin or to a third country that occupies the countries of origin—for example refugees from communist countries admitted by the United States;

(b) Demonstrate their sense of responsibility toward former allies—for example Moluccans (members of the dissolved Royal Netherlands East Indies Army) accepted by the Netherlands; Polish members of the Allied Forces admitted by Britain; and Southern Lebanese Army (SLA) soldiers accepted by Israel.

(c) Demonstrate their cooperation with current allies—for example the willingness of several Western countries to accept refugees from communist countries, partially in response to requests of the United States and Canada's willingness to accept Asian refugees from Uganda in tandem with Britain.

(d) Gain international respectability—for example Germany's uniquely liberal asylum/refugee policy (until 1992) was, at least partially, an attempt to atone for its World War II policies.

In addition, various countries of destination have adopted the 1951 Geneva Convention, and accepted refugees as part of the international refugee regimes. Compliance with the regime's norms may also be defined as a foreign policy consideration. It should likewise be noted that (a) the influence of the refugee regime has been limited (see chapter 1); and (b) compliance was influenced by other foreign policy and domestic considerations as well.[8]

The impact of the other socioeconomic factors has usually been weaker in the case of refugees than in that of non-refugee permanent immigrants of dissimilar composition. This happened because domestic opposition to refugees was mitigated by foreign policy considerations, and in particular by the linkage made between the immigration of refugees and security interests of the state. For example the conservatives in the United States (mostly Republicans and Southern Democrats), who tended to oppose dissimilar immigration, were much more supportive of immigration from communist countries due to the linkage made with security. In addition, as noted in chapter 1, much of the influence of the socioeconomic explanatory factors on refugee policy is brought to bear at an early stage, when deciding on whether to define the asylum seekers as refugees. Frequently, defining the asylum seekers as refugees already indicates that considerations of foreign policy have been more influential than racist attitudes and the dissimilar composition of immigration, and that pressures by the executive and by pro-immigration ethnic groups to liberalize immigration control policy have overcome domestic pressures to restrict it.

Social Conflicts and Industrial Unrest

Two partially overlapping factors that the theory mostly rejected were social conflicts and industrial unrest. Higham and Jones (in what is termed here the "national identity approach") argue that social cleavages, social unrest, and industrial unrest within American society fostered fears of losing national identity and of a national breakdown. This, in turn, produced nationalism and nativism (xenophobia).

The critique to this argument was both on theoretical and empirical grounds. Theoretically: (a) the "national identity" approach is unable to explain the fact that various countries have adopted similar immigration policies at the same time (see chapter 6); (b) the approach is vague with regard to identifying social conflicts and debates over national identity (see chapter 1); and (c) the link between industrial unrest and a restrictive immigration policy is problematic, because when large numbers of local workers are involved in strikes, employers are likely to recruit foreign workers in order to break the unity among local ones.[9]

Empirically, the argument relating *social cleavages* to restrictions on immigration lacks support in the U.S., British, and Dutch cases:

- While it is hard to define the main social conflicts in U.S. history, they would surely include the Civil War and the 1960s civil rights movement. In both cases immigration policy was mostly liberalized rather than restricted.
- Britain hardly experienced serious social conflicts (except for industrial unrest, dealt with later, and conflicts related to the immigrants themselves) during the past century. The main ethnic conflict, that is the Irish struggle for independence and later the Catholic–Protestant conflict in Northern Ireland, did not correlate with restrictions on immigration either. Nor did the abdication crisis of 1936 (which may be viewed as a debate over national identity).
- In the Netherlands, for the most part (with the exception of the 1918–1922 period), restrictions on immigration did not correlate with social conflicts or national debates in the Dutch society.

Germany seems to offer the strongest support for the social conflict theory, in particular the linkage between the attempts for "Germanization" during the end of the nineteenth century and the early twentieth century on the one hand, and restrictions on Polish immigrants on the other hand. In addition, it has been argued that the recent rise of the extreme-right was linked to German unification. However, even in these cases the linkage is debatable. The heightened nationalism of the late nineteenth century was related to the 1871 unification, but the peaks of nationalism (e.g. the restrictions on the use of the Polish language in Germany) did not correlate with the timing of restrictions on the importation of Polish labor (see chapter 5). After 1933, the emergence of the nationalist Nazi regime led to liberalization rather than to restrictions on labor migration. The 1969 social tensions coincided with a surge in labor recruitment. And with regard to German unification: (a) according to Westle and Niedermayer, the decline of the Republican party in the 1990 *Länder* elections was partly caused by Germany's reunification, which deprived it of one of its main issues; (b) the rise of extreme-right parties in Germany started in 1986, four years prior to reunification; and (c) extreme-right parties emerged in other European countries during the same time period, indicating that the causes of their rise are not particular to Germany.

The argument relating *industrial unrest* to restrictions on immigration does not accord with what happened in the United States, the Netherlands, and Germany, with the exception of the 1916–1923 period:

- The percentage of U.S. workers on strike does not correlate with U.S. immigration control policy between 1890 and 1981 (data is unavailable for the 1906–1915 period). No major restrictions were passed during the peak years of strikes. However, the main restrictions—the 1917 literacy test act and the 1921 and 1924 quota acts—did pass during a period of industrial unrest (1916–1922), although not during the peak years of it.
- The percentage of Dutch workers on strike does not correlate with Dutch immigration control policy between 1911 and 2000 with the exception of the 1918–1923 period. On the contrary: some of the peak years of strikes were also periods of relatively liberal immigration control policy. In particular, mass recruitment of foreign workers and the 1960–1971 recruitment contracts signed between the Dutch government and eight countries in the Mediterranean area followed the peak strikes of 1960 and "sharp tensions . . . in the labor market, where one wage claim followed another."[10]
- The percentage of German workers on strike does not correlate with German immigration control policy, with the exception of the post–World War I period and 1992. But the 1992 reform of asylum policy was clearly the product of an influx of asylum seekers.

Only in Britain did peak periods of strikes (1919, 1962, 1968–1971, and 1979–1982) coincide with restrictions on immigration. However, I could not find any indications of a causal link between the two factors. In addition, other restrictions—in 1905, 1914, 1965, and after 1984—did not coincide with large numbers of on strike.

One period that is an exception in this respect is 1916–1923, when industrial unrest did coincide with restrictions on immigration in various countries of destination. This is also the period highlighted by Higham and Jones with regard to the United States. However, two factors should be taken into consideration. First, this was also a period of economic instability and growing nationalism, both generated by the war. These two factors alone can explain the growing tendency to restrict immigration. And second, at least in the United States, immigrants (and particularly those in the IWW radical union) played an important role in the industrial unrest of that period. As I noted in chapter 1, I only reject the linkage between industrial unrest as a domestic conflict on the one hand, and restrictions on immigration on the other hand. I do, however, accept the argument that a substantial involvement of immigrants in industrial unrest might contribute to restrictions on immigration because: (a) immigrant militancy frightens the employers; (b) in some cases it is perceived as a domestic threat linked to external sources (hypotheses 4). This also explains the fact that many of the restrictions passed during the 1916–1923 period included greater supervision of aliens, especially those suspected of threatening domestic order; and (c) migrant involvement in strikes highlights the issue of immigration, and focuses public attention to the increasing permanency of the migrants. The same linkage between migrants' involvement in strikes and restrictions on immigration may have also influenced policies in the early 1970s: Castles and Kosak argue that the leading role of migrant workers in the 1973 strikes in Germany contributed to the ban on the entry of migrant workers.[11]

The Influence of Regional Integration on Immigration Control Policies of the Member States

This book focused on the immigration control policies of individual countries. But since the 1950s, a growing number of regional integration schemes established, or attempted to establish, common markets and the free movement of persons, thereby influencing the immigration control policies of the member states.[12] A rich literature deals with immigration policy and regional integration—particularly the European one—including Callovi, O'Keefee, Feldblum, Handoll, Miles and Thränhardt, Bigo, Overbeek, Brochmann, Guild and Niessen, Papademetrious, Bourdouvalis, Uçarer, Muus et al., Guild, MacLaughlin, Lahav, Koslowski, Martin, Geddes and Favell.[13] I offer elsewhere a more detailed analysis of labor mobility policy in regional integration.[14]

According to *hypothesis 6b*, regional integration schemes are likely to influence the immigration control policies of their member states in several ways:

(a) Regional integration liberalizes the policies of the member states toward immigration from the others;
(b) By facilitating free, or freer, movement of labor and persons among the member states, regional integration decreases the degree of control that states have over their own labor migration policies and their borders;
(c) Where free movement is achieved, regional integration contributes to harmonization between immigration control policies of the member states, and to the formation of a common "external immigration policy" toward immigrants from outside the region;
(d) This common external immigration policy is likely to be relatively restrictive.

Various regional integration schemes have attempted to achieve the free, or freer, movement of labor and persons among the member states, as part of a common market. Some of the attempts have been successful (e.g. the EEC/EC/EU, the Benelux Economic Union, and Nordic Community), while others experienced setbacks (e.g. the Economic Community of West African States (ECOWAS), the Economic Community of West Africa (CEAO), the Central African Customs and Economic Union (UDEAC), and the Economic Community of Central African States).

By facilitating free, or freer, movement of labor and persons among the member states, the successful regional integration schemes have decreased the degree of control the states have over their own labor migration policies and their borders. For example EU member states generally cannot prevent workers from other member states from seeking employment, and accepting employment offers made, even during recessions. Nor can they prevent nationals of other member states from crossing their borders. The situation has been different in the less successful regional integration schemes. Countries of destination—such as Nigeria and the Ivory Coast in ECOWAS, and Gabon in the Economic Community of Central African States—expelled migrant workers from other member states during periods of economic and/or political instability. Veteran member states have also delayed the implementation of the free movement of labor with regard to new member states (e.g. when Greece, Spain, Portugal, and Eastern European countries joined the EC/EU) for up to seven years.

Where free movement was achieved, regional integration contributed to harmonization between the immigration control policies of the member states, and to the formation of common external immigration policies toward immigrants from outside the region. The most advanced multilateral agreements on the free movement of labor and persons are the European ones. The freedom of movement for workers in the EEC/EC was mostly achieved between 1957 and 1968. The Benelux Economic Union and the Nordic Community also advanced the free movement of labor among their member states. The process leading to the free movement of persons within the EU, and more gradually toward a common external immigration policy, started with a series of intergovernmental meetings and with the 1986 Single European Act. It was moved forward by the 1990 Schengen Agreement, the 1992 Maastricht Treaty, and the 1997 Amsterdam Treaty; by declarations at European Council meetings in Rhodes (1988), Madrid (1989), Dublin (1990), Rome (1990), Corfu (1994), Cardiff (1998), Vienna (1998), Tampere (1999), Laeken (2001), and Seville (2002); and by additional intergovernmental meetings (e.g. the *Ad Hoc* Group on Immigration and Trevi).[15]

The Maastricht Treaty, the Amsterdam Treaty, and the European Council meetings in Tampere and Seville were major milestones in the process leading toward a common EU policy with regard to immigration from outside the Union. The Maastricht Treaty moved "external" immigration from *ad hoc* cooperation outside the treaty framework to more formal intergovernmental cooperation. It made immigration a matter of "common interest" for the EU, although it did not "super-nationalize" it yet.[16] The Amsterdam Treaty made immigration polices a full Community responsibility, and guided the Council to adopt, within a period of five years, directives about asylum, refugee, and immigration policies. Currently, the Council is expected to act on proposals from the Commission or on the initiative of a member state. But after May 1, 2004, the Commission will have an exclusive right of initiative. During the Tampere summit, the EU leaders decided to create an area of freedom, security, and justice in the EU, and to establish a Common European Asylum System by 2004. Immigration control policy was also a prominent subject during the 2002 EU Council meeting in Seville. The conclusions of that summit noted the need to speed up the current legislative work on the framing of a common policy on asylum and immigration. But they mostly focused on measures to combat illegal immigration and on the gradual introduction of integrated management of the EU's external borders.[17] To date, the EU has especially made progress toward cooperation and a common policy on asylum seekers and on illegal immigration, while advancement with regard to common labor migration and family reunification policies has been relatively limited.

The need for a common EU external immigration policy has been linked to the free movement of persons within the Union (i.e. "internal" immigration control policy). Geddes points out that "Free movement, immigration and asylum are clearly connected: free movement provisions raised the salience of external frontier control and internal security and impelled immigration and asylum co-operation."[18] Lavenex concludes, "action in asylum matters was from the beginning framed as a necessary 'compensation' measure for the safeguarding of internal security after the abolition of internal border controls in the single market."[19] And Uçarer notes, "many recognized that the abolishing of internal borders within the Union would invariably necessitate enforcing tougher controls on the Union's external borders."[20] The link between the two issues was expressed in the Treaty of Amsterdam, according to which the Council would adopt "measures aimed at ensuring the free movement of persons . . . in conjunction with directly related flanking measures with respect to external border controls, asylum and immigration."[21] And according to the Commission's Communication COM(2002)233, one of the major reasons for regarding external borders as a "priority question" is to "ensure mutual confidence between the member states which have abolished checks on persons and goods at their internal borders and thereby facilitate movement of travelers."[22]

The link between free movement within the EU and the Union's external policy has somewhat weakened over time, at least in legal terms. According to the Commission's Communication (COM(2000)757) of November 2000, "immigration and asylum matters . . . are now the subjects of specific Community policies and no longer simply complementary to those related to the free movement of persons within the Union."[23]

Studies have also recorded the restrictive nature of EU immigration control policies. The term "Fortress Europe" has been used in order to describe the tendency of the Union to move toward lowest common denominator policies, and of member states with relatively liberal policies or porous external borders to adopt more restrictive policies.[24] Also in the context of family reunification, the European Economic and Social Committee concluded that "a provision which had been conceived of as a framework of principles has become a lowest common denominator of the laws already applying in the Member States."[25]

In practice, the process of European integration involves various players, not all of whom support restrictive policies. Intergovernmental and Council negotiations, where governments have been represented by the national executives and by the Interior, Justice, and Immigration Ministries of the member states, did contribute to lowest common denominator immigration policies. But many Brussels-based pro-migrant NGOs also believe that more power for the Commission, European Court of Justice, and European Parliament could counteract these policies, and open social and political spaces for migrants.[26] A debate has also developed between human rights groups with regard to the impact of EU immigration policies. Amnesty International has argued that as a result of restrictive EU immigration measures, the number of refugees in the EU has dramatically fallen in recent years.[27] But the European Council on Refugees and Exiles (ECRE), a nongovernmental pressure group, disagreed with Amnesty, saying that the Tampere summit decisions assured the access of genuine refugees into the EU, and did not create a Fortress Europe.[28]

Finally, in accordance with the main theme of this book, the establishment of regional agreements on immigration and their impact on immigration policies of the member states are influenced by the *socio-economic factors* and *by the type of immigration*. For example I demonstrate elsewhere how the state of the economy and the size of the economic gap between the member states influence the likelihood of multilateral agreements on the free movement of labor.[29] And as is the case with the immigration policies of individual states, the policy of the EU with regard to illegal immigration has been influenced by the size of such immigration and by the threat of terrorism.[30] The impact of regional agreements on internal and external policies is also expected to differ according to the type of immigration:

Permanent immigration and naturalization The control over permanent immigration and naturalization is among the basic attributes of sovereignty. Therefore, member states are least likely to forego their jurisdiction in this regard. Currently, no regional multilateral agreement supercedes the right of the member states to determine which immigrants will be granted permanent immigrant status and citizenship.

Family reunification Member states are more likely to agree to migration for the purpose of family reunification than in the previous category because this right is already implemented by the countries of destination. In particular, countries tend to accept family reunification for the purpose of permanent settlement and naturalization where the person applying for reunification (the sponsor) is a citizen. Family reunification where the person applying for reunification is a noncitizen resident lawfully living in the country has also become common in countries of destination, and thus it may expand to common external policies of regional schemes. But the status of the immigrant would depend on the status of the sponsor, rather than automatically becoming a permanent resident and gaining citizenship.

Labor migration Various regional integration schemes, noted earlier, have attempted to achieve the free, or freer, movement of labor among their member states. The socioeconomic factors described in this book (particularly the state of the economy) influence, to some degree, the stability of the multilateral agreements and the labor migration policies of the member states. For example economic (and political) crises in 1983 and 1985 caused Nigeria to violate the spirit of the ECOWAS Treaty by expelling over two million (technically illegal) migrants. The economic crisis of the 1970s slowed, but did not reverse, the progress toward a free movement of labor and persons within the EC. The free movement of labor does not necessitate a common external labor migration policy, because it is possible to differentiate between *legal* migrant workers who originated in the region from those who came from third countries. But the creation of a unified labor market does increase the likelihood of a common migration policy of this kind in the longer term.

Asylum seekers and refugees Most major countries of destination take part in the refugee regime (based on the norms of the 1951 UN Convention on Refugees and the 1967 UN Protocol on Refugees), although the influence of this regime is limited in several aspects (see chapter 1). Some countries of destination also adhere to the norms of regional agreements on human rights and/or refugees, such as the EU's Charter of Fundamental Rights.[31] The combination of the refugee regime and of the free movement of persons enables asylum seekers who enter one member state to "shop around" among the other member states. This, in turn, increases the likelihood that the member states would harmonize their asylum policies and attempt to achieve a common asylum policy.

Illegal/undocumented immigration The free movement of persons within a region enables illegal migrants who enter one member state to easily move to other member states. Consequently, the internal free movement of persons increases the likelihood of the harmonization of immigration policies and a common external immigration control policy toward illegal immigration. Such a policy is likely to be relatively restrictive, as member states with relatively open external borders come under pressure to restrict immigration from outside the region.

Overall, since the 1950s, a growing number of regional integration schemes established, or attempted to establish, common markets and the free or freer movement of persons, thereby influencing the immigration control policies of the member states. Some of these attempts (in particular the European ones) have been successful, while others (notably the African ones) experienced setbacks, or remained limited to skilled labor. The most successful project of this type—the EEC/EC/EU—achieved the free movement of (most) labor by 1968. Since the mid-1980s, it also accomplished the free movement of persons, and is in the process of establishing common immigration policies with regard to asylum seekers and illegal immigrants from outside the Union.

In the context of this book, the influence of regional integration schemes on immigration control policies of the member states is still limited:

- First, with the exception of Europe, most other attempts to achieve free movement of labor and persons have suffered setbacks.
- Second, the movement of workers within the EC/EU has been relatively limited, and it has increasingly been composed of skilled labor. During the recession of the 1970s it was further discouraged by supporting the regions of origin through the regional policy. And when new members joined the Union, which could substantially increase the flow of migrant workers, transition periods of up to seven years were introduced before free movement of labor applied to them.
- Third, given the cultural similarities among the member states of the EU (at least at the 15-member stage), migration between them

was seldom restricted in the past, even before the establishment of the common market, with the exception of the great depression and the migration of Jews.

- Fourth, the member states of the EU still have jurisdiction over permanent migration policy and naturalization, even with regard to migrants from other EU members.
- Fifth, the movement toward a common external immigration policy for the EU has not been completed yet. And even when such common policies are achieved, the member states will still determine, in the foreseeable future, the number of immigrants (permanent, temporary, and to some degree asylum seekers) they wish to accept.
- Sixth, socioeconomic factors and the ensuing domestic political processes within the member states still influence the immigration policies of these countries and of the EU. For examples the resurgence of right-wing anti-immigrant parties in several EU states during the late 1990s and early 2000s substantially contributed to the recent saliency and restrictive character of EU immigration policies.[32]

Despite these caveats, regional integration schemes—at least the European ones—have influenced immigration control policies of their member states to some degree. EU policies have even affected the policies of Eastern European *candidate* states with regard to illegal immigration. In addition, the Union influences the immigration policies of its member states in several indirect ways:

- The economic criteria set by the Union (in the context of the EMU) influence the economies of the member states, and consequently their immigration policies;
- According to several scholars, European integration has exacerbated the fears of a loss of national identity, which contributed to the emergence of extreme-right anti-immigrant parties;
- Politicians in member states have occasionally promoted immigration control policies that were controversial at the domestic level by transferring the decision to the Union level.

Given the fact that the EU is a major destination for migrants, and that it is advancing toward a common external immigration control policy, the impact of regional integration on immigration policy is likely to increase in the future.

Global Patterns in Immigration Policy

The study emphasized the extraordinary similarity that has existed among the immigration control policies of the major Western countries of destination for over a century (*hypothesis 12*). During the 1870s–1880s, several countries restricted Chinese and other labor migration. Between 1890 and World War I, countries of destination attempted to block Eastern European and impoverished immigration, and restricted Japanese immigration. During the 1920s, various countries limited Eastern European immigration. Between World War I and World War II, countries of destination restricted immigration. During the 1960s, they mostly (with the exception of Britain and to some degree Switzerland) liberalized immigration policy in terms of numbers and/or composition. During the Cold War, most Western countries of destination also showed a preference for refugees from communism. In 1972–1974, Western European countries halted large-scale labor migration from outside Europe. During the mid-1970s, they attempted to encourage the return of the migrant workers to their home countries. Since 1979 and particularly since 1985, most countries of destination have attempted to restrict applications for asylum and to halt illegal immigration. And during the 1990s, there was a renewed tendency to accept migrant workers, but this time on a more limited and sectoral basis (e.g. in the agricultural and high-tech sectors).

I examined six alternative explanations for these similarities in immigration control policies: (a) a global hegemon that forces or persuades various countries to act in unison; (b) global or regional migration regimes and organizations; (c) interdependence between the immigration control policies of various countries; (d) emulation of immigration control policies of one country by other countries; (e) the world system approach; and (f) interdependence between the socioeconomic and foreign policy factors that lead to immigration control policies. I argued that (with the exception of the refugee regime and recently the EU) it is the last factor that explains most of the similarity among the immigration control policies (*hypothesis 13*). I then demonstrated how global economic cycles, shared migratory pressures, alliances that produce common foreign policy considerations, wars that receiving countries are involved in, and global ideological cycles between racism and liberalism have produced the similarities among immigration control policies in various receiving countries. For example according to hypothesis 1, recessions cause countries to accept fewer immigrants (i.e. to restrict immigration), while economic prosperity causes them to accept more immigrants (i.e. to liberalize immigration control policy). Since the economies of various countries of destination have become increasingly interdependent, global recessions have caused them to simultaneously restrict immigration, while global economic upturns have led them to simultaneously liberalize immigration. According to hypothesis 2, large-scale immigration of dissimilar racial or ethnic composition contributes to restrictions on immigration. Thus, common migratory pressures have caused various receiving countries, which share a common racial and ethnic preference system, to restrict immigration.

The interdependence between the socioeconomic and foreign policy factors explains most of the similarities among the immigration policies of the major countries of destination over time. In contrast, according to *hypothesis 14*, the structural factors of countries and their preference for permanent or temporary immigration, both of which are relatively stable, produce the cross-national differences between immigration policies at any given time (see figure 7.1). The structural characteristics—that is the economic structure and geopolitical position of a country—determine how the global economic cycle, alliances, wars, and common migratory pressures influence the immigration policy of a specific country. The country's population density and foreign policy considerations (derived from its geopolitical position) influence its preference for permanent or temporary migration, and consequently the type of immigration policy it will apply. For example high population density has caused Western European countries and Japan to prefer migrant workers, while low population density has induced the United States, Canada, and Australia to prefer permanent immigration. Consequently, economic prosperity would lead the former to recruit

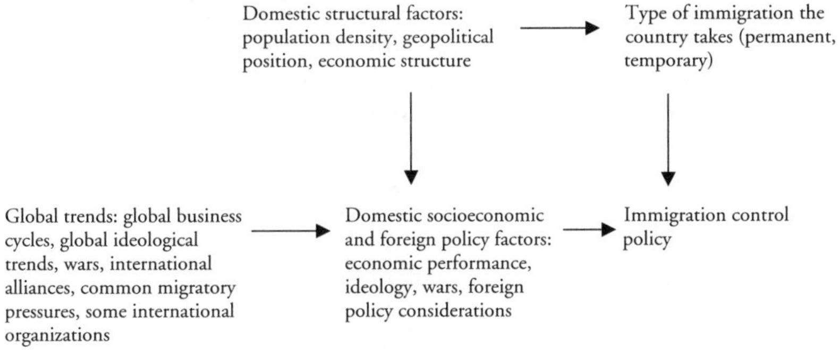

Figure 7.1 The factors determining similarities and differences between immigration control policies of various receiving countries

migrant workers, and the latter to accept permanent immigrants. Foreign policy considerations caused Britain to accept dissimilar New Commonwealth permanent immigration. Thus, the declining importance of the Empire and the Commonwealth, and the surge in dissimilar immigration, caused Britain to limit permanent immigration during the prosperous 1960s. In contrast, labor shortages caused most Western European countries to recruited migrant workers during the 1960s. Recruitment was stopped in 1973–1974, mainly as a result of the 1973 recession.

In Summary

Immigration control has emerged as a policy issue of ever increasing importance during the past two decades. A rich literature has also evolved, detailing the immigration policies of various countries. But the greatest weakness of most of this literature is, in my opinion, its limited theoretical grounding.

Some scholars doubt the possibility of constructing a theory capable of explaining immigration policies in various countries—countries that may differ in terms of culture, geography, economy, and political structure. I am among those who believe that constructing theories on immigration control policy is both possible and essential. Such theories must be based on refutable hypotheses, on ranking the various explanatory factors according to their relative importance, and on a comparative analysis of immigration control policies in various countries of destination.

Further studies could substantiate or refute the arguments presented here and augment their scope: studies that examine a greater variety of countries, including non-Western ones; those that use quantitative methods; and studies that analyze the influence of regional integration on immigration control policies of member states. It is comparative analyses, based on a variety of research strategies, which will enable us to understand the primary causes of immigration control policy.

Notes

Introduction

1. In October 2002, the United Nations Population Division estimated there were 175 million people residing outside their country of birth in 2000, double the number in 1975, and up from 120 million in 1990. This was equivalent to almost 3% of the world's population. The UN Population Division defines a migrant as someone outside her country of birth or citizenship for 12 months or more. These migrants include refugees and asylum seekers, foreign students, and other long-term visitors, unauthorized foreigners, and naturalized foreign-born citizens of Australia, Canada, and the United States (United Nations Population Division, 2002; *Migration News* 9(8)–10(1), August 2002–January 2003; *Global Development Briefing*, December 19, 2002).
2. Muus, 2001. This number underestimates the size of the foreign population in the EU, because it does not include migrants who had been naturalized.
3. *Migration News* 3(12), December 1996, based on U.S. Census Bureau data. See also Bouvier and Gardner (1986).
4. Only in France, the Netherlands, and Finland did natural increase (births minus deaths) exceed immigration.
5. Population stabilizes if fertility reaches 2.1 babies per woman. The overall EU fertility rate is 1.47, far below the replacement rate, with Sweden having the highest fertility rate in Europe of about 1.95, and Spain and Italy having some of the world's lowest fertility rates with 1.2–1.3 children per woman. Fertility rate in Canada is 1.5 (*Migration News* 9(7–10), July–October 2002).
6. In addition to the large Hispanic immigration, fertility in the United States also varies by race: 1.9 children for non-Hispanic white women, 2.1 for Black and Asian women, and 3.2 for Hispanic women. Twenty-one percent of the babies born in the United States in 2001 were Hispanic (*Migration News* 10(1), January 2003).
7. *New York Times*, July 28, 1993.
8. *Migration News* 4(3), March 1997; and 9(9), September 2002.
9. Illegal immigrants immigrate despite restrictions. However, the industrialized countries have the capacity to substantially limit illegal immigration. Even the large illegal immigration to the United States has been facilitated by

limited resources available for border control, partially a product of political pressure from pro-immigration interest groups. Thus, allowing illegal immigrants to enter a country by neglecting border control is essentially part of immigration policy (see Joppke, 1998b).

10. Zolberg (1989:406).
11. *Migration News* 9(12), December 2002.
12. This latter number might be somewhat misleading, because naturalization rates in Germany have been lower than in many other countries.
13. The United States did allow for the naturalization of large numbers of illegal/undocumented immigrants.

Chapter 1 A Theory of Immigration Policy

1. Husbands (1988).
2. Money (1999:26).
3. Fetzer (2000:15).
4. Beard and Beard (1944), Gorz (1970), Marshall (1973), Marx (1973, 1976), Castells (1975), Nikolinakos (1975), Castles and Kosack (1985), Miles (1986, 1987, 1989), and Bovenkerk et al. (1990, 1991). Piore (1979:42–43) also focuses on the nature of the economic system and on the struggle between various groups and classes in explaining immigration. However, he rejects several Marxist assumptions.
5. The studies of Divine (1957), Craig (1971), Zolberg (1981a), Hoffmann-Nowotny (1985), Shughart et al. (1986), LeMay (1987), Layton-Henry (1990, 1992), Hollifield (1992a), Freeman and Betts (1992), Freeman (1995), Joppke (1998b, 1999), and Money (1997, 1999) apply the domestic politics approach. However, many of them attribute changes in immigration policy not only to the state of the economy and to economic interest groups, but also to additional factors.
6. Husbands (1988).
7. Money (1999:6–7, 27–30).
8. Fetzer (2000:5–16). In contrast to the economic competition theory, marginality theory argues that recessions decrease the opposition to immigration and immigrants.
9. Higham (1955), Jones (1960), Herbert (1990), Brubaker (1992), Leitner (1995), and Kurthen (1995).
10. See Money, 1999.
11. Miller (1979), Miller and Papademetriou (1983), Teitelbaum (1984), Weiner (1985, 1990, 1993, 1995), Loescher and Scanlan (1986), Mitchell (1989, 1992), Bach (1990), Tucker et al. (1990), Salomon (1991), Hollifield (1992b), Miller (1992), Zolberg (1992), Hartigan (1992), Loescher (1996), Skran (1995), Teitelbaum and Weiner (1995), Koslowski (1998).
12. Meyers (2000).
13. Fitzgerald (1996:24–34).

14. Zolberg (1978:242).
15. Weiner (1985:446).
16. The full and more detailed list of themes is presented in the concluding chapter.
17. During the turn of the previous century it was mostly Eastern and Southern European immigration, and to a lesser degree Asian immigration, to WASP societies. After World War II it was mostly from the Third World to Western societies.
18. In some cases, the expectation of increased dissimilar migration, following past migration waves, is enough to generate pressures for restrictions.
19. See Hunt (1987:58, 69, 78–79, 139–40).
20. See Layton-Henry (1992), Zolberg (1989).
21. Zolberg (1983, 1981a).
22. Gurak and Caces (1992), Massy (1988, 1990), Massey et al. (1990, 1993).
23. The postwar state of the economy also influenced the transition from temporary labor migration to permanent migration.
24. Doomernik et al. (1997:25).
25. Regional integration schemes influence policies with regard to temporary labor migration. But they do not substantially influence immigration control policy with regard to permanent immigrants from other member states.
26. See Salomon (1991), Hartigan (1992), Loescher (1996), and Skran (1995). The influence of the international refugee regime can also be defined as a consideration of foreign policy.
27. See O'Connell (1970), Oppenheim (1955), Garcoa-Mora (1956:23–41), Krenz (1966), Nada (1981:449), Bevan (1986:214), Jankovic (1984:235), and Weis (1953)—all quoted in Plender (1988:394–95) as well as Amnesty International (2001).
28. Plender (1988:427–28).
29. Hartigan (1992). The refugee regimes and other types of multinational cooperation with regard to immigration are dealt with in a forthcoming study.
30. Immigrants of similar composition are usually welcomed as permanent immigrants, and are not defined as asylum seekers to begin with.
31. The "strong" versus "weak" dichotomy naturally oversimplifies the subtle influences of the various factors.
32. Castles and Kosak (1989).
33. On the difference between immigration control on the one hand, and immigrant policy or immigrant integration on the other hand, see Hammar (1985:7–9).
34. UN (1982).
35. For example, in 1960–1973 Europe, policymakers and the public believed that immigration was temporary. The same was true for the Bracero program between 1943 and 1963. In hindsight we know that they were wrong, because the former migrant workers in Europe did not return to

their countries of origin, and the Bracero program produced chain migration of permanent immigrants. But if one seeks to analyze the determinants of policy, it is necessary to look at what policymakers knew and believed at the time.

In practice, there was a prolonged transition as policymakers and the general public gradually came to realize that what they originally perceived to be a temporary migration had become a permanent feature of society. This happened in Europe during the 1970s and the early 1980s. Therefore, this study defines migration to Europe as temporary during the 1960s, as permanent in the 1980s–1990s, and as gradually shifting toward a status of permanent migration during the 1970s.

Chapter 2 Immigration Policies of the United States

1. LeMay (1987).
2. Quoted in Hutchinson (1981:31).
3. According to Zolberg (1983:23), the acts were designed by the Federalists to discourage the entry of democratic French, British, and Irish refugees.
4. LeMay (1987:53–54).
5. Higham (1955).
6. Jones (1960:156).
7. United States 37th Congress (1863:1029).
8. United States 38th Congress (1865:appendix 2). Quoted in Hutchinson (1981:50).
9. Hutchinson (1981:68–69).
10. Hutchinson (1981:77–93).
11. LeMay (1987).
12. Japanese immigration to the United States rose from 56 (excluding Hawaii) in 1870, to 24,000 in 1890, 72,000 in 1910, and 111,000 in 1920 (LeMay, 1987:62–63, 70).
13. United States 54th Congress (1896:2817–20). Quoted in Hutchinson (1981:117).
14. Quoted in Hutchinson (1981:128).
15. According to LeMay, the United States moved toward the "Pet-Door Era" in 1920.
16. The 1924 act set temporary quotas. These quotas became permanent in 1929, based on the 1920 census.
17. Hutchinson (1981:174–75).
18. Higham (1955:197).
19. Higham (1955:205–07).
20. The program was originally slated to end January 1919, but an extension was passed in January 1919 to extend it through June, and then to January 1, 1920. Additional temporary programs (not technically part of the original agreement) were implemented in February and April 1920, lasting until Wilson left office in March 1921 (Reisler, 1976; Fitzgerald, 1996).

21. Hutchinson (1981:169).
22. Most of the Mexicans repatriated were considered "illegal." However, many of them did not knowingly violate the law, but rather entered the United States at a time when the government's views on immigration were in flux, and new rules—or a new interpretation of old rules—were applied (Hoffman, 1974:2).
23. According to Hoffman (1974:38–39, 166–68), repatriations refer to cases where the immigrants left by themselves, with no cost to the government, and could apply to enter legally. Voluntary repatriations are defined as the return of aliens of their own volition, for whatever reason.
24. Quoted in Hutchinson (1981:219).
25. LeMay (1987:92), Reimers (1982:12).
26. Quoted in Morrison et al. (1983:407).
27. Divine (1957:66).
28. Dorsen et al. (1976:36, 55).
29. See Craig (1971), Reimers (1982), Calavita (1992).
30. The repeal of the Chinese Exclusion Act in 1943 was symbolic, and real numerical changes only came in 1965.
31. Kairys (1982:260).
32. U.S. Senate (1978:27).
33. Statement of Richard Feen, Special Consultant to the Office of the U.S. Coordinator for Refugee Affairs, quoted in Plender (1988:404).
34. United States 83rd Congress (1952:8083), Kraly (1990:79), Reimers (1982).
35. The parole power is technically that of the attorney general.
36. Reimers (1982:43).
37. LeMay (1987).
38. Over 200,000 Vietnamese came to America from 1975 to 1979, and after the "boat people" began to arrive in 1979, the administration committed itself to taking in 168,000 more refugees in 1980 (Reimers, 1982:41).
39. U.S. Congress, The Select Commission on Immigration and Refugee Policy (1981:44).
40. Kraly (1990).
41. *Migration News* 4(4–6), April–June 1997.
42. Before the IIRIRA, foreigners living unlawfully or in a Temporary Protected Status in the United States for more than seven years could apply to remain on grounds that their deportation would cause undue hardship to themselves or their U.S. families. Under IIRIRA, foreigners must live ten or more years in the United States, their deportation must cause "exceptional and extremely unusual hardship" to U.S. citizen or legal immigrant spouses, children, or parents, and there is an annual limit of 4,000 such adjustments per year (*Migration News* 4(8), August 1997).
43. *Migration News* 4(2–12), February–December 1997.
44. *Migration News* 4(1), January 1997; 4(9), September 1997; and 5(9–12), September–December 1998.

45. *Migration News* 6(8), August 1999.
46. *Migration News* 4(12), December 1997; 5(3), March 1998; 6(6), June 1999.
47. *Washington Post Weekly Edition*, July 4–10, 1994; *The Economist*, July 16, 1994.
48. *Migration News* 4(9), September 1997 and *Migration News* 5(11), November 1998.
49. The fear of growing Latin American immigration and changes in U.S. foreign policy priorities contributed to the restrictions on Western Hemisphere immigration.
50. LeMay (1987:115).
51. United States 88th Congress (1964:418).
52. *Migration News* 3(12), December 1996 and *Migration News* 4(2), February 1997.
53. *Migration News* 4(4), April 1997.
54. On U.S. policies with regard to highly skilled labor see Lowell (1999).
55. Calavita (1995:74–75); *Migration News* 5(9), September 1998.
56. *Migration News* 5(5), May 1998.
57. The policy of increasing the number of H-1B visas also generated substantial opposition. In 1997, e.g. the U.S. Department of Commerce released a report that concluded: "the emergence of a world-wide shortage of information technology (IT) workers indicates that US employers cannot rely on increased immigration or even outsourcing to foreign countries to meet any significant IT skill shortages. Instead, the United States—as well as other industrialized countries—will be forced to rely on policies and strategies directed at educating, training, and retraining their domestic work forces in IT skills." Other critics of the H-1B program, such as Professor Norm Matloff, of the University of California, Davis, have argued: (a) the employers have inflated the shortage estimates; (b) very selective hiring and overspecification of required skills, rather than the lack of programmers, is behind claims of programmer shortages; (c) U.S. employers, especially in the high-tech computer industry, misuse the H-1B program by asking for immigrants who are already working—sometimes illegally—for the employer, which files the petition on his behalf; and (d) American businesses bring in foreign skilled workers after having laid off skilled American workers, simply because they can get the foreign workers more cheaply (*Migration News* 4(10)–5(3), October 1997–March 1998).
58. *Migration News* 5(11–12), November–December 1998; and 8(3–8), March–August 2001.
59. The following section briefly deals with policy on foreign farm workers. For an in-depth discussion of this issue see Martin (1984, 1999, 2002) and Martin et al. (1995).
60. Martin (1999:179, 199).
61. *Migration News* 9(11) and 9(12) of November–December 2002.

62. As Briggs notes, the problems of determining the number of illegal immigrants are monumental. He further emphasizes several problems associated with using the number of illegal immigrants apprehended as an indicator of the magnitude of illegal immigration. But despite these gross deficiencies of the data on the apprehension of illegal immigrants, the U.S. General Accounting Office (GAO) was forced to conclude in 1982 that the apprehension statistics constitute the most comprehensive data on illegal aliens available, and these statistics have played an important role in a variety of policy decisions (Briggs, 1984:131–34).
63. *Migration News* 4(3), March 1997. Previous estimates put the number of illegal immigrants living in the United States in the range of 3–4 million, and increasing by about 100,000–300,000 annually (see *Migration News* 1(4)–1(5), May and June 1994).
64. *Migration News* 9(9), September 2002; 10(1), January 2003.
65. *Migration News* 1(3), April 1994.
66. *Migration News* 2(1), January 1995; 2(2), February 1995; 4(4), April 1997; 4(12), December 1997; 5(4), April 1998; 6(8), August 1999.
67. Quoted in Briggs (1984:170).
68. *Migration News* 3(11), November 1996; 4(2), February 1997; 4(4), April 1997; 5(8), May 1998; 5(11), November 1998.
69. *Migration News* 4(3), March 1997; 4(12), December 1997; and 5(4–5), April–May 1998.
70. *Migration News* 4(2–3) of February and March 1997; 4(9) of September 1997; 4(12) of December 1997; 5(4) of April 1998; 5(8) of August 1998; and 6(6) of June 1999.
71. *Migration News* 1(6), July 1994; 1(10), November 1994; 4(2–11), February–November 1997.
72. The section dealing with the recent plans to legalize the status of illegal immigrants residing in the United States is based on *Migration News* 9(8)–9(12) of August–December 2002.
73. The section about the impact of the September 11 attacks on U.S. immigration policy is mostly based on *Migration News* 9(10), 9(11), and 9(12) of October–December 2002 and on the text of the *Homeland Security Act of 2002*, unless indicated otherwise.
74. Justice Department officials reported that if they find a foreigner suspected of terrorism who has committed immigration violations, they would move to deport him, since immigration violations are easier to prove than criminal charges (*Migration News* 9(12), December 2002).
75. *New York Times*, April 25, 2003.
76. *Washington Post*, October 25, 2002.
77. *New York Times*, November 25, 2002; United States, White House Press Release (2002).
78. United States Senate. 2002. *Homeland Security Act of 2002*, section 441.
79. United States Senate. 2002. *Homeland Security Act of 2002*, section 402.

80. It is important to remember that while permanent immigration to the United States in the late 1980s and early 1990s constitutes an all-time high in gross numbers, it is still much smaller in comparison to the turn-of-the-century immigration as a percentage of U.S. population.
81. In 1898, the United States annexed Hawaii and in 1900 it granted the residents of Hawaii citizenship. In 1898 the United States took the Philippines and Cuba from Spain. In 1905 the United States started to handle the financial affairs of the Dominican Republic.
82. Sassen (1996b:70–71).
83. Craig (1971:40–48, 151), Fitzgerald (1996:190, 218).
84. Bennett (1963:173). The 1952 Act was not a restrictive act per se, but rather mostly a codification of previous legislation. But in the debate that developed after World War II between the supporters of the quota act (i.e. the restrictionist) and those who advocated its repeal (the pro-immigration group), the 1952 Act reflected the restrictionist stand.
85. Bennett (1963:179–80).
86. Bennett (1963:187).
87. While these examples provide some support for the argument with regard to the impact of wartime social conformity on pro-immigration liberals and ethnic groups, the argument should be further explored.
88. *New York Times*, July 28, 1993; *Newsweek*, August, 9, 1993.
89. See Zloberg (1983:28).
90. It is extremely difficult to define the main social conflicts in American history. In discussions I conducted with several scholars of American politics, it was agreed that the Civil War and the civil rights movement fit the definition of a social conflict. Other periods suggested included the 1770s, 1890s, 1920s–1930s, and 1980s.
91. The termination of the Bracero program in 1964, and the 1965 amendment that applied quantitative restrictions to the Western Hemisphere, restricted immigration. But the latter, and to some extent also the former, were part of a legislative package that generally liberalized immigration policy. Moreover, to the best of my knowledge there is no indication that the social conflicts of the 1960s contributed to any of these policy changes.
92. Higham (1988:6–7). In addition, one long-term effect of the Civil War was to consolidate federal government control over immigration policy. But this did not necessarily produce a restrictive policy: during the decade that followed the Civil War, immigration policy was notably liberal.
93. A bill by Representative Seaman to prevent the immigration of criminals and paupers died in committee in 1847; Representative Levin failed to prevent an act protecting immigrants arriving on ships in 1847; Representative Levin's bill to extend the naturalization period to 21 years failed in late 1849 or early 1850 (Hutchinson, 1981:35–38).
94. LeMay (1987:33).
95. Higham (1988:7) does refer to this aspect, although in the context of the general crisis in the American society: "With the old parties dissolving and

the bonds of national unity strained to the breaking-point, the American Party offered a way of championing national homogeneity."

Chapter 3 Immigration Policies of Britain

1. Plender (1988:65–66).
2. Plender, ibid.
3. The similarity between the immigrants and the local population is stated in the Royal Commission on Population's report of 1949, quoted in Thomas Edward Smith (1981b:92). The foreign policy considerations are dealt with later.
4. Rees (1979:69–70).
5. Layton-Henry (1985:98).
6. Rees (1979:71).
7. Plender (1988:75).
8. Rees (1979:71).
9. Unemployment in 1905 was still low in comparison to what it was in the late 1880s or the 1920s and 1930s.
10. Layton-Henry (1985).
11. Rees (1979:72), Layton-Henry (1985:75–76).
12. Plender (1988:75–76).
13. During the December 1916–October 1922 period, Lloyd George of the Liberal Party served as prime minister, with a cabinet consisting largely of Conservatives.
14. Smith (1981b:91–92).
15. Layton-Henry (1989:61).
16. Foot (1965:116–18), Rees (1979:73–75), Smith (1981b:97), Layton-Henry (1989:61).
17. Foot (1965:118–19).
18. Foot (1965:124–26).
19. Layton-Henry (1989:61).
20. Layton-Henry (1989:65), Smith (1981b:101).
21. Great Britain, Office of Information (1987:1).
22. The policy was also changed so that no one Commonwealth country was to receive more than 15% of the vouchers issued in category A, thus eliminating any possibility of substantial direct recruitment of Indians and Pakistanis by industry (Smith, 1981b:108).
23. Layton-Henry (1985:93, 104), Solomos (1993:69), Hansen (2000:195).
24. Layton-Henry (1992:84–85), Solomos (1993), Steiner (2000:102), Hansen (2000:194).
25. Layton-Henry (1985), Smith (1981b).
26. Rees (1979:88), Studlar (1979:90), Layton-Henry (1992:53–54).
27. The influence of the two factors is elaborated on in the section "factors shaping British immigration policy—conclusions."

28. Great Britain, Office of Information (1987:16).
29. Layton-Henry (1992:86).
30. Layton-Henry (1992:58–59, 156).
31. Layton-Henry (1992:156–57).
32. The National Front gained 16.3% of the vote in the West Bromwich by-elections, although it fared poorly in the 1974 elections. In 1976, the National Front reached 15% in several May 1976 municipal elections, and secured a number of seats. And in 1977 it reached its peak, gaining 19.2% of the vote in the Bethnal Green and Bow County constituency in the elections to the Council of Greater London (Kitschelt, 1995; Hansen, 2000:223).
33. Layton-Henry (1992:94, 158, 183).
34. Smith (1981b:121–22).
35. Layton-Henry (1992:157).
36. See Messina (1989:128), Hansen (2000:211).
37. For details see Hansen (2000:232).
38. "Settled" is defined in Britain as being free from restrictions according to immigration laws (Plender, 1986:531).
39. Plender (1986:559).
40. Hansen (2000:230–31).
41. Mullins (1987:435–36), Layton-Henry (1992:205), Kaye (1994:151).
42. Layton-Henry (1989:71–73).
43. Steiner (2000:109), Kaye (1994:152).
44. Layton-Henry (1992:207).
45. Rogers (1992).
46. Freeman (1992).
47. Steiner (2000:118–19).
48. *Times*, March 14, 1995.
49. The tests are most frequently used for those coming from South Asia and Africa.
50. *The Guardian*, March 29, 1995; *Daily Telegraph*, June 16, 1995 and January 8, 1996; *Press Association Newsfile*, June 16, 1995; *Financial Times*, March 18, 1996.
51. *Migration News* 4(6), June 1997; 5(3), March 1998; Fiddick (1999).
52. *Guardian*, July 26, 1999.
53. *Migration News* 5(3)–6(4), March 1998–April 1999. With the return of Hong Kong to China in 1997, these rights applied to only 150,000–200,000 residents, and thus the government felt that immigration from these territories was not a threat.
54. *Migration News* 7(1), January 2000.
55. Fiddick (1999).
56. The description of the 1997–2000 measures is based on *Migration News* 4(9), September 1997; 4(12), December 1997; 5(1), January 1998; 5(5), May 1998; 5(11), November 1998; 6(1), January 1999; 7(2), February 2000; 7(9), September 2000; and 8(1), January 2001.

57. *Migration News* 5(8)–7(5), August 1998–May 2000.
58. Ireland has been the traditional source of migrant labor to Britain, even before joining the EU.
59. *Migration News* 2(4), April 1995; 6(12), December 1999; 8(10), October 2001.
60. *Migration News* 3(6), June 1996; 8(1), January 2001.
61. *Migration News* 7(6), June 2000.
62. *Migration News* 7(10), October 2000.
63. *Migration News* 9(1), January 2002.
64. *Migration News* 8(10), October 2001.
65. *Migration News* 7(6), June 2000; 8(4), April 2001.
66. *Migration News* 8(7), July; 8(10), October 2001.
67. As noted, the categories of asylum seekers and of illegal immigration sometimes overlap.
68. Home Office, *Immigration and Nationality Department Report* (1986) and *Runnymede Trust Bulletin*, no. 196 (1986). Quoted in Layton-Henry (1992:205).
69. Studlar (1979).
70. Money (1997:701–04).
71. Britain's joining the EU may have also contributed to the decline in the number of work permits issued to non-EU workers.
72. The Ugandan Indians were British citizens, and thus eligible to settle in Britain, but their arrival generated local opposition, and their immigration would have been blocked if not for humanitarian and foreign relations considerations. The Greek Cypriots refugees were admitted as short-term visitors, but later the time limit on their stay was removed.
73. According to the Office of Information data, these were the only countries whose citizens needed a visa in 1897 (Great Britain, Office of Information (1987:18); Smith (1981b:107)).
74. Center for Research and Ethnic Relations, quoted in *Socialist Review*, 1995.
75. *Financial Times*, October 27, 1995.
76. Cesarani and Kushner (1993).
77. What one may describe as British social conflicts and debates over national identity do not compare with those in the United States, Germany, or France. The 1936 abdication crisis, which shocked the British public and might be viewed as a debate over national identity, did not influence British immigration policies.

Chapter 4 Immigration Policies of the Netherlands

1. The section dealing with Dutch immigration policy until World War II is mostly based on Caestecker and Moore (1998) and on Fields (1932).
2. Pre–World War II emigration from the Netherlands exceeded immigration to that country between 1865–1874, 1880–1900, 1903–1913, 1919–1921, 1924–1925, and 1934–1944 (data from Mitchell 1992:145–52).

3. Entzinger (1985:54), Hoffmann-Nowotny (1985:209).
4. Kuijer and Steenbergen (1999:17), Bennekom et al. (2000).
5. Act of June 4, 1858; State Journal No. 46.
6. Art. 2 of the Royal Decree of July 27, 1887; State Journal No. 141.
7. Fields (1932:677), Caestecker and Moore (1998:61).
8. Lucassen (1998:51).
9. Data with regard to the volume of immigration is based on Mitchell (1992:148–54).
10. Accurate data with regard to unemployment rates is unavailable for the period prior to 1911. However, according to Thorp et al. (1926), the period 1898–1900 was one of prosperity.
11. Caestecker and Moore (1998:60–61).
12. Caestecker and Moore (1998:61–62).
13. Royal Decree of August 11, 1920 (State Journal No. 699), Royal Decree of December 12, 1922 (State Journal No. 671), and Art. 27 of the Regulations regarding Foreigners, amplifying Art. 438 of the Criminal Code, revised by the Royal Decree of March 31, 1922 (State Journal No. 164). Quoted in Fields (1932:677).
14. Caestecker and Moore (1998:62–65).
15. Fields (1932:677).
16. Caestecker and Moore (1998:66–67, 75–77).
17. Caestecker and Moore (1998:73–90).
18. Penninx et al. (1994), Beyer (1979:114), Vellinga (1993:148), Bovnekerk (1979:118).
19. Entzinger (1985:52; 1987:95), Penninx et al. (1994:9). Indonesia won its independence from the Netherlands in 1949. Refugees started arriving from New Guinea at the end of the 1950s when Indonesia announced its plans of annexation.
20. Penninx (1984:349).
21. Entzinger (1985:52), Penninx (1984:345–46), Penninx et al. (1994:9).
22. Bovenkerk (1979:119–21), Entzinger (1985:52), Penninx et al. (1994:9). By 1977, the Moluccans numbered 40,000.
23. Bennekom et al. (2000).
24. Penninx et al. (1994:9–10).
25. Entzinger (1985:64–66), Plender (1988:408–09). The Royal Decree of January 10, 1974 created an additional category of "persons entitled to asylum." These are persons who for humanitarian reasons cannot reasonably be required to return to their country of origin, considering the political situation there. Members of this group are also known as persons with "B" status, as opposed to persons admitted as refugees who have "A" status (Plender, 1988:413, 448, no. 157)
26. Bovenkerk (1979:128), Beyer (1979:117).
27. Penninx et al. (1994:172), Voerman and Lucardie (1992:37). Voerman and Lucardie argue that the Farmers Party had ambivalent attitudes toward parliamentary democracy, but was not an anti-immigration party.

28. Bovenkerk (1979:129).
29. According to SOPEMI (1983:59) data, the number of foreign workers in the Netherlands was 163,400 in 1974; 176,000 in 1975; 180,500 in 1976; 187,000 in 1977; 196,400 in 1978; and 182,300 in 1979. According to Entzinger (1985:60, 66), when recruitment dropped after 1973, jobseekers continued to come spontaneously and some were still granted the necessary permits after arrival (see also Beyer, 1979:117).
30. These included cases where (a) a sufficient supply of labor exists for the work concerned; (b) the maximum number of workers allotted to the enterprise is exceeded; (c) the worker originates from a country with which the Netherlands has not concluded an agreement on recruitment, and a sufficient supply of labor is available from the countries with which such agreements have been concluded; (d) the worker is under 18 or over 35 years of age; (e) there is no suitable housing available; and more (see Plender, 1986:531–32, 551; Plender, 1988:318).
31. WRR (*Wetenschappelijke Raad voor het Regeringsbeleid*), 1979, *Ethnic Minorities* (The Hugue: State Publishers), quoted in Entzinger (1985:64).
32. In addition, in November 1975, the government declared a general amnesty for illegal immigrants who could prove that they had resided and worked in the Netherlands for at least one year (Entzinger, 1985:66–67; Plender, 1986:553; Amersfoort, 1999:147). Some 15,000 former illegal immigrants took advantage of this opportunity, half of them Turks or Moroccans (Nicolaas and Sprangers, 2001:16).
33. Amersfoort (1999:149), Amersfoort and Penninx (1994:136), Vellinga (1993:154), Penninx (1986:965), Bovenkerk (1979:130).
34. Bovenkerk (1979:130–31).
35. Bennekom et al. (2000), Vellinga (1993:154), UN (1998:107).
36. Bovenkerk (1979:125).
37. De Vries (1981), Penninx (1984:350), Penninx et. al (1994:32), Amersfoort (1999:145).
38. Entzinger (1985:68).
39. Penninx (1984:346), Entzinger (1985:63–64).
40. Entzinger (1985:70–77; 1994:100), Penninx (1984:352–56); Pennix et al. (1994:160–61), Amersfoort (1999:136).
41. Penninx et al. (1994:166–67), Jacobs (1998:351). The modified law was introduced on January 1, 1985.
42. In August 1980, in reaction to a renewed flow of immigrants, the Dutch government required Surinamese to obtain visas in order to enter. Three months later, in November 1980, the Netherlands renewed its bilateral Settlement Treaty with Surinam, but the privileged position of Surinamese entrants was revoked (Entzinger, 1985:65; Amersfoort, 1999:149).
43. Entzinger (1985:64, 70), Amersfoort (1999:148).
44. Entzinger (1985:78), Amersfoort and Surie (1987).
45. This section is based on Entzinger (1985:83), Husbands (1988), Voerman and Lucardie (1992), and Penninx et al. (1994:173).

46. Nicolaas and Sprangers (2001:4–7). If family members (e.g. of a labor migrant) immigrate in the *same year* as the labor migrant, these family members are considered to be accompanying family members.
47. Amersfoort and Penninx (1994:135).
48. Nicolaas and Sprangers (2001:4–7).
49. Doomernik et al. (1997:28); *Migration News* 6(8), August 1999.
50. Amersfoort (1999:148), Doomernik et al. (1997:28), Kuijer (1993), Nicolaas and Sprangers (2001:4), SOPEMI (1998:141).
51. *Migration News* 6(8), August 1999; 6(1), January 1999.
52. SOPEMI (2001:213).
53. *Radio Netherlands*, June 14, 2002; *Economist*, July 4, 2002. The Center–Right coalition collapsed in October 2002, less than 100 days after taking power, when the List Pim Fortuyn party disintegrated.
54. 1996 was an exception, with only 22,200 immigrants applying for asylum.
55. *BBC News*, June 13, 2002.
56. Bennekom et al. (2000:1) note that some of the immigrant workers from Greece, Spain, and Portugal in the 1960s in fact were fleeing the dictatorial regimes of their countries of origin.
57. Amersfoort (1999:150), Doomernik et al. (1997:38).
58. Doomernik et al. (1997:38), Penninx et al. (1994:36).
59. Freeman (1992:1156), Doomernik et al. (1997:39), Amersfoort (1999: 151). In addition to these new acts and regulations, the growing restrictive character of Dutch asylum policy was also manifested by the rapid increase in the percentage of the visa applications refused: from 12.5% in 1986 to 46% in 1993, and 40% in 1994 (Doomernik et al., 1997:34).
60. SOPEMI (2001:309).
61. The description of the 1994 policies is based on data from *Migration News* 1(4), May 1994; 1(5), June 1994; 2(2), February 1995; 3(11), November 1996; Doomernik et al. (1997:34–39), USCR (1997, 1998), Muus (1997), *IRR News*, May 1, 1994, and Bennekom et al. (2000:4). The same year, the Netherlands also enacted the General Equal Treatment Act of March 2, 1974—the main provision in the general law against racial discrimination (ECRI, 1998).
62. Amersfoort (1999:151–53).
63. See table 4.3 and Muus (1997).
64. Doomernik et al. (1997:34). While the Act was being debated in Parliament, The Dutch Refugee Council estimated that as many as 40% of all new asylum seekers would not be allowed to apply under it (*Migration News*, 2(2), February 1995).
65. *Migration News* 4(1), January 1997; 5(12), December 1998. In December 1998, the Dutch parliament voted to remove deportation bans on the removal of rejected asylum seekers to northern Iraq, northern Sudan, and parts of Somalia. In contrast, the Netherlands introduced automatic bans on the return of rejected asylum seekers from the Democratic Republic of

Congo and Angola, and banned the deportation of ethnic Albanians from Kosovo (USCR, 1999).

66. *Sri Lanka Monitor*, September 1997. The Dutch Foreign Affairs Minister concluded that the situation in Colombo is safe for Tamils, and quoting the UNHCR, he argued that those repatriated from other European nations in 1996 and 1997 encountered no problem in Sri Lanka.
67. SOPEMI (1998:143–44), Bennekom et al. (2000:4).
68. The following description of the 1997–2000 measures is based on data from *Migration News* 4(12), December 1997; and 8(8), August 2001; SOPEMI (1998:143; 1999:182), and USCR (1999, 2000).
69. According to Vink (2001:14), the basic principles of the Aliens Act 2000 were already laid down in the 1998 government coalition agreement between the Labor Party (PVDA), the Liberal Party (VVD), and the Democrats (D66).
70. SOPEMI (2001:77, 213), Nicolaas and Sprangers (2001:3), *Migration News* 7(5), May 2000, USCR (2001).
71. *Radio Netherlands*, June 14, 2002.
72. *Migration News* 5(10), October 1998, Autonoom (2000), *Radio Netherlands*, June 14, 2002.
73. SOPEMI (2001:214).
74. *Migration News* 7(11), November 2000.
75. Autonoom (2000).
76. Bennekom et al. (2000:2). Also according to Muus (1998): "The majority of asylum seekers who have to depart from the country, leave only their registered address, while their destination remains unknown. Partly they will have left the country for other (European) destinations, but a growing number of asylum seekers who have lost their case go into hiding and continue their stay in the Netherlands illegally."
77. *Radio Netherlands*, June 14, 2002, Autonoom (2000), *Migration News* 3(8), August 1996.
78. *Migration News* 2(2), February 1995.
79. According to *Migration News* 2(2), February 1995 and *Migration News* 7(2), February 2000, legalization according to the "six-year rule" started in 1993/1995. But according to Autonoom (2000), an unwritten rule on that matter already existed for almost 20 years, a result of small legalization campaigns in the 1980s.
80. Autonoom (2000).
81. Ibid.
82. Amersfoort and Penninx (1994:145).
83. Amersfoort (1999:160–61).
84. *Migration News* 1(5) of June 1994 and 2(2) of February 1995, USCR (1997, 1998), Amersfoort (1999:161), Autonoom (2000).
85. *Migration News* 3(8), August 1996.
86. Amersfoort (1999:160–63), Doomernik et al. (1997:52), Bennekom et al. (2000:5), USCR (1999). On October 7, 1998, a court in The Hague ruled

that the linkage law contravenes the 1953 European Convention on Social and Medical Assistance. The Ministry of Social Affairs appealed the decision (USCR, 1999).

87. *Christian Science Monitor*, October 21, 1997.
88. *Migration News* 4(12), December 1997, SOPEMI (1998:143).
89. *Migration News* 5(5), May 1998, USCR (1999).
90. SOPEMI (2001:214).
91. *Migration News* 7(11), November 2000.
92. *Migration News* 8(1), January 2001.
93. SOPEMI (2001:77), *Radio Netherlands*, June 14, 2002.
94. *Migration News* 8(6), June 2001.
95. Nicolaas and Sprangers (2001:7, 19), *Migration News* 7(5), May 2000, SOPEMI (2001:213).
96. Nicolaas and Sprangers (2001), SOPEMI (2001:213).
97. SOPEMI (2001:213), The Netherlands, Central Bureau of Statistics (2002a).
98. SOPEMI (2001:210–12), The Netherlands, Central Bureau of Statistics (2002a,b).
99. This section is based on Husbands (1988), Voerman and Lucardie (1992), Penninx et al. (1994:173), Stephen Roth Institute (1999), and *Migration News* 1(6), June 1994.
100. J. van Donselaar attributed the losses of the extreme-right to changes in the law on voting (Stephen Roth Institute, 1999).
101. *Migration News* 9(8–11) of August–November 2002. The growing anti-immigrant feelings were also reflected outside Parliament: while in 1980 there were only 22 cases reported of harassment and violence against immigrants, in 1994 there were more than 1,000 such incidents (Van Donselaar, 1996:7–10, quoted in Amersfoort, 1999:159).
102. Amesfoort and Surie (1987:174).
103. See Bovenkerk (1979), Entzinger (1985), Doomernik et al. (1994:10), Amersfoort (1999).
104. In 1965, between 83 and 100% of immigrants from the Mediterranean area were male. In contrast, by 1985, only 51% of the new immigrants from Turkey and 47% of those from Morocco were men (Penninx et al., 1994:44–45).
105. *Nota buitenlandse werknemers* (1970:6), quoted in Amersfoort and Surie (1987:178).
106. The Memorandum on Aliens Policy, quoted in Entzinger (1985:64).
107. Entzinger (1985:59), Amersfoort and Penninx (1994:136–37), Amersfoort (1999:143). Amersfoort and Penninx argue that scarcely anyone grasped the impact on immigration of granting Dutch citizenship to the inhabitants of Surinam and the Netherlands Antilles.
108. Amersfoort (1999:135–36), Amersfoort and Penninx (1994:134).
109. Penninx et al. (1994:9).

110. Amersfoort (1999:143).
111. Penninx (1984:349).
112. Amersfoort (1999:150).
113. Amersfoort and Penninx (1994:134).
114. Amersfoort (1999:150).
115. Penninx et al. (1994:16).
116. *Migration News* 4(12) of December 1997 and 5(12) of December 1998.
117. Doomernik et al. (1997:26–27).
118. These immigrants, too, were referred to as "repatriates" (Doomernik et al., 1997:8).
119. Caestecker and Moore (1998:63–64).
120. Doomernik et al. (1997:56).
121. Caestecker and Moore (1998:61).
122. Rowen (1985).
123. *Economist*, January 6, 2003.
124. Voerman and Lucardie (1992).
125. *Economist*, January 6, 2003.
126. Vellinga (1993:149).

Chapter 5 Immigration Policies of Germany

1. According to the 1910 census, out of the 1,259,873 foreigners residing in Germany, 667,159 were from Austria-Hungary; 144,175 from the Netherlands; 137,697 from Russia; and 104,204 from Italy (Herbert, 1990:21).
2. Esser and Korte (1985:166), Katzenstein (1987:211).
3. Esser and Korte (1985:166), Herbert (1990:20, 93).
4. Herbert (1990:93–94).
5. Herbert (1990:100–06).
6. Herbert (1990:121–23).
7. Herbert (1990:127–28), Martin (1995:197), *Migration News* 2(5), May 1995.
8. Herbert (1990:128). The Nazi regime did force or encourage the departure of certain ethnic groups.
9. Ethnic German expellees numbering 430,000 were absorbed by Austria.
10. Münz (2001:7800–01), Rudolph (1994:115), Reimann and Reimann (1979:63), Esser and Korte (1985:169).
11. Münz (2001:7801).
12. Münz (2001:7801), Rudolph (1994:115).
13. Martin (1995:198).
14. Westle and Niedermayer (1992:84–85).
15. Miller and Martin (1982), Martin (1995).
16. Miller (1986:71).
17. Esser and Korte (1985:170, 178), Plender (1986:550).

18. Plender, ibid., Herbert (1990:231), Rudolph (1994:121).
19. Arendt, "Ausländische Arbeiter sind kein Ballast," *Süddeutsche Zeitung*, March 30, 1971, quoted in Herbert (1990:230–31).
20. German *Bundestag*, seventh session, January 18, 1973:11, quoted in Herbert (1990:234).
21. Mehrländer (1979).
22. "Italiener in der deutschen Industrie—Ergebnis eines Experiments," *Frankfurter Allgemeine Zeitung*, October 21, 1959, quoted in Herbert (1990:211).
23. Esser and Korte (1985:170), Herbert (1990:214–15), Joppke (1999:67).
24. Hoskin and Fitzgerland (1989:98).
25. Martin (1995:201), Esser and Korte (1985:180).
26. Herbert (1990:231).
27. Herbert (1990:233), Esser and Korte (1985:180, 194), O'Brien (1996:53).
28. Herbert (1990:222, 225).
29. "Unbeliebte Gastarbeiter," *Abendzeitung Nürnberg*, May 5, 1966, quoted in Herbert (1990:226–27).
30. Westle and Niedermayer (1992:84–85).
31. Herbert (1990:228).
32. Münz et al. (1997:40–42), Martin (1998a:492).
33. Esser and Korte (1985:182), Herbert (1990:248), O'Brien (1996:51, 54).
34. Herbert (1990:248–49), O'Brien (1996:55).
35. In the "Indian Case" the court ruled that an Indian whose residence permit had been renewed since 1961 could not simply be denied further renewal; after that time, authorities had to justify the refusal to renew residence permits of established foreigners (Joppke, 1998; *Migration News* 5(7), July 1998).
36. Joppke (1999:73).
37. O'Brien (1996:55–56), Herbert (1990:249).
38. Esser and Korte (1985:183).
39. Plender (1988:315), Herbert (1990:247–48), O'Brien (1996:51).
40. Esser and Korte (1985:186).
41. The 1990 reform of the Aliens Act abolished the one-year waiting period for the spouses of second-generation foreigners, but also made it more difficult for new entrants to acquire residence and family unification rights (*Migration News* 5(7), July 1998).
42. Quoted in O'Brien (1996:87).
43. Martin (1995:203–04), O'Brien (1996:81–83), Thrändhardt (1996:212).
44. The foreign population does not include the ethnic Germans, who gained German citizenship upon arrival.
45. Martin (1995:189–90).
46. Martin (1995).
47. UNHCR (2001:145, 155).
48. Plender (1986:558).

49. Katzenstein (1987:233).
50. Data with regard to the restrictive measures is based on Katzenstein (1987:232), Thränhardt (1996:212–13), O'Brien (1996:85), Martin (1995:193, 213–14), UNHCR (2001:61), *New York Times*, May 27, 1993, Freeman (1992:1156), Rudolph (1994:123), and Angenendt (1997).
51. The section about German policy toward Bosnian asylum seekers/refugees is based on Thränhardt (1999:41–42) and on *Migration News* 3(1–10), January–October 1996. The section about German policy toward Kosovar asylum seekers is based on *Migration News* 5(4), April 1998; 5(9), September 1998; 6(7), July 1999; 6(10), October 1999; 7(4), April 2000. The section about the liberalization of immigration policy with regard to Bosnian and Kosovar asylum seekers/refugees during 2000–2001 is based on EFMS (2001) and on *Migration News* 7(12), December 2000; 8(3), March 2001; 8(4), April 2001; 8(7), July 2001.
52. The number of asylum seekers originating from the former Yugoslavia was: 74,900 in 1991; 115,400 in 1992; 73,500 in 1993; 30,400 in 1994; 34,500 in 1995; 24,800 in 1996; 31,000 in 1997; 35,000 in 1998; and 31,500 in 1999. Only in 1996 did the number of asylum applicants from Turkey surpass that from the former Yugoslavia, and in 1993 the number of asylum applicants from Romania approximately equaled that from the former Yugoslavia. In all other years, the former Yugoslavia was the main source of asylum seekers to Germany (UNHCR, 2001:32, 61, 101).
53. There were also 50,000–70,000 Croatian refugees in Germany. But most of them return home at a relatively early stage (*Migration News* 3(3), March 1996).
54. Under German law, the sixteen interior ministers have considerable discretion in arranging for the return of Bosnians (*Migration News* 3(3), March 1996).
55. Bavaria was the first state to forcibly repatriate Bosnians, starting in 1997 (*Migration News* 9(9), September 2002).
56. *Migration News* 7(7), July 2000; 8(11), November 2001.
57. Thränhardt (1999:44).
58. Martin (1995:194–95).
59. The quotes of politicians' statements with regard to the need to limit illegal immigration are from *Migration News* 4(9), September 1997; 5(1), January 1998; 5(5), May 1998; 5(9), September 1998; 7(4), April 2000; 8(7), July 2001; 9(7), July 2002.
60. *Migration News* 2(2), February 1995.
61. Data with regard to the 1994–1998 laws that restricted the number of asylum seekers/illegal immigrants is based on *Migration News* 1(5), June 1994; 1(6), July 1994; 4(12), December 1997; 5(2), February 1998; 5(6), June 1998.
62. Data on the attempts to block illegal immigration coming though its eastern borders is based on *Migration News* 3(1), January 1996; 4(7), July 1997;

5(6), June 1998; 5(10), October 1998. This immigration included not only Eastern Europeans, but also immigrants from Third World countries (e.g. Afghanistan and Sri Lanka) who arrive though Eastern Europe.

63. Data on German–Polish cooperation is based on *Migration News* 2(5), May 1995; 4(5), May 1997; 4(12), December 1997; 6(2), February 1999.
64. The Union allows for greater freedom of movement among its member states at the cost of a tighter boundary around all of them (*Radio Free Europe*, January 9, 2001).
65. In April 1998, the Austrian interior minister threatened to withdraw support for the entry of the Czech Republic and Hungary unless they tightened visa requirements and border controls (*Migration News* 5(6), June 1998).
66. Martin (1995:194–95).
67. Plender (1988:315–16).
68. *Migration News* 4(2), February 1997; 4(12), December 1997; 7(2), February 2000; 8(6), June 2001.
69. Hönekopp (1997:173).
70. Martin (1998:27).
71. Rudolph (1994:14).
72. *Migration News* 8(12), December 2001.
73. This sum was later revised to $140 million, paid to the returning Vietnamese and to the Vietnam government.
74. *Migration News* 1(8), September 1994; 2(2), February 1995; 2(5), May 1995; 2(7), July 1995; 2(12), December 1995; 3(6–8), June–August 1996; 4(1), January 1997.
75. Münz (2001:7802).
76. Münz (2001:7802), Martin (1995:215–16), Rudolph (1994:118).
77. Only in 1967–1969 did *Aussiedler* migration from Czechoslovakia outnumber that from Poland.
78. Some of these ethnic Germans will still be able to immigrate legally into Germany within the framework of family unification (Münz, 2001:7803; *Migration News* 10(1), January 2003).
79. Some of those who fail the test later come to Germany as family members of someone who successfully claimed *Aussiedler* status (Münz, ibid.).
80. Münz (2001:7802–03); Martin (1995:216–17); Thränhardt (1996:215); *Migration News* 3(2–8), February–August 1996; 3(12), December 1996; 4(3), March 1997; 4(8), August 1997; 5(1–3), January–March 1998; 6(12), December 1999; 7(7–8), July–August 2000; 10(1), January 2003
81. SOPEMI (2001:170), *Migration News* 5(2), February 1998; 7(2), February 2000.
82. The section dealing with the debate over the employment of EU labor in the German construction industry is based on Thränhardt (1999:43) and on *Migration News* 1(8), September 1994; 2(1), January 1995; 2(7), July 1995; 2(12), December 1995; 3(1–12), January–December 1996; 4(1–12),

January–December 1997; 5(7), July 1998; 6(7), July 1999; 7(2), February 2000.

83. SOPEMI (1999:292; 2001:320).
84. Starting in 1991, the European Commission advanced a proposal (COM(91)230, later amended to COM(93)225), which would ensure that EU workers seeking employment in other EU nations would receive the same pay and conditions as local employees as of the first day they are employed abroad. The proposal was opposed by the United Kingdom, Ireland, and Portugal, but it gained additional support due to German complaints of "social dumping" in its construction industry. I deal with this topic elsewhere (Meyers, forthcoming (a)).
85. According to one employer's calculation, the total cost of employing a German construction worker was $57 per hour, about four times the cost of a Portuguese worker (*Migration News* 2(7) of July 1995). According to *Migration News* 2(12) of December 1995, the Portuguese earn about DM8–10 per hour, the Poles earn about DM4 per hour, while the British workers earn an hourly wage comparable to the Germans of DM30 per hour. According to *Migration News* 3(7) of July 1996, British and Irish workers were earning between DM22 and 35 an hour and getting twice what they would at home, but far less than the DM65 labor cost of a German. Thränhardt (1999:43) estimated that a German construction worker earned about 20DM per hour and cost the employer about 40DM per hour, probably more than twice the cost of a foreign worker.
86. Estimates with regard to the number of unemployed German construction workers vary between 140,000 and 400,000.
87. The subcontracting agreements had already started in the early 1980s.
88. Martin (1998:27–29), Martin (1995:217–220), Hönekopp (1997), Rudolph (1994:124–25).
89. According to Martin (1995, 1998) their numbers were over 128,000 during 1991, about 200,000 in 1992 and 1993, and 150,000 in 1994.
90. The programs are reciprocal, but almost no German workers have gone to one of the neighboring eastern countries participating in the program.
91. According to Hönekopp's revised calculation (1997:174–75), East Europeans as percentage of total foreign were 11.8% in 1992, 10.8% in 1993 and 9.5% in 1994.
92. According to Hönekopp's revised calculation (1997:174–75), they constituted 1.1% of the total employees in 1992 and 0.9% in 1994.
93. Hönekopp (1997).
94. *Migration News* 4(10) and 4(11), October–November 1997.
95. *Migration News* 7(4), April 2000.
96. *Migration News* 7(6), June 2000.
97. Similar transition periods were also implemented with regards to several other states that joined the EC/EU in earlier periods, such as Portugal and Spain.

98. *Migration News* 8(12), December 2001; 9(1), January 2002.
99. *Migration News* 7(4–11), April–November 2000; 8(6–9) June–September 2001; 10(2), April 2003.
100. See Meyers (forthcoming, (b)).
101. *Migration News* 7(4–6), April–June 2000; 8(2–3), February–March 2001.
102. In comparison, the United States issued more than 10,000 six-year H-1B visas a month during recent years.
103. *Migration News* 7(8), August 2000; 7(11–12), November–December 2000; 8(2–9), February–September 2001; 8(11), November 2001; 9(1–5), January–May 2002; 10(2) April 2003.
104. *Migration News* 7(4–12), April–December 2000; 8(2–4), February–April 2001.
105. Martin (1995:213).
106. *Migration News* 6(8), August 1999; 7(4), April 2000; 7(8), August 2000; 7(11), November 2000; 8(1), January 2001; 8(3), March 2001; 8(9), September 2001.
107. This section is based on data from *Migration News* 1(4), May 1994; 1(7), August 1994; 2(1), January 1995; 2(6), June 1995; 3(4), April 1996; 3(5), May 1996; 3(12), December 1996; 4(5), May 1997; 4(12), December 1997; 5(6), June 1998; 6(2), February 1999; 6(3), March 1999; 6(6), June 1999; 6(9), September 1999; 8(6), June 2001.
108. *Migration News* 4(12), December 1997.
109. This book generally deals with immigration control policy rather than with citizenship policy. The latter is also influenced by partisan factors to a greater degree than the former, for reasons explained in Meyers (forthcoming (b)). Nevertheless, I do describe here the changes in Germany's citizenship policy because of their link to its immigration control policy, and particularly to the concept, which prevailed until recently, that Germany "is not a country of immigration."
110. Brubaker (1992).
111. The differentiation between ethnic Germans and other foreigners still exists. However, during the 1990s, Germany restricted the migration of ethnic Germans, while liberalizing citizenship policy with regard to other foreigners residing in Germany.
112. *Migration News* 3(8), August 1996, Martin (1995:209).
113. SOPEMI (1999:265).
114. Between 1973 and 1994, about 1.5 million foreigners became German citizens, but 1.1 million of them were ethnic Germans (*Migration News* 1(5), June 1994; 3(8), August 1996; Martin 1995:196; Brubaker, 1987).
115. Martin (1995:209–10), O'Brien (1996:94), *Migration News* 3(8), August 1996.
116. The Center for Turkish Studies in Essen. Summarized in *Migration News* 1(10), November 1994.
117. *Migration News* 3(8), August 1996.
118. *Migration News* 2(2), February 1995.

119. *Migration News* 1(5), May 1994; and 1(10), November 1994, O'Brien (1996:113).
120. *Migration News* 5(11), November 1998.
121. The description of the reform in the citizenship law is based on *Migration News* 5(11), November 1998; 6(2), February 1999; 6(4), April 1999; 6(6), June 1999.
122. German women average only 1.35 children.
123. *Migration News* 4(3), March 1997; 7(11), November 2000; 8(5), May 2001.
124. According to the 1993 paper, this could be achieved with: (a) annual quotas on immigration that would not discriminate on the basis of the country of origin; (b) once the immigrants arrived in Germany, they would have to be integrated in a process that involves mutual adaptation and respect; (c) permanent immigrant status should be granted after five years of residence (*Migration News* 1(4), May 1994).
125. The description of the 2002 immigration law is based on *Migration News* 8(9), September 2001; 8(12), December 2001; 9(1), January 2002; 9(4–5), April–May 2002; 10(1), January 2003.
126. The bill was approved in the *Bundesrat* with representatives of the state of Brandenburg casting both yes and no votes.
127. *Migration News* 8(3), March 2001; 8(11), November 2001; 9(1), January 2002; 9(4), April 2002; 10(1), January 2003; 10(2), April 2003.
128. *Migration News* 8(6), June 2001.
129. This section is based on data from *Migration News* 8(10), October 2001; 8(11), November 2001; 9(1), January 2002; 9(4), April 2002.
130. Data on extreme-right parties in Germany is mostly based on Veen et al. (1993:11–12). Additional sources include: Husbands (1988:711–20; 1992:275–77), Ignazi (1992:17), Westle and Niedermayer (1992:86), Jackman and Volpert (1996:520), EREPS (2002), and *Migration News* 1(10), November 1994; 5(5), May 1998; 5(6), June 1998.
131. Arzheimer (2002).
132. As is usually the case, it could be argued that the supply of legal and illegal foreign labor caused the employers to reduce wages, and that if foreign labor was unavailable, wages would increase enough for Germans to seek employment in some of these sectors.
133. *Migration News* 7(4), April 2000.
134. Martin (1998b:29).
135. Based on data from Hönekopp (1997:174–75) for the years 1989–1994.
136. See Meyers (forthcoming (a)),
137. The foreign worker programs initiated in the early 1990s also include measures aimed at preventing the immigration of East European foreign workers from turning permanent. But these measures were already included in the programs when they were initiated.
138. See Herbert (1990:226–27).
139. Martin (1975:202).

140. Thränhardt (1996:204, 208–09).
141. O'Brien (1996:84). According to Thränhardt (1996:208), the association treaty, which would have provided for free labor movement up to 1986, was not implemented because of the rising unemployment in Western Europe since 1974. But it does not seem feasible to cut down severely the numbers of Turks under existing treaties and political relations.
142. *Migration News* 9(6), June 2002.
143. Hönekopp (1997:171).
144. Martin (1998:27).
145. Martin (1995:193).
146. Rudolph (1994:122–23).
147. Thränhardt (1996:212), Faist (1994:57).
148. *Financial Times*, October 6, 1992. Quoted in Martin (1995:193).
149. *Migration News* 1(9), October 1994.
150. While unemployment rates were relatively high, some scholars, nevertheless, argue that Germany needed the ethnic German refugees for economic reasons. Rudolph (1994:117) writes: "The successful integration of millions of refugees from the East during the first decade after World War II has sometimes been referred to as the genuine economic miracle of Germany. However, there was no magic at all. The specific framework for this growth scenario was a perfect matching of the structure of opportunities and economic incentives, on the one hand, with the skills and attitudes of individuals on the other. In contrast to popular reviews, the production capacity of West German industry that had been enlarged enormously during the war was only marginally reduced by bombs. The most serious bottleneck in the early postwar period was labor, and in this situation the German refugees were an important economic resource."
151. Münz (2002:7801–02).
152. Gugel (1990:118 ff.), quoted in Thränhardt (1996:214).
153. *Migration News* 5(2), February 1998; 7(8), August 2000; 8(7), July 2001.
154. *Migration News* 3(3) and 3(4), March–April 1996; Thränhardt (1999:36–38).
155. Martin (1975:202).
156. See Thränhardt (1996), O'Brien (1996).

Chapter 6 Global Patterns in Immigration Control Policy

1. Between 1894 and 1897, the Congress of the United States increased the head tax and attempted to pass the literacy test (both measures were aimed at limiting impoverished immigration from Eastern Europe); the Australian states of New South Wales, Western Australia, and Tasmania introduced a dictation test in order to restrict Japanese immigration, while Queensland signed an agreement with Japan for the same purpose (Charteris, 1927); the House of Lords in Britain passed bills aimed at limiting Eastern

European Jewish immigration; Canada passed the Alien Labor Act; and Sweden required aliens to register every year (Field, 1932:680).

Between 1905 and 1908, the United States, Australia, and Canada limited Japanese immigration; Australia started employing the "white Australia policy," which used administrative means to restrict immigration, and repatriated the Kanakas; the Canadian Parliament passed several laws restricting the immigration of indigent and diseased persons; Britain passed the Aliens Immigration Act; France attempted to regulate the inflow of migrant labor; and Germany strengthened the control on Polish workers and reinstated compulsory rotation.

2. Receiving countries limited permanent immigration: Britain passed the Aliens Restriction Act the day following the outbreak of the war; the United States passed acts that introduced the literacy test and authorized the president to control the entry of persons whose presence was deemed to endanger public safety; Australia banned German immigration until 1925; and several countries introduced passport and visa requirements. Receiving countries also restricted former immigrants in various ways: Britain and Australia interned German immigrants; the United States and the state of South Australia changed German place-names; and Sweden passed the Deportation Act of 1914 and deported immigrants.
3. The United States implemented the first Bracero migrant labor program; Germany forced Poles, Hungarians, and Belgians to work in its war economy; and France recruited migrant workers (including colonial ones). In addition, colonial seaman were employed in Britain, and formed settlements in several port cities during World War I (Layton-Henry, 1985:91).
4. Between 1919 and 1924, most of the receiving countries restricted immigration: the United States passed the 1921 and 1924 national origins quota act, deported communist immigrants, created the Border Police, and ended the first Bracero program; Australia implemented administrative quota restrictions on immigrants from Southern Europe; Britain passed the 1919 Aliens Restriction Act, which reaffirmed the 1914 act of the same name; Germany deported Polish workers and closed the frontier to potential migrant workers; Canada prohibited the immigration of Mennonites, Doukhbours, Hutterites, and most East Indians, effectively barred Asian immigration, and required visas; the Netherlands applied strict registration requirements to aliens; and Switzerland raised the minimum residency for naturalization from two to six years.
5. However, Sweden required aliens to obtain a labor permit in 1927, and American consular officers began denying visas to most Mexicans in August 1928.
6. The United States deported and encouraged the voluntary departure of Mexicans, restricted Filipino immigration, used administrative means to deny entry to impoverished Mexicans and Europeans, applied the contract labor laws to small professional groups, and made illegal entry a punishable crime; Australia terminated the assisted passage program and strictly applied

the "white Australia policy"; Germany restricted the employment of migrant labor and closed the German–Polish frontier to such migrants; France curbed labor migration, placed a ceiling on the number of foreigners employed in certain professions and industrial sectors, imposed sanctions on employers of illegal migrant workers, offered financial incentives to foreigners who agreed to leave, and expelled Italian and Polish foreign workers; Canada prohibited the immigration of Asians; and Switzerland enacted the 1931 law on the residency and settlement of aliens (ANAG) and the parliamentary implementation order of 1933 (ANAV) (Hoffman-Nowotny and Killias, 1979:50).

7. Australia renewed the assisted passage program, Britain passed the 1937 Empire Settlement Act, and Nazi Germany recruited migrant labor.
8. On the one hand, several receiving countries expanded the recruitment of foreign labor: the United States established the Bracero program with Mexico and a migrant labor program with West Indian countries; Britain employed migrant workers from their colonies; Germany exploited forced and slave labor; and Sweden abolished work permit requirements for all Nordic nationals. On the other hand, the receiving countries strengthened their controls on permanent immigration, and some of them interned aliens from enemy countries: the United States added new deportable classes, passed the 1940 Alien Registration Act, authorized consular officers to refuse visas to aliens who endangered the public safety, and detained persons of Japanese origin in relocation centers; Britain announced a series of Aliens Orders and interned Jewish refugees from Europe; Australia interned enemy aliens; and France strengthened controls on immigrants and restricted the liberties of aliens in France. In contrast, Sweden accepted Scandinavian and Baltic refugees, and the United States repealed the Chinese Exclusion Act.
9. European policy during the same period can be divided into two phases. Between 1945 and 1955, Europe was still recovering from the war, and labor migration was still limited in scope. The exceptions were Sweden and Britain, which already recruited migrant workers prior to 1956. Most immigration during that period was of a permanent nature, including refugees from the former Netherlands East Indies to the Netherlands, East European German refugees to Germany, New Commonwealth immigrants to Britain and Algerians to France. France and to some extent Germany and Belgium attempted to facilitate the immigration of permanent immigrants of similar origin. During the second phase, between 1956 and 1972 (with the exception of 1966–1968), Western European countries recruited large numbers of migrant workers, mostly from Southern Europe and North Africa.
10. The number of work permits issued by the Netherlands, and the number of foreign workers in that country, continued to grow until 1978.
11. For example, the United States passed the 1986 Simpson-Mazzoli act (IRCA), expanded its Border Patrol along the border with Mexico, doubled

the number of its asylum officers, and introduced new procedures aimed at limiting the number of asylum seekers and making the process more efficient; Britain required visitors from several Asian and African countries to obtain visas; implemented the 1993 Asylum and Immigration Appeals Act, which gave officials greater capacity to prevent the filing of questionable claims and to deport those whose applications had been denied; and passed the Asylum and Immigration Act of 1996, which barred welfare benefits to asylum seekers who did not apply for asylum in the United Kingdom upon arrival; Australia tightened the process by which people already there might apply for asylum, took steps to curb illegal immigration, and cracked down on "sham marriages"; Canada reformed its asylum processing procedures, required refugee applicants to be fingerprinted and pay a fee, and stationed immigration officers at airports overseas; Germany set penalties on employers of illegal immigrants, and in 1993 it amended its constitution and passed a law that severely restricted asylum right; France imposed penalties on employers of illegal immigrants and deported such immigrants; Sweden made it more difficult to obtain political asylum, imposed a visa requirement on Cubans, and announced that it would refuse to accept asylum seekers from several Eastern European countries; the Netherlands passed legislation aimed at reducing the number of asylum seekers, has been detaining rejected asylum seekers until their deportation; and tightened its border controls against illegal immigration; and EU members adopted legislation that would prevent persons from applying for asylum if they entered via a safe third country.

12. For example, Australia introduced the Structured Selection Assessment System (SSAS) in 1973, the Numerically-Weighted Multi-Factor Assessment System (NUMAS) in 1979, and announced its intention to "shift away from some of the family category into the skilled area" in 1996; Canada introduced a point system in 1967, and unveiled a ten-year program to attract more business immigrants from Taiwan in 1994; the United States gave preference to skilled labor, professionals, and investors in the 1990 Immigration Act; and Britain created an entrepreneurial business immigration category in 1994 (Hawkins, 1991:105; Jenness, 1974; *Migration News* 1(7), August 1994; 1(5), June 1994). During recent years, Britain, Germany, the United States, and other countries have devised programs to recruit high-skill foreign workers for their IT industry.
13. See Meyers (1994), Meyers (forthcoming (a)).
14. Attempts by the ILO to effect immigration control policies with regard to migrant workers have failed. To some degree, the ILO influences policies on migrant workers already residing in the country of destination (e.g. social security, trade union membership, and cultural rights), but these relate to immigrant policy, rather than to immigration control policy.
15. Meyers (forthcoming (a)).
16. Plender (1988:69–70).

17. Plender (1988:74).
18. Layton-Henry (1992:31).
19. Doomernik et al. (1997:35).
20. IRR News, May 1, 1994; Doomernik et al. (1997:34).
21. Hawkins (1991:105, 144–45).
22. Haas (1992:3–4).
23. Hawkins (1991:101–02, 142).
24. The influence of epistemic communities on immigration policies does warrant further study.
25. The description of the world system theory is based on Wallerstein (1972, 1974a,b), Hopkins and Wallerstein (1982), Viotti and Kauppi (1987), Kondratieff (1979), Miller and Denemark (1993), and Petras (1981).
26. Morawska (1990), Sassen (1990), Petras (1981), Portes and Walton (1981).
27. Massey et al. (1993).
28. Sassen (1990:21).
29. Viotti and Kauppi (1987:416–18). See, e.g., Skocpol (1977) and Gourevitch (1978).
30. Brubaker (1992:22).
31. Zolberg (1981a,b).
32. Portes and Walton (1981:49–90), Castells (1975).
33. This hypothesis is explored only in the global context, and is not numbered according to the hypotheses in chapter 1.
34. Husbands (1988).
35. Miles and Kay (1994:23).
36. Zolberg (1989:414–15).
37. The British 1914 Aliens Restriction Act gave the Home Secretary powers to prohibit aliens from entering the country and to deport them; the Swedish Deportation Act of 1914 allowed the government to impose a regulatory system in emergency situations, which led to a series of expulsions; a revision of the Swiss federal constitution granted the federation the authority to control aliens; the Immigration Act of 1918 in the United States authorized the president to control the arrival and departure in time of war or national emergency of any persons whose presence was deemed contrary to public safety; and in the Netherlands, a central registration of foreigners was installed, and the executive obtained powers to intern aliens if they were threatening domestic order in 1918.
38. For example, Switzerland's emergency law was turned into a regular law in 1931–1934; Britain's 1914 Aliens Restriction Act was renewed in 1919 and served as the basis for immigration regulation (not including Commonwealth citizens) until 1971; and Sweden's wartime emergency measures were integrated and made more permanent by the 1927 Aliens Act. Passports and visa requirements, which were introduced in many receiving countries during World War I, became a permanent feature of immigration policy.
39. Grant (1916); London (1910 and 1946), quoted in Higham (1955:156, 172).

40. Gould (1920); Burr (1922); Huntington (1924), quoted in Higham (1955:273–74).
41. Congressional Record, May 11, 1952:5102. Quoted in Reimers (1982: 25–26).
42. Tobin (1989:49).
43. Australia's and Canada's skill- and language-based selection systems still retain, in practice, some preference for European immigrants.
44. Reimers (1982:33).
45. Much of Whitlam's statement also referred to foreign policy considerations. The Prime Minister's Foreign Policy Statement, House of Representatives, Canberra, May 24, 1973. Quoted in Hawkins (1991:94).
46. Studlar (1979:91), Layton-Henry (1992:83).
47. *New York Times*, October 18, 1991.
48. The degree to which trade and immigration are substitutes for one another is a matter of debate among economists. According to Collins et al. (1997), there has been little empirical research on the issue of whether trade and factor flows have in fact been substitutes, e.g., trade in goods is a substitute for the migration of labor. Using 700 data indicators from the United States and Europe between 1870 and 1940, they conclude that trade and migration were not substitutes in the North Atlantic economy and that policymakers did not treat them as substitutes (*Migration News* 5(2), February 1998).
49. Vernon Briggs (1995) divides U.S. immigration and trade policy into three periods: mass immigration and high tariffs from the 1780s until 1914; low immigration and high tariffs from 1914 until 1965; and mass immigration and low tariffs since 1965 (*Migration News* 5(2), February 1998). Also according to this division, U.S. trade and immigration policies did not coincide prior to 1914.
50. For the link between the state of the economy and trade policies see Gallarotti (1985) and McKeown (1983:89–91).
51. Britain recruited migrant workers prior to the rise in New Commonwealth immigration. The Netherlands, which also had a low unemployment rate, accepted refugees from Indonesia starting in 1946, and thus did not require migrant workers during the early postwar period.
52. Canada, too, admitted Ugandan Asians, Chileans, and Lebanese, in addition to the refugees from communist regimes. However, in accepting Ugandan Asians it followed Britain (see Kubat, 1993b:36).
53. The Ugandan Indians were British citizens, and thus eligible to settle in Britain. The Greek Cypriot refugees were admitted as short-term visitors, but later the time limit on their stay was removed.
54. The actual differentiation is between permanent dissimilar immigration and temporary dissimilar immigration. In addition, France and the Netherlands also accepted permanent immigration for reasons of foreign policy. Both these issues are dealt with later.
55. Money (1999).

56. See Ragin (1991:327–28).
57. LeMay (1987:7).
58. Higham (1955).
59. Tobin (1989:32).
60. Australia, National Population Inquiry Report of 1975:742.
61. Amersfoort (1999:135–36).
62. Germany has accepted Germans, Israel has accepted Jews, and France accepted Italian, Spanish, and Portuguese Catholics after World War II.
63. Britain accepted a large volume of permanent dissimilar immigration from the New Commonwealth due to foreign policy considerations.
64. The Netherlands accepted a large number of permanent immigrants from its colonies and former colonies, including 300,000 refugees from the Dutch East Indies/Indonesia between 1946–1962/1963, and 142,000 immigrants from Surinam and the Dutch Antilles between 1970 and 1980. These immigrants were Dutch citizens, who were granted Dutch nationality due to the Netherlands colonial policy, i.e., for foreign policy considerations. In addition, many of the refugees from the Dutch East Indies/Indonesia were culturally oriented toward the Netherlands, which facilitated their rapid assimilation into Dutch society, while other colonial immigrants (i.e. Moluccans and those from Surinam and the Dutch Antilles) were viewed as temporary. Between the early 1960s and 1973 the Netherlands also recruited migrant workers from Mediterranean countries, the number of which grew during this period by 133,000. After 1973 the number of Mediterranean immigrants continued to grow faster than that of immigrants from Surinam and the Dutch Antilles (except for 1975), but these were mostly family members of former migrant workers. In addition, Dutch employers recruited workers from other EEC/EC member states.
65. The United States had major migrant worker programs in 1917–1922 and in 1943–1963. But only in 1953–1961, was the annual number of temporary migrant workers larger than the number of permanent immigrants.
66. Colonial immigration is viewed here as foreign.
67. See Ragin (1991).

Chapter 7 Summary and Conclusions

1. See introduction, n. 9.
2. A third factor, which also influences immigration control policy to some degree, mostly as an intervening variable, is the political process leading to policymaking. I deal with this aspect elsewhere (Meyers, forthcoming (b)).
3. Foot (1965), Money (1997).
4. The continued preferential treatment given to Cuban immigrants is also the product of domestic pressures from Cubans living in the United States.
5. Surges in illegal immigration from Mexico also led to attempts to block such migration in the 1950s ("Operation Wetback"), 1974 (the amendment

to the Farm Labor Contractor Registration Act), 1986 (IRCA), and during the 1990s. But the fact that illegal immigration also undermines the sovereignty of the state, and on the other hand, the fact that Mexican immigration is becoming increasingly similar to U.S. population (the Hispanic community just turned into the largest ethnic minority in the country) differentiate between the case of illegal immigration and permanent legal immigration.

6. During the mid-nineteenth century, Germans and Irish were viewed by the predominantly WASP population as dissimilar, and attempts were made to restrict their immigration.
7. In Israel, doubts regarding the Jewish origins of some immigrants from the former USSR led to intensified screening of such immigrants and to pressures to restrict their immigration during the 1990s.
8. See, e.g. Hartigan (1992).
9. As long as the foreign workers do not play a leading role in the industrial unrest.
10. Vellinga (1993:149).
11. Castles and Kosack (1989).
12. This topic is dealt with only in this chapter, and not in the country chapters.
13. Callovi (1990, 1992), O'Keefee (1992), Feldblum (1994), Handoll (1995), Miles and Thränhardt (1995), Bigo (1996), Overbeek (1996), Brochmann (1996), Guild and Niessen (1996), Papademetriou (1996), Bourdouvalis (1997), Uçarer (1997), Muus et al. (1997), Guild (1998), MacLaughlin (1998), Lahav (1998), Koslowski (1998, 2000), Martin (1999), Geddes (2000a,b), Favell (2000).
14. Meyers (forthcoming (a)).
15. The Amsterdam Treaty was signed on October 2, 1997, and entered into force on May 1, 1999. The Schengen agreement included most EU member states. It served as a prototype for EU immigration control policies, and was later incorporated into the EU legal framework with the Treaty of Amsterdam.
16. Geddes (2000a:86–100).
17. European Council (2002), Statewatch (2002).
18. Geddes (2000b).
19. Bigo (1996), Huysmans (1995), Lavenex (2000).
20. Uçarer (1997:291).
21. European Union (1997: Art. 61).
22. European Commission (2002:4).
23. European Commission (2000:5).
24. See Carlier and Vanheule (1994), Feldblum (1994), Overbeek (1996), MacLaughlin (1998), Martin (1999), Geddes (2000a).
25. European Economic and Social Committee (2002:108).
26. Geddes (2000b), Lavenex (2000).
27. Amnesty International (2001).

28. *Radio Free Europe*, October 18, 1999.
29. Meyers (forthcoming (a)).
30. See *European Commission* (2002).
31. On the contrary, Yundt (1989) demonstrates that the Organization of American States only had a limited involvement with Central American refugee issues during the 1980s.
32. *Radio Free Europe*, June 18, 19, and 21, 2002.

Bibliography

Amersfoort, Hans van. 1999. "Migration Control and Minority Policy: The Case of the Netherlands," in Grete Brochmann and Tomas Hammar, eds., *Mechanisms of Immigration Control: A Comparative Analysis of European Regulation Policy*. Oxford: Berg, 135–68.

Amersfoort, Hans van and Rinus Penninx. 1994. "Regulating Migration in Europe: The Dutch Experience, 1960–92," in Mark Miller, ed., Strategies for Immigration Control: An International Comparison. *The Annals of the American Academy of Political and Social Science*. Volume 534(July):133–46.

Amersfoort, Hans van and Boudewijn Surie. 1987. "Reluctant Hosts: Immigration into Dutch Society, 1970–1985," *Ethnic and Racial Studies* 10(2) April:169–85.

Amnesty International. 2001. *The Dublin Convention*. http://www.amnesty.ie/act/refug/dc.shtml.

Angenendt, Steffen. 1997. *Deutsche Migrationspolitik in neuen Europa*. Opladen: Leske Budrich.

Arzheimer, Kai. 2002. "Extreme Right Parties in Germany: An Overview," in EREPS, http://cidsp.upmf-grenoble.fr/guest/ereps/analysis.htm.

Australia, National Population Inquiry. 1975. *Population Projections for the States and Territories of Australia, Components of Population Growth and Sex-Age Composition. Research Report 1, Vol. 2*. Canberra: Australian government Publishing Service.

Australian Population and Immigration Council. 1977. Green Paper, *Immigration Policies and Australia's Population*. Quoted in Freda Hawkins. 1991. *Critical Years in Immigration: Canada and Australia Compared*. Montreal: McGill-Queen's University Press, 2nd edition:xxxiv.

Autonoom Centrum. 2000. "Illegalized Migrants in the Netherlands," in Kein Mench ist Illegal (ed.), *Without Papers in Europe*, http://www.noborder.org/without/holland.html.

Bach, Robert L. 1990. "Immigration and U.S. Foreign Policy in Latin America and the Caribbean," in Robert W. Tucker, Charles B. Keely, and Linda Wrigley, eds., *Immigration and U.S. Foreign Policy*. Boulder, Colorado: Westview Press, 123–49.

Bade, Klaus J. and Myron Weiner, eds. 1997. *Migration Past, Migration Future: Germany and the United States*. Providence: Berghahn Books.

Beard, Charles A. and Mary R. Beard. 1944. *A Basic History of the United States*. New York: Doubleday, Doran & Co.

Bennekom, Willem van et al. 2000. *Comparative Study of Member States on Immigration Law, with Special Reference to Deportation and Administrative Detention: Report on the Netherlands*. Centre for Migration Law, University of Nijmegen. January.

Bennett, Marion T. 1963. *American Immigration Policies: A History*. Washington D.C.: Public Affairs Press.

Beyer, Gunther. 1979. "The Benelux Countries: Belgium, The Netherlands, Luxemburg," in Daniel Kubat, ed., *The Politics of Migration Policies: The First World in the 1970s*. New York: Center for Migration Studies, 107–25.

Bigo, Didier. 1996. *Polices en Réseaux: L¥expérience Européenne*. Paris: Presses de Science Po.

Bohning, W.R. 1984. *Studies in International Labor Migration*. London: MacMillan.

——.1978. *Migration for Employment Project: Elements of a Theory of International Migration and Compensation*. Geneva: International Labor Organization.

Bourdouvalis, Chris. 1997. "The European Union and the Immigration Problem: Small Steps and Possible Solutions," in Emek M. Uçarer and Donald J. Puchala, eds., *Immigration into Western Societies: Problems and Politics*. London: Pinter, 266–80.

Bouvier, Leon F. and Robert W. Gardner. 1986. "Immigration to the U.S.: The Unfinished Story," *Population Bulletin* 41(4):3–50.

Bovenkerk, Frank. 1979. "The Netherlands," in Ronald E. Krane, ed., *International Labor Migration in Europe*. New York: Praeger, 118–32.

Bovenkerk, Frank, Robert Miles, and Gilles Verbunt. 1991. "Comparative Studies of Migration and Exclusion on the Grounds of 'Race' and Ethnic Background in Western Europe: A Critical Appraisal," *International Migration Review* 25(2) Summer:375–91.

——. 1990. "Racism, Migration and the State in Western Europe: A Case for Comparative Analysis," *International Sociology* 5(4) December:475–90.

Briggs, Vernon. 1995. "Mass Immigration, Free Trade, and the Forgotten American Worker," *Challenge* May–June:37–44.

——. 1984. *Immigration Policy and the American Labor Force*. Baltimore: John Hopkins University Press.

Brochmann, Grete. 1996. *European Integration and Immigration from Third Countries*. Oslo: Scandinavian University Press.

Brochmann, Grete and Tomas Hammar, eds. 1999. *Mechanisms of Immigration Control: A Comparative Analysis of European Regulation Policy*. Oxford: Berg.

Brubaker, Rogers W. 1992. *Citizenship and Nationhood in France and Germany*. Cambridge, Massachusetts: Harvard University Press.

Burr, Clinton Stoddard. 1922. *America's Race Heritage*. New York: The National Historical Society.

Caestecker, Frank and Bob Moore. 1998. "Refugee Policies in Western European States in the 1930s: A Comparative Analysis," *IMIS-Beiträge* 7, March.

Institut für Migrationsforschung und Interkulturelle Studien (IMIS), Universität Osnabrück.

Calavita, Kitty. 1995. "U.S. Immigration and Policy Responses: The Limits of Legislation," in Wayne Cornelius, Philip Martin, and James Hollifield, eds., *Controlling Immigration: A Global Perspective*. Stanford, California: Stanford University Press, 55–82.

——. 1992. *Inside the State: The Bracero Program, Immigration, and the I.N.S.* London: Routledge.

Callovi, Giuseppe. 1992. "Regulation of Immigration in 1993: Pieces of the European Community Jig-Saw Puzzle," *International Migration Review* 26(2):353–72.

——. 1990. "Immigration and the European Community," *Contemporary European Affairs* 3:17–38.

Carlier, Jean-Yves and Dirk Vanheule. 1994. "Belgian bricks for Fortress Europe: Comment on the New Refugee Law after a Judgment of the Cour d'Arbitrage," *International Journal of Refugee Law* 6(3):323–44.

Castells, Manuel. 1975. "Immigrant Workers and Class Struggles in Advanced Capitalism: The Western European Experience," *Politics and Society.* 5(1):33–66.

Castles, Stephen and Godula Kosack. 1989. "Immigrant Workers and Trade Unions in the German Federal Republic," in Stephen Castles, ed., *Migrant Workers and the Transformation of Western Societies.* Ithaca: Cornell University.

——. 1985. *Immigrant Workers and Class Structure in Western Europe.* New York: Oxford University Press.

Cesarani, David and Tony Kushner, eds. 1993. *The Internment of Aliens in Twentieth Century Britain.* Special issue of the *Journal of Immigrants and Minorities.* London: Frank Cass.

Charteris, A.H. 1927. "Australian Immigration Policy," *International Conciliation*, no. 235, December:517–36.

Collins, Williams J., Kevin H. O'Rourke, and Jeffrey Williamson. 1997. *Were Trade and Factor Mobility Substitutes in History?* NBER WP 6059. June.

Cornelius, Wayne, Philip Martin, and James Hollifield. 1995. *Controlling Immigration: A Global Perspective.* Stanford, California: Stanford University Press.

Craig, Richard B. 1971. *The Bracero Program: Interest Groups and Foreign Policy.* Austin: University of Texas Press.

De Vries, Marlene H. 1981. "The 'Second Generation' of Immigrants in Education and on the Labor Market," *Planning and Development in the Netherlands* 13(1):59–79.

Divine, Robert A. 1957. *American Immigration Policy, 1924–1952.* New Haven: Yale University Press.

Donselaar, J. Van and C. Nelissen. 1982. "De deelname v an racistische politieke partijen aan de Kamerverkeizingen van 1981," *Intermediair* (Amsterdam) 18. Quoted in Entzinger, 1985:83.

Doomernik, Jaroen et al. 1997. *A Migration Policy for the Future.* Brussels: Migration Policy Group.

Dorsen, Norman, Paul, Bender, and Burt Neuborne. 1982. *Political and Civil Rights in the United States—1982 Supplement.* Boston: Little, Brown.

——. 1976. *Political and Civil Rights in the United States.* Boston: Little, Brown and Company.

ECRI (European Commission against Racism and Intolerance). 1998. *Report on the Netherlands.* CRI (98) 49. Strasbourg. June 15.

EFMS (Academic Institute at the University of Bamberg, European Forum for Migration Studies). 2001. "Interior Ministers allow Kosovar refugees to stay," May, http://www.uni-bamberg.de/~ba6ef3/dmai01_e.htm.

Entzinger, Han B. 1987. "Shifting Paradigms: An Appraisal of Immigration in the Netherlands," in Heinz Fassmann and Rainer Münz, eds., *European Migration in the Late Twentieth Century.* Edward Elgar:93–112.

——. 1985. "The Netherlands," in Tomas Hammar, ed., *European Immigration Policy: A Comparative Study.* Cambridge, England: Cambridge University Press, 50–88.

——. 1981. "Research on Ethnic Minorities and Its Contribution to Policy Development," *Planning and Development in the Netherlands* 13(1): 81–91.

EREPS. 2002. "The Extreme Right Vote in Germany: Summary Table 1949–2000," http://cidsp.upmf-grenoble.fr/guest/ereps/analysis.htm.

Esser, Hartmut and Hermann Korte. 1985. "Federal Republic of Germany," in Tomas Hammar, ed., *European Immigration Policy: A Comparative Study.* Cambridge, England: Cambridge University Press, 165–205.

Europa. 1993–2000. *The Europa World Year Book.* London: Europa Publications.

European Commission. 2002. *Towards Integrated Management of the External Borders of the Member States of the European Borders. COM(2002)233.* Brussels: May 7.

——. 2000. *Communication from the Commission to the Council and the European Parliament on a Community Immigration Policy. COM(2000)757.* Brussels: November 22.

European Council. 2002. *Presidency Conclusions: Seville European Council 21 and 22 June 2002.*

European Economic and Social Committee. 2002. "Opinion of the Economic and Social Committee on the Amended Proposal for a Council Directive on the Right to Family reunification COM(2002) 225." ESC(2002)857. July 17. *Official Journal* C 241/108-9. October 7.

European Union. 1997. *Treaty Establishing the European Community, as Amended by the Treaty of Amsterdam,* http://europa.eu.int/eur-lex/en/treaties/selected/ livre214.html

Faist, Thomas. 1994. "How to Define a Foreigner? The Symbolic Politics of Immigration in German Partisan Discourse, 1978–1992," in Martin Baldwin-Edwards and Martin A. Schain, eds., *The Politics of Immigration in Western Europe.* London: Frank Cass and Company, 50–71.

Fassmann, Heinz and Rainer Münz, eds. 1994. *European Migration in the Late Twentieth Century.* Edward Elgar.

Favell, Adrian. 2000. "Immigration Politics in Europe," *ECPR News* 11(2) Spring, http://www.essex.ac.uk/ecpr/publications/ecprnews/spring2000/features.htm.

Feldblum, Miriam. 1994. "Fortress Europe, Fortress America," *Peace Review* 6(1) Spring:25–31.

Fetzer, Joel S. 2000, *Public Attitudes towards Immigration in the United States, France and Germany*. New York: Cambridge.

Fiddick, Jane. 1999. *Immigration and Asylum*, Research Paper 99/16. House of Commons, Home Affairs Section, February 19.

Fields, Harold. 1932. "Closing Immigration Throughout the World," *The American Journal of International Law* 26:671–99.

Fitzgerald, Keith. 1996. *The Face of the Nation: Immigration, the State, and the National Identity*. Stanford, California: Stanford University Press.

Flora, Peter. 1987. *State, Economy, and Society in Western Europe 1815–1975*. Frankfurt: Campus Verlag.

Foot, Paul. 1965. *Immigration and Race in British Politics*. Harmondsworth, England: Penguin Books.

Freeman, Gary P. 1995. "Modes of Immigration Politics in Liberal Democratic States," and "Rejoinder," *International Migration Review* 29(4):881–902, 909–13.

——. 1992. "Migration Policy and Politics in the Receiving States," *International Migration Review* 26(4) Winter:1144–67.

Freeman, Gary P. and Katharine Betts. 1992. "The Politics of Interests and Immigration Policymaking in Australia and the United States," in Gary P. Freeman and James Jupp, eds., *Nations of Immigrants*. Melbourne: Oxford University Press, 72–88.

Gallarotti, Giulio M. 1985. "Toward a Business Cycle Model of Tariffs," *International Organization* 39(1) Winter:155–88.

Geddes, Andrew. 2000a. *Immigration and European Integration: Towards Fortress Europe?* Manchester: Manchester University Press.

——. 2000b. "The Europeanization of Migration," in Adrian Favell ed., "Immigration Politics in Europe," *ECPR News* 11(2) Spring, http://www.essex.ac.uk/ecpr/publications/ecprnews/spring2000/features.htm.

Gorz, Andre. 1970. "Immigrant Labor," *New Left Review* 61.

Gould, Charles W. 1920. *America, A Family Matter*. New York: Scribner.

Gourevitch, Peter. 1978. "The International System and Regime Formation: A Critical Review of Anderson and Wallerstien," *Comparative Politics* 10(April):419–38.

Grant, Madison. 1916. *The Passing of the Great Race or the Racial Basis of European History*. New York: Scribner.

Great Britain, Home Office. 1986. *Immigration and Nationality Department Report, 1986*. HMSO.

Great Britain, Office of Information of the Foreign and Commonwealth Office. 1987. *Immigration into Britain: Notes on the Regulation and Procedures*, no. 62/87. London: Office of information.

Great Britain, Royal Commission on Population. 1949. *Report*. London: Her Majesty's Stationery Office.

Gugel, Günther. 1990. *Ausländer—Aussiedler—Übersiedler. Fremdenfeindlichkeit in der Bundesrepublic Deutschland.* Tübingen: Verein für Friedenspädagogik.

Guild, Elspeth. 1998. "Competence, Discretion and Third Country Nationals: The European Union's Legal Struggle with Migration," *Journal of Ethnic and Migration Studies* 24(4):613–26.

Guild, Elspeth and Jan Niessen. 1996. *The Developing Immigration and Asylum Policies of the European Union.* Den Haag: Kluwer Law International.

Gurak, Douglas T. and Fe Caces. 1992. "Migration Networks and the Shaping of Migration Systems," in Mary M. Kritz, Lin Lean Lim, and Hania Zlotnik, eds., *International Migration Systems.* Oxford: Clarendon Press, 150–76.

Haas, Peter M. 1992. "Introduction: Epistemic Communities and International Policy Coordination," *International Organization* 46(1) Winter:1–36.

Hammar, Tomas, ed., 1985. *European Immigration Policy: A Comparative Study.* Cambridge, England: Cambridge University Press.

Handlin, Oscar. 1957. *Race and Nationality in American Life.* Boston: Little Brown.

Handoll, John. 1995. *Free Movement of Persons in the EU.* Chichester: Wiley.

Hansen, Randall. 2000. *Citizenship and Immigration in Post-War Britain.* Oxford: Oxford University Press.

Hartigan, Kevin. 1992. "Matching Humanitarian Norms with Cold, Hard Interests: The Making of Refugee Policies in Mexico and Honduras, 1980–89," *International Organization* 46(3) Summer:709–30.

Hawkins, Freda. 1991. *Critical Years in Immigration: Canada and Australia Compared.* Montreal: McGill-Queen's University Press.

Herbert, Ulrich. 1990. *A History of Foreign Labor in Germany, 1880–1980.* Ann Arbor: The University of Michigan Press.

Higham, John. 1955/1988. *Strangers in the Land: Patterns of American Nativism, 1860–1925.* New Brunswick: Rutgers University Press.

Hoffman, Abraham. 1974. *Unwanted Mexican Americans in the Great Depression: Repatriation Pressures, 1929–1939.* Tucson: University of Arizona Press.

Hoffmann-Nowotny, Hans-Joachim. 1985. "Switzerland," in Tomas Hammar, ed., *European Immigration Policy: A Comparative Study.* Cambridge, England: Cambridge University Press, 206–36.

Hoffmann-Nowotny, Hans-Joachim, and Martin Killias. 1979. "Switzerland," in Ronald E. Krane, ed. and trans., *International Labor Migration in Europe.* New York: Praeger, 45–62.

Hollifield, James F. 1992a. *Immigrants, Markets and States.* Cambridge, Massachusetts: Harvard University Press.

———. 1992b. "Migration and International Relations: Cooperation and Control in the European Community," *International Migration Review* 26(2) Summer:568–95.

Hönekopp, Elmar. 1997. "The New Labor Migration as an Instrument of German Foreign Policy," in Rainer Münz and Myron Weiner, eds., *Migrants, Refugees and Foreign Policy.* Providence: Berghahn Books, 165–81.

Hopkins, Terence K. and Immanuel Wallerstein. 1982. *World-Systems Analysis: Theory and Methodology*. Berkeley: Sage.

Hoskin Marilyn and Roy C. Fitzgerald. 1989. "German Immigration Policy and Politics," in Michael C. LeMay, ed., *The Gatekeepers: Comparative Immigration Policy*. New York: Praeger, 95–118.

Hunt, Michael H. 1987. *Ideology and U.S. Foreign Policy*. New Haven: Yale University Press.

Huntington, Ellsworth. 1924. *The Character of Races as Influenced by Physical Environment, Natural Selection and Historical Development*. New York: Scribner.

Husbands, Christopher T. 1988. "The Dynamics of Racial Exclusion and Expulsion: Racist Politics in Western Europe," *European Journal of Political Research* 16(6):701–20.

Hutchinson, Edward P. 1981. *Legislative History of American Immigration Policy 1798–1965*. Philadelphia: University of Pennsylvania Press.

Huysmans, Jef. 1995. "Migrants As a Security Problem: Dangers of 'Securitizing' Societal Issues," in Robert Miles and Dietrich Thränhardt, eds., *Migration and European Integration: The Dynamics of Inclusion and Exclusion*. London: Pinter.

Ignazi, Piero. 1992. "The Silent Counter-Revolution: Hypotheses on the Emergence of Extreme Right-Wing Parties in Europe," *European Journal of Political Research* 22(1) July:3–34.

International Labor Office. *Yearbook of Labor Statistics*. Geneva.

Jackman, Robert W. and Karin Volpert. 1996. "Conditions Favoring Parties of the Extreme-Right in Western Europe," *British Journal of Political Science* 26:501–21.

Jacobs, Dirk. 1998. "Discourse, Politics and Policy: The Dutch Parliamentary Debate About Voting Rights for Foreign Residents," *International Migration Review* 32(2) Summer:350–73.

Jenness, R.A. 1974. "Canadian Migration and Immigration Patterns and Government Policy," *International Migration Review* 8(1).

Jones, Maldwyn Allen. 1960. *American Immigration*. Chicago: University of Chicago Press.

Joppke, C. 1999. *Immigration and the Nation-State: The United States, Germany and Great Britain*. New York: Oxford University Press.

——. 1998a. *Challenge to the Nation-State: Immigration in Western Europe and the United States*. New York: Oxford University Press.

——. 1998b. "Why Liberal States Accept Unwanted Immigration," *World Politics* 50(2) January:266–93.

Kairys, David. 1982. *The Politics of Law: A Progressive Critique*. New York: Pantheon Books.

Katzenstein, Peter J. 1987. *Policy and Politics in West Germany*. Philadelphia: Temple University Press.

Kaye, Ronald. 1994. "Defining the Agenda: British Refugee Policy and the Role of Parties," *Journal of Refugee Studies* 7(2/3):144–59.

Kitschelt, Herbert. 1997. *The Radical Right in Western Europe: A Comparative Analysis*. Ann Arbor: University of Michigan Press.

Kondratieff, N.D. 1979. "The Long Waves in Economic Life," *Review* 2(4) Spring:519–62. (The article originally appeared in the *Archiv fur Sozialwissenschaft and Sozialpolitik*, LVI (3), 1926:573–609.)

Koslowski, Ray. 2000. *Migrants and Citizens: Demographic Change in the European State System*. Ithaca: Cornell University Press.

——. 1998. "EU Migration Regimes: Established and Emergent," in Christian Joppke, ed., *Challenge to the Nation State: Immigration in Western Europe and the United States*. Oxford: Oxford University Press.

Kraly, Ellen Percy. 1990. "U.S. Refugee Policies and Refugee Migration Since World War II," in Robert W. Tucker, Charles B. Keely, and Linda Wrigley, eds., *Immigration and U.S. Foreign Policy*. Colorado: Westview Press, 73–98.

Krane, Ronald E., ed. 1979. *International Labor Migration in Europe*. New York: Praeger.

Kubat, Daniel. 1993a. *The Politics of Migration Policies: Settlement and Integration—The First World in the 1990s*. New York: Center for Migration Studies.

——. 1993b. "Canada: Immigration's Humanitarian Challenge," in Kaniel Kubat, ed., *The Politics of Migration Policies: The First World into the 1990s*. New York: Center for Migration Studies.

——, ed. 1979. *The Politics of Migration Policies: The First World in the 1970s*. New York: Center for International Studies.

Kuijer, Aldo 1993. "Recent Changes in Dutch Immigration, Nationality and Anti-Discrimination Law," in Philip J. Muus, ed., *Migration, Immigrants and Policy in the Netherlands. Recent Trends and Developments*. Report for the Continuous Reporting System on Migration (SOPEMI) of the OECD, Amsterdam (CEMIO/UvA).

Kuijer, Aldo and J.D.M. Steenbergen. 1999. *Nederlands Vreemdelingenrecht* [Dutch Immigration Law]. Utrecht: Nederlands Centrum Buitenlanders NCB, 4th edition.

Kurthen, Hermann. 1995. "Germany at the Crossroads: National Identity and the Challenges of Immigration," *International Migration Review* 29(4): 914–38.

Lahav, Gallya. 1998. "Immigration and the State: The Devolution and Privatization of Immigration Control in the EU," *Journal of Ethnic and Migration Studies* 24(4): 675–94.

Lavenex, Sandra. 2000. "Refugees in an 'Area of Freedom, Security and Justice,'" in Adrian Favell, ed., "Immigration Politics in Europe," *ECPR News* 11(2) Spring, http://www.essex.ac.uk/ecpr/publications/ecprnews/spring2000/features.htm.

Layton-Henry, Zig. 1992. *The Politics of Immigration: Immigration, "Race" and "Race" Relations in Post-war Britain*. Oxford, London: Blackwell.

——. 1990. *The Political Rights of Migrant Workers in Western Europe*. London: Sage Publications.

——. 1989. "British Immigration Policy and Politics," in Michael C. LeMay, ed., *The Gatekeepers: Comparative Immigration Policy*. New York: Praeger, 59–94.

——. 1985. "Great Britain," in Tomas Hammar, ed., *European Immigration Policy: A Comparative Study*. Cambridge: Cambridge University Press, 89–126.

——. 1984. *The Politics of Race in Britain*. London: George Allen & Unwin.

Leitner, Helga. 1995. "International Migration and the Politics of Admission and Exclusion in Postwar Europe," *Political Geography* 14(3):259–78.

LeMay, Michael C. 1989a. *The Gatekeepers: Comparative Immigration Policy*. New York: Praeger.

——. 1989b. "U.S. Immigration Policy and Politics," in Michael C. LeMay, ed., *The Gatekeepers: Comparative Immigration Policy*. New York: Praeger, 1–22.

——. 1987. *From Open Door to Dutch Door: An Analysis of U.S. Immigration Policy Since 1820*. New York: Praeger.

Loescher, Gil. 1996. *Beyond Charity: International Cooperation and the Global Refugee Crisis*. New York: Oxford University Press.

Loescher, Gil and John A. Scanlan. 1986. *Calculated Kindness: Refugees and America's Half-Open Door, 1945 to the Present*. New York: The Free Press.

London, Jack. 1911/1946. *South Sea Tales*. New York: Macmillan.

——. 1910. *Revolution and Other Essays*. New York: Macmillan.

Lowell, B. Lindsay, ed. 1999. *Foreign Temporary Workers in America: Policies that Benefit the U.S. Economy*. Quorum Books.

Lucassen, Leo. 1998. "The Great War and the Origins of Migration Control in Western Europe and the United States (1880–1920)," in Anita Bocker et al., eds., *Regulation of Migration: International Experiences*. Amsterdam: Het Spinhuis Publishers, 45–72.

MacLaughlin, Jim. 1998. "Racism, Ethnicity and Multiculturalism in Contemporary Europe: A Review Essay," *Political Geography* 17(8) November: 1013–24.

Marshall, Adriana. 1973. *The Import of Labor: The Case of the Netherlands*. Rotterdam: Rotterdam University Press.

Martin, Michael T. 1999. " 'Fortress Europe' and Third World Immigration in The Post–Cold War Global Context," *Third World Quarterly* 20(4) August:821–37.

Martin, Philip L. 2002. "Mexican Workers and U.S. Agriculture: The Revolving Door," *International Migration Review* 36(4):1124–42.

——. 1999. "California's Farm Labor Market and Immigration Reforms," in B. Lindsay Lowell, ed., *Foreign Temporary Workers in America: Policies that Benefit the U.S. Economy*. Quorum Books, 179–207.

——. 1998a. "Book Review: German Immigration Literature," *International Migration Review* 32(2) Summer:491–94.

——. 1998b. *Germany: Reluctant Land of Immigration*. American Institute for Contemporary German Studies, The Johns Hopkins University, German Issues No. 21.

Martin, Philip L. 1995. "Germany: Reluctant Land of Immigration," in Wayne Cornelius, Philip Martin, and James Hollifield, eds., *Controlling Immigration: A Global Perspective*. Stanford, California: Stanford University Press, 189–226.

——, ed. 1984. *Migrant Labor in Agriculture: An International Comparison*. Berkeley: Giannini Foundation.

Martin, Philip L. and Mark J. Miller. 1994. "European–American Immigration Convergence: A Conference Report," *International Migration Review* 28(3) Fall:591–94.

Martin, Philip L. et al., eds. 1995. *Immigration Reform and U.S. Agriculture*. Berkeley: University of California Press.

Marx, Karl. 1976. *Capital*, Vol. 1. Harmondsworth: Penguin.

——. 1973. *Grundrisse: Foundations of the Critique of Political Economy*. Harmondsworth: Penguin.

Massey, Douglas S. 1990. "The Social and Economic Origins of Immigration," in *Annals of The American Academy of Political and Social Sciences* 520, July:60–72.

—— 1988. "Economic Development and International Migration in Comparative Perspective," *Population and Development Review* 14(3) September:383–414.

Massey, Douglas S. et al. 1993. "Theories of International Migration: A Review and Appraisal," *Population and Development Review* 19(3) September:431–66.

Massey, Douglas S. et al. 1990. *Return to Aztlan: The Social Process of International Migration from Western Mexico*. Berkeley: University of California Press.

McKeown, Timothy J. 1983. "Hegemonic Stability Theory and the 19th Century Tariff Levels in Europe," *International Organization* 37(1) Winter:73–91.

Mehrländer, Ursula. 1979. "Federal Republic of Germany," in Daniel Kubat, ed., *The Politics of Migration Policies: Settlement and Integration—The First World in the 1990s*. New York: Center for Migration Studies, 145–62.

Messina, Anthony. 1989. *Race and Party Competition in Britain*. London: Clarendon Press.

Meyers, Eytan. Forthcoming (a). *Multilateral Cooperation in International Labor Mobility*.

——. Forthcoming (b). *The Politics of International Immigration Policy*.

——. 2000. "Theories of International Immigration Policy," *International Migration Review* 34(4):1245–82.

——. 1994. "European Immigration Regimes in a Comparative Perspective," paper presented at the Ninth International Conference of Europeanists, Chicago, March 31–April 2.

Miles, Robert. 1989. *Racism*. London: Routledge.

——. 1987. *Capitalism and Unfree Labour: Anomaly or Necessity?* London: Tavistock.

——. 1986. "Labour Migration, Racism and Capital Accumulation in Western Europe since 1945," *Capital and Class* 28:49–86.

Miles, Robert and Diana Kay. 1994. "The Politics of Immigration to Britain: East–West Migrations in the Twentieth Century," in Martin Baldwin-Edwards and Martin A. Schain, eds., *The Politics of Immigration in Western Europe,* special issue of West European Politics. London: Frank Cass and Company, 17–32.

Miles, Robert and Dietrich Thränhardt, eds. 1995. *Migration and European Integration: The Dynamics of Inclusion and Exclusion.* London: Pinter.

Miller, Mark J. 1992. "Evolution of Policy Modes for Regulating International Labor Migration," in Mary M. Kritz, Lin Lean Lim, and Hania Zlotnik, eds., *International Migration Systems.* Oxford: Clarendon Press, 300–14.

——. 1986. "Policy Ad-Hocracy: The Paucity of Coordinated Perspectives and Policy," *Annals of The American Academy of Political and Social Sciences* 485, May:64–75.

——. 1979. "Reluctant Partnership: Foreign Workers in Franco-Algerian Relations, 1962–1979," *Journal of International Affairs* 33(2):219–38.

Miller, Mark J. and Robert A. Denemark. 1993. *Migration and World Politics: A Critical Case for Theory and Policy.* New York: Center for Migration Studies.

Miller, Mark J. and Philip L. Martin. 1982. *Administering Foreign-worker Programs: Lessons from Europe.* Lexington, Massachusetts: Lexington Books.

Miller, Mark J. and Demetrios G. Papademetriou. 1983. "Immigration and U.S. Foreign Policy," in Miller and Papademetriou, eds., *The Unavoidable Issue: U.S. Immigration Policy in the 1980s.* Philadelphia: Institute for the Study of Human Issues.

Mitchell, Brian. R. 1992. *International Historical Statistics: Europe 1750–1988.* New York: Stockton Press, 3rd edition.

Mitchell, Christopher, ed. 1992. *Western Hemisphere Immigration and United States Policy.* University Park, Pennsylvania: The Pennsylvania State University Press.

——. 1989. "International Migration, International Relations and Foreign Policy," *International Migration Review* 23(3):681–708.

Money, Jeannette. 1999. *Fences and Neighbors: The Political Geography of Immigration Control.* Ithaca: Cornell University Press.

——. 1997. "No Vacancy: The Political Geography of Immigration Control in Advanced Industrial Countries," *International Organization* 51(4) Autumn: 685–720.

Morawska, Ewa. 1990. "The Sociology and Historiography of Immigration," in Virginia Yans-McLaughlin, ed., *Immigration Reconsidered: History, Sociology and Politics.* New York: Oxford University Press, 187–240.

Morrison, Samuel Eliot, Henry Steele Commager, and William E. Leuchtenburg, eds. 1983. *A Concise History of the American Republic.* Tel Aviv: Zmora Bitan Publishers.

Mullins, David. 1987. "Events and Trends in Race Relations: July–December 1986," *New Community* 13(3) September:435–41.

Muus, Philip. 2001. "International Migration and the European Union, Trends and Consequences," *European Journal on Criminal Policy and Research* 9(1) Spring:31–49.

——. 1998. "Migration, Immigrants and Policy in the Netherlands," *Recent Trends and Developments, SOPEMI Report*. Utrecht: ERCOMER.

——. 1997. "International Migration to the Netherlands: Recent Trends as Observed in the Provisional SOPEMI-Netherlands 1996 Report," MERGER (the newsletter of the Netherlands and Ethnic Relations Group For European Research), 4(1), http://www.ercomer.org/merger/vol4no1/intmignl.html.

Muus Philip et al., eds. 1997. *Free Movement for Non-EC Workers Within the European Community*. Utrecht: Centrum Buitenlanders.

Münz, Rainer. 2001. "International Migration by Ethnic Germans," *International Encyclopedia of the Social & Behavioral Sciences*. Amsterdam: Elsevier Science, 7799–804.

Münz, Rainer and Ralf Ulrich. 1997. "Changing Patterns of Immigration to Germany: 1945–1995," in Klaus J. Bade and Myron Weiner, eds., *Migration Past, Migration Future: Germany and the United States*. Providence: Berghahn Books, 65–119.

Münz, Rainer and Myron Weiner, eds. 1997. *Migrants, Refugees and Foreign Policy*. Providence: Berghahn Books.

The Netherlands, Central Bureau of Statistics. 2002a. External Migration by Country of Birth, in www.cbs.nl.

——. 2002b. Statistics Netherlands Press Release, "Immigration Sharply Down," PB02-219, in www.cbs.nl.

Nicolaas, Han and Arno Sprangers. 2001. "Migration Motives of Non-Dutch Immigrants in The Netherlands," paper for EAPS Population Conference, Helsinki, Finland. June 7–9.

Nikolinakos, Marios. 1975. "Notes Toward a General Theory of Migration in Late Capitalism," *Race and Class* 17(1) Summer:5–18.

O'Brien, Peter. 1996. *Beyond the Swastika*. London: Routledge.

O'Brien, Phillip. 1975. "A Critique of Latin American Theories of Dependency," in Ivar Oxaal, Tony Barnett, and David Booth, eds., *Beyond the Sociology of Development: Economy and Society in Latin America and Africa*. London: Routledge and Kegan Paul, 7–29.

O'Keefee, David. 1992. "The Free Movement of Persons and the Single Market," *European Law Review* 17(1): 3–19.

Overbeek, Henk. 1996. "L'Europe en quête d'une politique en matière de migration: les contraintes de la mondialisation et de la restructuration des marchés du travail," *Etudes Internationales* 27(1) March:53–80.

Papademetriou, Demetrios. 1996. *Coming Together or Pulling Apart? The European Union's Struggle with Immigration and Asylum*. Washington, DC: Carnegie Endowment for International Peace.

Penninx, Rinus. 1986. "International Migration in Western Europe Since 1973: Developments, Mechanisms and Controls," *International Migration Review* 20(4):951–72.

——. 1984. "Research and Policy with Regard to Ethnic Minorities in the Netherlands; An Historical Outline and the State of Affairs," *International Migration* 22(4):345–66.

Penninx, Rinus et al. 1994. *The Impact of International Migration on Receiving Countries: The Case of the Netherlands*. The Hauge: NIDI.

Petras, Elizabeth McLean. 1981. "The Global Labor Market in the Modern World-Economy," in Mary M. Kritz, Charles B. Keely, and Silvano M. Tomasi, eds., *Global Trends in Migration*. New York: The Center for Migration Studies of New York, 44–63.

Piore, Michael J. 1979. *Birds of Passage: Migrant Labor and Industrial Societies*. New York: Cambridge University Press.

Plender, Richard. 1988. *International Migration Law*. Dordrecht: Martinus Nijhoff.

——. 1986. "Recent Trends in National Immigration Control," *International and Comparative Law Quarterly* 35:531–66.

Portes, Alejandro. 1981. "Modes of Structural Incorporation and Present Theories of Labor Immigration," in Mary M. Kritz, Charles B. Keely, and Silvano M. Tomasi, eds., *Global Trends in Migration*. New York: The Center for Migration Studies of New York, 279–97.

Portes, Alejandro and John Walton. 1981. *Labor, Class, and the International System*. New York: Academic Press.

Ragin, Charles C. 1991. "Comments," in Pierre Bourdieu and James S. Coleman, eds., *Social Theory for a Changing Society*. Boulder, Colorado: Westview Press.

Rees, Tom. 1979. "The United Kingdom," in Daniel Kubat, ed., *The Politics of Migration Policies*. New York: Center for Migration Studies, 67–91.

Reimann Horst and Helga Reimann. 1979. "Federal Republic of Germany," in Ronald E. Krane, ed., *International Labor Migration in Europe*. New York: Praeger Publishers, 63–87.

Reimers, David M. 1982. "Recent Immigration Policy: An Analysis," in Barry R. Chiswick, ed., *The Gateway: U.S. Immigration Issues and Policies*. New York: University Press of America, 13–53.

Reisler, Mark. 1976. *By the Sweat of Their Brow: Mexican Immigrant Labor in the United States, 1900–1940*. New York: Greenwood Press.

Rogers, Rosmarie, 1992. "The Future of Refugee Flows and Policies," *International Migration Review* 26(4) Winter:1112–43.

——. ed. 1985. *Guests Come to Stay, the Effects of European Labor Migration on Sending and Receiving Countries*. Boulder: Westview.

Rowen, Herbert H. 1985. "Low Countries, The Netherlands," in the *Encyclopedia Britannica*. Chicago: Encyclopedia Britannica.

Rudolph, Hedwig. 1994. "Dynamics of Immigration in a Nonimmigrant Country: Germany," in Heinz Fassmann and Rainer Münz, eds., *European Migration in the Late Twentieth Century*. Edward Elgar, 113–26.

Salomon, Kim. 1991. *Refugees in the Cold War: Towards a New International Refugee Regime*. Lund: Lund University Press.

Sassen, Saskia. 1996a. "Beyond Sovereignty: Immigration Policy Making Today," *Social Justice* 23(3) Fall:9–20.

Sassen, Saskia. 1996b. *Losing Control—Sovereignty in an Age of Globalization*. New York: Columbia University Press.

——. 1990. *The Mobility of Labor and Capital: A Study in International Investment and Labor Flow*. Cambridge: Cambridge University Press.

Shughart, William F., Robert D. Tollison, and Mwangi S. Kimenyi. 1986. "The Political Economy of Immigration Restrictions," *Yale Journal of Regulation* 51:79–97.

Skocpol, Theda. 1977. "Wallerstein's World Capitalist System: A Theoretical and Historical Critique," *American Journal of Sociology* 82, March: 1075–90.

Skran, Claudena M. 1995. *Refugees in Inter-War Europe: The Emergence of a Regime*. Oxford: Clarendon Press.

Smith, Thomas Edward, ed. 1981a. *Commonwealth Migration: Flows and Policies*. London: Macmillan Press.

——. 1981b. "Commonwealth Migration to and from the United Kingdom," in Thomas Edward Smith, ed., *Commonwealth Migration: Flows and Policies*. London: Macmillan, 89–131.

Socialist Review. 1995. Issue 192, December, http://website.lineone.net/~socrev2text/pubs/sr192/morgan.htm.

Solomos, John. 1993. *Race and Racism in Britain*. London: Macmillan, 2nd edition.

SOPEMI. Organization for Economic Co-operation and Development (OECD), *Trends in International Migration: Continuous Reporting System on Migration, Annual Reports*. Paris: OECD Publications Service.

Soysal, Yasemin. 1994. *The Limits of Citizenship*. Chicago: The University of Chicago Press.

Statewatch. 2002. *EU Presidency Conclusions at the Seville European Council 21–22 June*. http://www.statewatch.org/news/2002/jun/14seville.htm.

Steiner, Niklaus. 2000. *Arguing About Asylum: The Complexity of Refugee Debates in Europe*. New York: St. Martin's Press.

Stephen Roth Institute for Anti-Semitism and Racism, Tel Aviv University. 1999. "Anti-Semitism Worldwide 1998/9: Netherlands," http://www.tau.ac.il/Anti-Semitism/asw98-9/nether.html.

Studlar, Donley T. 1979. "Great Britain," in Ronald E. Krane, ed., *International Labor Migration in Europe*. New York: Praeger Publishers, 88–117.

Teitelbaum, Michael S. 1984. "Immigration, Refugees, and Foreign Policy," *International Organization* 38(3) Summer:429–50.

Teitelbaum, Michael S. and Myron Weiner. 1995. *Threatened Peoples, Threatened Borders: World Migration and U.S. Policy* (New York: Norton).

Thorp, Willard Long et al. 1926. *Business Annals*. New York: National Bureau of Economic Research.

Tobin, Gregory. 1989. "Australian Immigration Policy and Politics," in Michael C. LeMay, ed., *The Gatekeepers*. New York: Praeger, 23–58.

Thränhardt, Dietrich. 1999. "Germany's Immigration Policies and Politics," in Grete Brochmann and Tomas Hammar, eds., *Mechanisms of Immigration*

Control: A Comparative Analysis of European Regulation Policy. Oxford: Berg, 29–58.
——, ed. 1996. *Europe: A New Immigration Continent*. Münster: Lit Verlag.
Tucker, Robert W., Charles B. Keely, and Linda Wrigley, eds. 1990. *Immigration and U.S. Foreign Policy*. Boulder, Colorado: Westview Press.
Uçarer, Emek M. 1997. "Europe's Search for Policy: The Harmonization of Asylum Policy and European Integration," in Emek M. Uçarer and Donald J. Puchala, eds., *Immigration into Western Societies: Problems and Politics*. London: Pinter, 281–309.
United Nations. Department of International Economic and Social Affairs. 1998. *International Migration Policies*. New York: United Nations Publications.
——. 1982. *International Migration Policies and Programs: A World Survey*. New York: United Nations Publications.
United Nations Population Division. 2002. *International Migration Report 2002*. ESA/P/WP.178. November.
UNHCR, Population Data Unit. 2002. "Number of Asylum Applications Submitted in 30 Industrialized Countries, 1992–2001," http://www.unhcr.ch/cgi-bin/texis/vtx/home?page=statistics.
——. 2001. *Asylum Applications in Industrialized Countries: 1980–1999*. Geneva, November.
United States Census Bureau. 2001. *Time Series of Intercensal State Population Estimates*. http://eire.census.gov/popest/data/counties/tables/CO-EST2001-12/CO-EST2001-12-00.php.
United States Committee for Refugees (USCR). 2001. Country Report: Netherlands 2001. http://www.refugees.org/ world/countryrpt/europe/2001/netherlands.htm.
——. 2000. Country Report: Netherlands 2000. http://www.refugees.org/world/countryrpt/europe/2000/netherlands.htm.
——. 1999. Country Report: Netherlands 1999. http://www.refugees.org/world/countryrpt/europe/1999/netherlands.htm.
——. 1998. Country Report: Netherlands 1998. http://www.refugees.org/world/countryrpt/europe/1998/netherlands.htm.
——. 1997. Country Report: Netherlands 1997. http://www.refugees.org/world/countryrpt/europe/1997/netherlands.htm.
United States 88th Congress. 2nd Session. 1964. House, Subcommittee No. 1 of the Committee on the Judiciary, *Immigration: Hearings*. Washington D.C.: The U.S. Government Printing Office, 1964:418. Quoted in Reimers:35.
United States 83rd Congress. 1952. *Congressional Record* 98. Washington D.C.: U.S. Government Printing Office.
United States 54th Congress. 2nd Session. 1897. *Congressional Record* 29. Washington D.C.: U.S. Government Printing Office.
United States 54th Congress. 1st Session. 1896. *Congressional Record* 28. Washington D.C.: U.S. Government Printing Office.

United States 48th Congress. 1884. *Congressional Record* 15. Washington D.C.: U.S. Government Printing Office.

United States 38th Congress. 1865. *Congressional Globe.* Washington D.C.: U.S. Government Printing Office.

United States 37th Congress. 1863. *Congressional Globe.* Washington D.C.: U.S. Government Printing Office.

United States Congress. House. Committee of the Judiciary. 1990. Serial No. 54. *Processing of Soviet Refugees.* Washington D.C.: U.S. Government Printing Office.

United States Congress, The Select Commission on Immigration and Refugee Policy. 1981. *U.S. Immigration Policy and the National Interest.* Washington D.C.: U.S. Government Printing Office, April 30.

United States Congress. Senate. Committee on the Judiciary. 1986. S. HRG 99-798. *Midyear Consultations on Refugee Programs For Fiscal Year 1986.* Washington D.C.: U.S. Government Printing Office.

United States Department of Commerce. 1949–2002. *Statistical Abstract.* Washington D.C.: U.S. Government Printing Office.

United States Department of Commerce. 1975. *Historical Statistics of the United States—Colonial Times to 1970.* Washington D.C.: U.S. Government Printing Office.

United States Department of Labor. 2002a. Foreign Labor Statistics: Comparative Civilian Labor Force Statistics, Ten Countries, http://www.bls.gov/fls.

——. 2002b. Foreign Labor Statistics: Unemployment Rates in the European Union and Selected Member Countries, Unadjusted by BLS, 1990–2002, http://www.bls.gov/fls.

——. 1942. *Strikes in 1941.* Washington D.C.: U.S. Government Printing Office.

——. 1937. Strikes in the United States: 1880–1936. Washington D.C.: U.S. Government Printing Office.

——. 1927. *Handbook of Labor Statistics.* Washington D.C.: U.S. Government Printing Office.

——. 1904. *Bulletin.* Washington D.C.: U.S. Government Printing Office.

——. 1896. *Bulletin.* Washington D.C.: U.S. Government Printing Office.

United States Department of State. Bureau of Public Affairs. 1988. *Current Policy No. 1103, Proposed Refugee Admissions for FY 1989.* Washington D.C.: U.S. Government Printing Office.

United States, Immigration and Naturalization Service (INS). 2002. *Homeland Security Act of 2002.* http://news.findlaw.com/cnn/docs/terrorism/hsa2002.pdf.

——. 1978. *The West Indies (BWI) Temporary Alien Worker Program, 1943–1977.* Washington D.C.: GPO. Table 2 quoted in Briggs, 1984:100.

——. *Statistical Yearbook of the Immigration and Naturalization Service.*

United States. White House Press Release. 2002. "President Bush Signs Homeland Security Act," November 25. http://www.whitehouse.gov/news/releases/2002/11/20021125-6.html.

Veen Hans-Joachim, Norbert Lepszy, and Peter Mnich. 1993. *The Republikaner Party in Germany: Right-Wing Menace or Protest Catchall?* Westport, Connecticut: Praeger.

Vellinga, Menno. 1993. "The Benelux Countries: Divergent Paths toward Restrictive Immigration," in Daniel Kubat, ed., *The Politics of Migration Policies: Settlement and Integration—The First World in the 1990s*. New York: Center for Migration Studies.

Vink, Maarten. 2001. "The Limited Europeanization of Domestic Asylum Policy: EU Governments and Two-Level Games." Paper prepared for the First YEN Research Meeting on Europeanisation, Workshop IV, "Europeanisation of Domestic Politics," November 2 and 3, 2001, Siena, Italy.

Viotti, Paul R. and Mark V. Kauppi. 1987. *International Relations Theory: Realism, Pluralism, Globalism*. New York: MacMillan.

Voerman, Gerrit and Paul Lucardie. 1992. "The Extreme Right in the Netherlands," *European Journal of Political Research* 22(1) July:35–54.

Wallerstein, Immanuel. 1974a. *The Modern World-System: Capitalist Agriculture and the Origins of the European World-Economy in the Sixteenth Century*. New York: Academic Press.

——. 1974b. "The Rise and the Future Demise of the World Capitalist System: Concepts for Comparative Analysis," *Comparative Studies in Society and History* 16(4) September:387–415.

——. 1972. "Three Paths of National Development in the Sixteenth Century," *Studies in Comparative International Development* 7(2) Summer:95–101.

Weiner, Myron. 1995. *The Global Migration Crisis: Challenge to States and to Human Rights*. New York: HarperCollins College Publishers.

——. 1993. *International Migration and Security*. Boulder, Colorado: Westview Press.

——. 1990. "Asian Immigrants and U.S. Foreign Policy," in Robert W. Tucker, Charles B. Keely, and Linda Wingley, eds., *Immigration and U.S. Foreign Policy*. Boulder, Colorado: Westview Press, 192–213.

——. 1985. "On International Migration and International Relations," *Population and Development Review* 11(3) September:441–55.

Westle, Bettina and Oskar Niedermayer. 1992. "Contemporary Right-Wing Extremism in West Germany," *European Journal of Political Research* 22(1) July:83–100.

Whipple, Leon. 1927. *The Story of Civil Liberty in the United States*. New York: Vanguard Press.

Yundt, Keith W. 1989. "The Organization of American States and Legal Protection to Political Refugees in Central America," *International Migration Review* 23(2) Summer:201–18.

Zolberg, Aristide R. 1992. "Labor Migration and International Economic Regimes: Bretton Woods and After," in Mary M. Kritz, Lin Lean Lim, and Hania Zlothik, eds., *International Migration Systems*. Oxford: Clarendon Press, 315–34.

Zolberg, Aristide R. 1989. "The Next Waves: Migration Theory for a Changing World," *International Migration Review* 23(3) Fall:403–30.

——. 1983. "Contemporary Transnational Migrations in Historical Perspective: Patterns and Dilemmas," in Mary M. Kritz, ed., *U.S. Immigration and Refugee Policy*. Lexington, Massachusetts: Lexington Books, 15–51.

——. 1981a. "International Migrations in Political Perspective," in Mary M. Kritz, Charles B. Keely, and Silvano M. Tomasi, eds., *Global Trends in Migration: Theory and Research on International Population Movements*. New York: Center for Migration Studies, 3–27.

——. 1981b. "Origins of the Modern World System: A Missing Link," *World Politics* 23(2):253–81.

——. 1978. "International Migration Policies in a Changing World System," in William H. McNeill and Ruth Adams, eds., *Human Migration, Patterns and Policies*. Bloomington: Indiana University Press, 241–86.

Newspapers

BBC News, http://bbc.co.uk. June 13, 2002. "EU Ministers Agree to Fortify Borders"

Christian Science Monitor. October 21, 1997. "Tailor's Tale Wins Sympathy but No Reprieve by Dutch"

Daily Telegraph. January 8, 1996. "Howard Takes Asylum Message to Pakistan"

——. June 16, 1995. "Howard to Bar Sham Marriages"

The Economist. January 6, 2003. "Survey: Netherlands," http://www.economist.com/ surveys

——. July 4, 2002. "The Legacy of Pim Fortuyn," http://www.economist.com/agenda

——. July 16, 1994. "America's Least Wanted":23–24

Financial Times. March 18, 1996. "Home Office Plans Could Increase Deportations"

——. October 27, 1995. "Howard Digs In on Hong Kong Passports"

——. October 6, 1992. "Tensions Rise as the Economy Weakens"

Global Development Briefing. December 19, 2002. "International Migration Day," http://db.ngo.ru/info.nsf/MigrantIndex/NT00003186

The Guardian. March 29, 1995. "Targets of the Genetic Inquisition"

Migration News. 1994–2003. Edited by Philip Martin. Internet edition. University of California, Davis [Migration News summarizes the most important immigration and integration developments of the preceding month. http://migration.ucdavis.edu]

New York Times. April 25, 2003. "Fearful, Angry or Confused, Muslim Immigrants Register," http://www.nytimes.com/2003/04/25/international/worldspecial/25REGI.html

——. November 25, 2002. "Bush Signs Bill for New Dept. and Picks Ridge as Its Secretary"

Newsweek. August 9, 1993. "America: Still a Melting Pot?":8–23

Press Association Newsfile. June 16, 1995. "Anger at Plans for Tougher Immigrant Marriage Laws"

Radio Free Europe. June 21, 2002. "EU: Summit to Focus on Immigration," http://www.rferl.org/nca/features/2002/06/21062002084229.asp

——. June 19, 2002. "EU: Seville Summit to Focus Largely on Immigration Issues," http://www.rferl.org/nca/features/2002/06/19062002152043.asp

——. June 18, 2002. "EU: Prodi Welcomes Putting Immigration on Top of Summit Agenda," http://www.rferl.org/nca/features/2002/06/18062002152435.asp

——. January 9, 2001. "East/West: Analysis From Washington—Illegal Migration and International Politics," http://www.rferl.org/nca/features/2001/01/09012001104317.asp

——. October 18, 1999. "EU: Leaders Agree to Fight Illegal Immigration, Organized Crime," http://www.rferl.org/nca/features/1999/10/F.RU.991018120306.html

Radio Netherlands Wereldomroep. June 14, 2002. "Dutch Tighten Rules for Immigration," http://www.rnw.nl/hotspots/html/dut020614.html

Sri Lanka Monitor. September 1997. "Holland to Deport Tamils," http://brcslproject.gn.apc.or/slmonitor/september97

The Times. March 14, 1995. "Benefit Cuts Aim is to Deter Bogus Asylum Seekers"

The Washington Post Weekly Edition. October 25, 2002. "Immigration Logic"

——. July 4–10, 1994. "Different Strokes for Different Refugees"

Index

- Laws and acts are indexed under the country that enacted them. For example, the Chinese Exclusion Act is indexed under "United States, Chinese Exclusion Act."
- All political parties are indexed under "political parties." All unions are indexed under "trade unions."